This book given to

_____

on the occasion of

_____

Presented by

_____

Date

_____

Watching the Clock

260 Meditations from Real Life

EDWARD GRUBE

CPH.
SAINT LOUIS

In thanksgiving to God for Renee—
a faithful, loving, and patient wife for more than 25 years

All Scripture quotations, unless otherwise indicated, are taken from the HOLY BIBLE, NEW INTERNATIONAL VERSION®. NIV®. Copyright © 1973, 1978, 1984 by International Bible Society. Used by permission of Zondervan Publishing House. All rights reserved.

Scripture quotations marked KJV are from the King James or Authorized Version of the Bible.

Copyright ©1999 Concordia Publishing House
3558 S. Jefferson Avenue, St. Louis, MO 63118-3968
Manufactured in the United States of America

1   2   3   4   5   6   7   8   9   10   09 08 07 06 05 04 03 02 01 00

Contents

Before You Begin ...

Watching the Clock contains 260 brief devotions—ideal for a year's worth of weekly workdays when you're most likely to watch the clock. Schedule—or at least spare—five minutes of your break or lunch to refresh yourself with reminders of God's love. I hope that each meditation will leave you smiling, grinning, or perhaps groaning. You'll find a little light humor and lots of Gospel—both integrated into things you observe or experience in everyday life.

If your church conducts children's sermons, the messages may include some type of object lesson. Have you noticed that the entire congregation—not only the children—pays attention during the presentation? We adults enjoy the same lively, illustrated "sermons" as children. Why not look for object lessons in everyday life?

Nearly anything can remind us of Jesus and His uncommon love. Whether it's watches or sidewalks, car washes or funeral homes, crash dummies or loons, these items can trigger an opportunity to recall what God has done for us. So look around. Look at the walls, floors, kitchen, and cabinets. Look out the window. Open your wallet or purse and inspect your pockets. What you find has potential to give you a spiritual boost—by the power of the Holy Spirit, of course. I pray this book will help too.

Speaking of the Spirit's power, you'll want to tap into it regularly. These devotions mean nothing without it. Take a few moments after each reading to thank God for His mercy and grace. Ask Him to strengthen your faith. Ask Him to help you narrow the gap between spiritual matters and the "rest of the world." In reality, God is truly in the world even if He isn't of this world. The same is true of Christians. However, we might need an occasional nudge and a timely Bible passage to remind us of that fact. You'll find both in this book. Each daily meditation includes a recommended Scripture reading, and appropriate Bible passages are included within each message.

May God bless your meditations. May you come as close to God as He is to you.

Ed Grube

1
Watching the Time

Joshua 10:6–13

WE LOOK AT IT OFTEN EACH DAY. Perhaps that's why we call timepieces "watches." We constantly watch our watches—watching for the precise time to begin or end something. Or simply watching time pass oh-so-quickly or ever-so-slowly—the difference between waiting for your turn in the dentist's chair or the interminable time remaining before you escape from it. Sometimes time is on our side. Sometimes not. At times we may envy God, whose existence is timeless. No clocks to punch, no deadlines, no dead times. But can this God of ours really understand what it's like to live in the dimension of time?

From Old Testament days on to our present day, our timeless Lord has lowered Himself to time on our terms. Once, He literally made time stand still to deliver His people from their enemies. Consider this account from Joshua 10:12–13:

> *On the day the LORD gave the Amorites over to Israel, Joshua said to the LORD in the presence of Israel: "O sun, stand still over Gibeon, O moon, over the Valley of Aijalon." So the sun stood still, and the moon stopped, till the nation avenged itself on its enemies, as it is written in the Book of Jashar. The sun stopped in the middle of the sky and delayed going down about a full day.*

"The Day the Sun Stood Still" sounds like a science fiction movie (of course, it was called "The Day the Earth Stood Still"!). But who needs fiction when we have the real thing from God's own Word? Time and again, God used time to shower His love and blessings on us.

God sent His Son at just the right time to live for a time among people. And His Son spent a tormented three hours—less than a half-day's work (unless you're hanging on a cross)—pouring out His life to save us from our sins. Then it was over. But it began again. New life. Endless life. A life we'll share free of those little regulators hugging our wrists, clinging to our walls, or glowing softly on our nightstands.

May God speed that day when time really flies—flies away for good. Time will stand still again as we enjoy the victory Christ won on that fatal and fabulous weekend so long ago. Until that time, may God keep your faith strong and eternal.

2

Take It from Smokey

Exodus 3:1–10

R EMEMBER THE SLOGAN broadcast by the spokesbear for the National Forest Service? Not only was he right, he also had something in common with Moses, spokesperson for God.

"Only you can prevent forest fires," said Smokey. Moses might have laughed because what he saw defied all logic. Exodus 3:2 tells the story: "There the angel of the LORD appeared to him in flames of fire from within a bush. Moses saw that though the bush was on fire it did not burn up."

Understandably, Moses was curious about this incident. As Moses inched closer, the burning bush started talking to him. The flaming shrub was really God in disguise. God had a hot message for Moses. He wanted Moses to serve Him with fervent, fiery passion. You may know the rest of the story—how Moses led God's people out of slavery to the land God had promised. But that's another story. Let's not forget Smokey.

While we can't consider Smokey some furry theologian, the truth of his slogan applies to spiritual matters, as well as to forest fires. We can indeed snuff out the Spirit's fire. And the devil (uncharacteristically?) is willing to help extinguish the blaze. We can keep our Bibles closed, skip church, neglect prayer, live self-centered lives, refuse to forgive others, develop self-reliant intellect, and forfeit hope in difficult times.

Frightening as that prospect is, God has promised that "neither height nor depth, nor anything else in all creation, will be able to separate us from the love of God that is in Christ Jesus our Lord" (Romans 8:39). God has sent the Holy Spirit to set Christians on fire with the Word of God and the love of Jesus. Nobody can extinguish our spiritual fire without our consent.

We need not fear that God will stop loving us. Nor should we worry that Jesus will somehow take back the salvation that He won on the cross. No matter how we anger or disappoint God, He always stands ready to forgive and keep the fire burning in our soul. The Holy Spirit fans the flames of faith with God's Word as we hear and read it.

So keep on burning. Let your smoke get in other people's eyes so they see your fire too. Tell them how they, too, can burn with passion and desire that last forever.

3

Waiting to Record

3 John 5–11

On a scale of one to 10, how would you rate your proficiency with technology? Think of one as owning your VCR for six years and it's still flashing 12:00. Think of 10 as having successfully programmed the VCR to record a full month of shows that you'll miss because you're watching other programs. Good thing this devotion won't be as difficult to understand as your VCR manual!

We humans compare favorably with VCRs. We record in our minds and hearts much of what happens around us. Acquaintances, observations, experiences, and desires often play the role of program, while our behavior plays back that which we've recorded. Our behavior or lifestyle becomes a function of what we've seen, heard, or fantasized. God has something to say about that in 3 John 11:

> Dear friend, do not imitate what is evil but what is good. Anyone who does what is good is from God. Anyone who does what is evil has not seen God.

Christians are tuned to record the "good from God." Like VCRs, we're woefully unable to tune to the right "station" ourselves. But the Holy Spirit programs us with suitable channels. We're tuned to God's love through the life, death, and resurrection of Jesus Christ. We record His life in our very souls, and just as a videotape sucks up every pixel on the screen, we are equipped to imitate our Savior and God. Just as the tape is a duplicate of the original program, we are copies of Jesus.

What does it mean to be a copy of Jesus—to be an "imitator" of Him? First, it means that we're filled to overflowing with God's grace and mercy. Second, that overflow is meant to spread like oil over all with whom we come in contact. Third, as imitators, we want to know and do what God the Father asks of us. We want to serve Him. We want to hate sin.

The Holy Spirit has filled each of us with faith. Some of us may be half-hour shows while others may run for two hours. Whatever the degree of faith, we Christians are part of an eternal series that the Producer will never cancel. God has recorded His Son's goodness and righteousness on us. We have the power to do much more than flash 12:00 the rest of our lives. And that's a long, long time!

4

A Way Out

Luke 21:29–36

THE FIRE WAS ESPECIALLY SMOKY AND HOT. The hotel's guests crawled through the hallway until they saw the faint glow of an exit sign—the door to a stairway and escape! Those who made it to the fresh air gratefully recalled the room instructions that normally are so easy to ignore. "Locate the nearest exit before occupying the room." Such a simple task. Look down the hallway for the familiar exit sign, and mark it in your memory. Sadly, not all the guests heeded the advice. When the heat was on, their cool was off.

How good for us that Jesus gave safety instructions! In Luke 21:36, He says, "Be always on the watch, and pray that you may be able to escape all that is about to happen, and that you may be able to stand before the Son of Man."

This valuable counsel may sound a bit ominous. But if we're not offended or frozen in fright over common safety warnings, then this Word from God need not lurk on the dark side either. Just as we need to prepare ourselves for fire, we also need to be ready to "escape all that is about to happen."

What is "about to happen"? Nothing short of the end of the world. (Just what you needed to lighten up your day!) "Now wait," you may say. "Nobody escapes the end of the world. Everyone will see God face to face—believers and unbelievers alike."

Yes, it's true that Judgment Day will fully involve all creation. But if you're reading this book, be confident that you will escape God's wrath. No, this book doesn't contain an asbestos shield; you're probably reading it because you're a Christian. Maybe a very strong one. Maybe a very feeble one. One thing is certain, however; you're equipped for escape. The Holy Spirit has brought the Gospel into your heart where it flourishes or, perhaps frequently, fumbles. But if you know Jesus Christ died for your sins and rose for your victory, then you're prepared to escape.

When the final trumpets sound and all around you quakes and burns, look for the exit sign. It will look just like Jesus. It will glow gloriously through the flames and smoke. You're sure to make a safe exit in the arms of Christ.

Bleep Bleep

Romans 3:10–20

W HEN YOU THINK ABOUT IT, car horns often are the equivalents of mechanical expletives, aren't they? They should go "Bleep! Bleep!" instead of "Beep! Beep!" Too bad we can't delete them like they sometimes do profanity on public broadcasts.

Car horns often react to our steering-wheel evil. They let us know when we've done something wrong—or at least when someone accuses us of derelict driving. Next time you hear a horn bleeping at you, think about Romans 3:20, which says, "Therefore no one will be declared righteous in His sight by observing the law; rather, through the law we become conscious of sin."

God's Law is like a car horn. It accuses us, and its accusations are always accurate. The Law points out every way we err. Sometimes it makes us feel guilty; at other times it fuels our anger. If we're in the right mood (or should we say the *wrong* mood?), the Law makes us want to give up—give up trying to meet God's uncompromising demands for perfect obedience.

The only way to avoid the bleeping horns that expose our sins is never to be born. Too late for that now. But that's okay because there is a better option. Jesus silenced the horns. He quieted them when every sin for every time blared in His ears as He hung on the cross and died. No doubt it was a very silent Sunday when He left the tomb to visit His faulty friends, whom He had every right to honk at. We're among those friends, too, but we need not fear retribution. Jesus brings only His cheer and love.

You say you still hear horns blaring? That's the devil honking. He's like those impatient drivers who bellow at you even when you're obeying the law. Satan wants to keep you feeling guilty. He wants you to be more like him. When he honks, do what you do to impatient drivers. (Well, maybe not.) Get out of his way. Let the devil race by you. Your leader is Jesus Christ, Satan slayer and silencer of the Law's bleeping horns. Jesus loves you and will take you where you're going. And you'll get there exactly when He expects you.

6

Guilty but Blameless

1 Corinthians 1:4–9

APPARENTLY THE NEWS ANNOUNCER thought nothing was peculiar when she reported that a counselor pled "guilty but blameless" to charges that she had bilked an agency of nearly $1 million. The counselor claimed to be suffering from drug misuse and other emotional disorders that drove her to cheat on her billing. Good thing justice is blind. It probably wouldn't want to see things like this!

Before we get too self-righteous, we need to think of ourselves. We can be exceptionally good at assigning blame, especially when assigning it to others. We also can be deplorably good at blaming ourselves and suffering the guilt that accompanies blame. No one can deny that there is plenty of blame to go around because so much is wrong with life.

Let's not get mired in the slop of hopelessness, though. The apostle Paul said, "He will keep you strong to the end, so that you will be blameless on the day of our Lord Jesus Christ" (1 Corinthians 1:8). Maybe there is such a situation as "guilty but blameless"!

Everyone is guilty of sin whether they admit it or not. Believers fall into that category, too, and we have nothing better than flimsy excuses to proffer. That's okay because we don't need excuses. We have something better. We have Jesus Christ.

Guilty though we are, we also are blameless. Remember our Counselor? Jesus cleared us of guilt so God will find us blameless when He judges the world. God will not think it ironic that believers are both guilty and blameless. He knows what happened to our guilt. He knows that we store up a new batch of sin every day of our imperfect lives on earth. He hears us when we beg His pardon day after day for the sake of Jesus, who suffered, died, and defeated sin's power for us. God declares us blameless every day, though we're as guilty as sin.

Judged blameless, we have some responsibilities. Chief among them is the call to forgive others freely—to declare them blameless—regardless of fault. Because God unfairly holds us blameless, we are free to forgive and extend to others that same grace. Even if they neither deserve nor ask for it.

Justice is indeed blind. Good thing God is just.

7
Almost Persuaded

Acts 26:1–32

SOME PEOPLE BUY NEWSPAPERS only for the ads. It's hard to understand, but then the ads are probably as believable as the news! At least they have something good to say, and they usually say it in large letters. Just look at the car ads in any major newspaper. They advertise shockingly low prices for the car of your dreams. But instead of decimal points, the ads usually have * ** *** **** ***** behind them. Each asterisk leads you to microscopic print secluded somewhere on the page. Each stands for limitations on the deal. Those ads can nearly persuade normal but suspicious buyers, while those less skeptical make the cost of the ads justifiable.

Ancient King Agrippa was the target of some classy advertising by Paul. He listened to eloquent, honest testimony, yet Agrippa was more likely to buy a dream car direct from the Saturday morning ads than he was to believe the truth. Agrippa said, " 'Do you think that in such a short time you can persuade me to be a Christian?' " Paul replied, "Short time or long—I pray God that not only you but all who are listening to me today may become what I am, except for these chains" (Acts 26:28–29).

How persuasive are you? Do you place Jesus on a pedestal wherever you go? Would you succeed in the advertising world as a walking billboard? Hard questions, aren't they? Yet we can tap the same source of confidence that Paul had 2,000 years ago. The Holy Spirit is the highest-powered ad agency in the universe, and He wants us to work for Him.

What a product we have to sell! Who wouldn't want it? Do you feel your enthusiasm growing? You want to throw down this book and get right out there and … Wait a minute. We need to get real. If Paul couldn't persuade Agrippa, how can we expect success?

We can't expect success—at least not a success that we can always see. As you talk and act as a Christian, people will take notice. Some will want to know more, and there's your big chance. Some people will ignore you. Others will think your news is too good to be true. Don't let that discourage you. Proclaim Jesus' love for the world in BIG LETTERS. And you don't need a single asterisk!

8

Change

Numbers 23:15–21

HOW WOULD YOU DEFINE CHANGE? *Change* is … *Change* is … Having trouble? The best definition of *change* is found in your pocket or purse. You know, two dimes and a nickel? The book *Future Shock* claimed that even *change* is changing, and it is right. You have to spend five times as much money to get the same change that you received 10 years ago.

Sometimes change is bad. Newspapers report changes that adversely affect people—crimes, accidents, obituaries, and the scores of your favorite losing team, to name a few. You easily could add to the list with more personal accounts of unwanted changes—jobs lost, marriages broken, health failing, relatives rebelling, etc.

Sometimes change is only what you make of it. The Internet is widely assailed as a tool of those who wish to poison hearts and minds. Yet that same Internet carries many Christian sites that unite believers and evangelize. The same could be said of books, magazines, television, nuclear energy, and the supermarket.

The Scriptures speak often of change—and changelessness. Consider this from Numbers 23:19–20: "God is not a man that He should lie, nor a son of man, that He should change His mind. Does He speak and then not act? Does He promise and not fulfill? I have received a command to bless; He has blessed, and I cannot change it."

God is no "small change." In fact, He isn't change at all. God is never bad nor is He neutral. While some may foster evil in His name, He doesn't support them. God keeps His promises. He's proved that many times—through Noah, Abraham, Jesus, and (insert your name).

You have the blessing of God. The devil and his agents would love to hear God curse sinners and give up on them. God knows we deserve it! Despite sinfulness, God refuses to give up sinners if they cling to Him with even the smallest fleck of faith. And no one can change that.

What Good News we have because we know that God's love doesn't change! But because God doesn't change, we should. God's love through Jesus Christ changes us, drives us to hate sin and live the way He wants us to live.

Next time some coins cross your palm, think about the change Jesus brought to you. Thank Him for it. Now that really makes some sense.

Act of God

Psalm 100:1–5

THE ARKANSAS LEGISLATURE didn't like the terminology, so they struck it from common use in legal documents. An "act of God," they said, gives God a bad name for something He didn't do.

They replaced the term with "act of nature," though they might have shown more candor and termed such random destruction "acts of Satan." Perhaps they thought it risky to offend him too.

"Why, God?" is a common question after disasters, natural or human-made. The emotions of a tragic moment tempt people either to blame or to question God. We know that terror and destruction afflict the world. Evil events are the result of sin, and we can expect calamity and adversity to affect believers and nonbelievers alike. (Keep in mind that God showers both with blessings too.)

The psalmist says, "For the LORD is good and His love endures forever; His faithfulness continues through all generations" (Psalm 100:5). Our good God has not shielded us from the consequences of sin. Rather, He uses those occasions to draw us closer to Himself.

The Old Testament contains many examples of how God faithfully cared for His people though they were beset with grief and distress. He demonstrated His power by strengthening the Israelites throughout their four centuries of slavery. (Talk about getting physically and mentally prepared for an arduous trip in the wilderness!) When the Israelites were threatened with annihilation from myriad enemies, God always saved a few of the faithful to carry His Word and promise to future generations. How precious that Word became when endangered with extinction! People clung desperately to it because it was the only possession they had.

Later, we marvel at God's promise come true in the birth of baby Jesus. We hear how He lived a perfect life—for our sake. Then, tragedy. He was wrongfully executed, but it was for our sake. The sky turned black on that Friday. The earth quaked, and the temple suffered major damage to its finest curtain. Then all was quiet. God's Son was dead.

But not for long. Some distraught women discovered the truth in the quiet hours a couple days after the horrific spiritual storm. An empty tomb. A living Jesus. A promise of eternal life. Now there's an act of God!

10

Ladders

Genesis 28:10–17

SOME SAY IT'S BAD LUCK to walk under a ladder. To me, it seems more risky to climb one. There was that crisp, fall day when I climbed to the roof bent on relieving the gutters of their collection of crisp color. I got up just fine, but the ladder wouldn't let me down. It stood there and defied me, teasing me to enjoy fall on its terms. It wasn't until my family returned from shopping and encouraged me (with raucous laughter) that I had the shame, er ... courage, to descend.

As much as ladders cause me nightmares, Jacob had sweet dreams about his. Perhaps he hoped to dream of a fluffy pillow and a downy bed as he arranged the rock beneath his head. You probably know the story. Jacob saw angels walking up and down the ladder, and the Lord Himself was at the top.

God gave Jacob something better than a pleasant dream. He gave Jacob a vision for the future. Jacob could be certain that his days on the run would end. God said, "I am with you and will watch over you wherever you go, and I will bring you back to this land. I will not leave you until I have done what I have promised you" (Genesis 28:15). Jacob, a scheming, cheating sinner, received God's personal attention. Undoubtedly, Jacob repented of his sins. While he might fear his relationships with brother Esau, Jacob's dream assured him of God's forgiveness.

How often do we climb ladders in fear? We fall into deep pits of sin (many of which we dug personally) and struggle vainly to escape to higher living. Jacob's story suggests something different: Rest in the middle of your clash with sin. Rest on Jesus. He's at the top of our ladder with comfort and promise.

Jesus knows our sinfulness, and He accepts our repentance. What a life He has planned for us! His blessings began even before we were born when He knew who we were and what we needed. He has watched us fall to sin, and He's repeatedly picked us up with His love and forgiveness. We continue through life confident that we belong to Him, right now, here on earth. And we look forward to that day when He will take us up that ladder to heaven. And we'll never come down either.

Leave Your Message at the Tone

Nehemiah 1:5–7

ALEXANDER GRAHAM BELL invented the telephone. Some evidence suggests that his teenage son was an inventor too. Tradition hints that he developed the first busy signal! As you have experienced, telephones have been busy ever since.

Recent years have seen a proliferation of area codes as the number of devices using telephone technology increases beyond the imagination of communications engineers. Today you can call almost anyplace. Just the other day I must have misdialed and reached a number on the ocean floor. There was a crab on the other end of the line. Which brings us to the subject of answering machines.

It's a bit hard to believe that answering machines were invented by someone who didn't want people to miss a call. More likely, the inventor didn't want to answer the phone during dinner. Think for a moment (before the phone rings) about what it would be like if God used an answering machine. We would face the same uncertainty and anxiety we experience when we trust an important message to a tiny audiotape. Will God check for messages? Did I speak clearly enough? Will He check caller ID to see if He should pay attention to me?

The Bible is our 411 for calls to God. Psalm 4:3 says, "Know that the LORD has set apart the godly for Himself; the LORD will hear when I call to Him."

Perhaps your calls to the Lord are frequent, or maybe you call Him only when you need something special. Regardless of how often you talk to God, He always recognizes your voice. Believers always get God's personal attention, even if the conversation seems one-sided. God invites, welcomes, and commands our calls, though we can be cranky, distracted, demanding, unreasonable, distrustful, and whiny.

One benefit of daily, routine calls on God is that we get to say things we might not think of during a crisis. Opportunity abounds to express our gratitude for His love and forgiveness. We can tell Him how much we appreciate all those blessings that He continues to send, though sometimes we take them for granted. We can chat about the problems others have and ask Him to give them a call.

Call God often. Listen for His calls too. The Operator is waiting.

Grow Down

Matthew 18:1–4

HAVE YOU DISCOVERED the secret of staying young? Lie about your age! Of course, there are those who look forward to growing old(er) and finally reaching their eternal rest. (Then again, some employees have achieved that while still living.) The Bible is an excellent source of information about living forever. The mystery isn't in finding ways to grow older but in ways to grow younger.

It wasn't in the context of living forever or finding a fountain of youth that Jesus spoke the words of Matthew 18:3, unless, of course, we realize that the disciples were acting like children. Instead of telling them to grow up, however, Jesus said they should grow down. Actually, He said, "I tell you the truth, unless you change and become like little children, you will never enter the kingdom of heaven."

The message is clear. Disciples need to adopt the genuine humility of children. Children have much about which to be humble. The beauty of that humility is that they're naively modest about it. They are not consciously aware of their humility, so they live naturally with the condition. You don't hear them saying things such as "It's with great humility that I accept this racy, red bicycle on my birthday." They simply ride off with a smile stretching from training wheel to training wheel.

That's how we are called to live with the faith God gives us. Grow down and act like a kid who just got the gift she has always wanted. Free of thoughts about being deserving or undeserving, worthy or unworthy, we can romp and carouse in the generosity of God's love and blessings. We joyously accept our role in life because nothing could be better than living with the special gift that never grows old—the gift of salvation and eternal life.

True humility probably involves a little selfishness. Oh, not the bad kind, rather a selfishness that approaches a gift-giver with bold confidence, assured that a gift is forthcoming. That's exactly how we can approach God. Despite how bad we've been, we can approach the lap of our heavenly Father, knowing that He won't reject us—that He wants us to come to Him in faith.

Grow down. You won't have to lie about your age to keep from growing old. In truth, you're getting younger every day. You're growing down until that time when you'll be born again, never to grow old.

13
Window Decorations

Joshua 2

THEY COME IN MANY SIZES and designs depicting everything from hummingbirds to flying fish to the skyline of beautiful, downtown Holyrood, Kansas (a general store dwarfed by colossal waves of grain). Sun catchers make a statement. Occasionally, they evoke statements too—such as when the little suction cups malfunction in the middle of the night and you think an invader is crawling through your window!

What sun catcher would you design to tell the world you believe in Jesus? What would you want Jesus to see when He returns on Judgment Day?

The Old Testament relates the story of a prostitute named Rahab whose fame involved protecting some spies. She hung something in her window—something that would save her life when Israel invaded and destroyed Jericho. It's found in Joshua 2:17–18a: "The men said to her, 'This oath you made us swear will not be binding on us unless, when we enter the land, you have tied this scarlet cord in the window through which you let us down.' "

Rahab's red rope identified her as someone to be saved. It made a statement both to the invading army and to herself. Every time she looked out her window, she saw that scarlet ribbon shimmering in the sun or standing in joyful contrast to cloudy gloom. She believed the army would come and victoriously destroy the evil that surrounded her.

While we might wish to announce our Christianity to passersby via sun catchers, we might consider the way we live as the best window dressing. Our lifestyle provides a window to our soul. When others hear how we talk, see how we act, notice how we forgive, and accept how we love, they can't help but see the Son shining on these symbols of His influence in our lives.

Like Rahab, we expect something of an invasion. Jesus will come back, and at His Word, every wicked and evil thing will be utterly destroyed—except us. Jesus will see our scarlet cord and recognize us as numbered among those cleansed by His blood. He will recall how He brought us to faith and how we harbored Him in our heart, waiting for the day when He would return to make life better.

Hang something in the window of your soul. A big, bright thankful heart would be a good way to begin.

14
See Food

Luke 24:1–29

I EMBRACE A DEFINITE PREFERENCE for a see-food diet. I eat nearly every food I see. If only we could treat food like we treat people and avoid those that disagree with us! It seems the only wise move is to adopt a diet. At the very least, it'll make us gain weight more slowly.

The Bible contains many references to food. We might say food really is the way to a person's heart as we note how Jesus served thousands a satisfying meal while they listened to Him preach. Food was a daily reminder of God's menu of love when He daily fed morsels of manna to the children of Israel. And instead of feeding the birds, Elijah was fed by them as God took care of his physical needs. Of course, who can forget the bread and wine—the body and blood—at Jesus' last meal with the disciples?

Two men, citizens of Emmaus, enjoyed one particular see-food platter as they ate with a stranger. Luke says, "When He was at the table with them, He took bread, gave thanks, broke it and began to give it to them. Then their eyes were opened and they recognized Him, and He disappeared from their sight" (Luke 24:30–31). The mysterious "He" was Jesus. What made this experience so remarkable was not the eerie disappearance of Jesus after the meal, but the eye-popping revelation when He prayed and served the bread. The two men saw Jesus. Now that's our kind of see food!

Obviously, the Lord's Supper provides a regular feast that keeps our eyes focused on the Savior. Jesus supplies us with another kind of food too. Words. His words in the Bible. They're not the kind of words we're forced to eat. (We do enough of that!) Instead, we experience their sweet-sour character as we consume them to nurture our souls. God's sour words sear our souls like acid when they reveal how willingly we gorge ourselves on sin. Then, like delicacies from an opulent French menu, God heaps our plate with fresh words of forgiveness and refreshing renewal.

We may describe God's menu using mouth-watering terms, but Jesus kept it simple. He compared Himself to bread, widely known as the "staff of life." And what delicious bread He is! He gives sight to the soul, revealing to eyes once blind that He is our living God. Finally—a diet worth keeping!

How Old Are We?

Genesis 1:26–31

T HE OLDER WE GET, the more things ache. Especially new ideas. Here is one of them: In 1997, scientists discovered a skull and leg bone in Kenya that not only startled them, but caused them to rethink some treasured ideas about the age and evolution of humans. Mounting evidence suggests that humans started looking and acting like humans sooner than was thought humanly possible.

Here is another scientific fact: A 1997 survey of scientists disclosed that only 40 percent believe in some kind of god. Furthermore, this percentage remains unchanged from a 1916 survey. What has changed, however, is public reaction. In 1916, the public was shocked and alarmed. Today, it barely scores an emotional ripple.

But back to our age. The discovery in Kenya may tug at our spiritual nerves and grate on our scriptural intellect, but perhaps we should find some ironic comfort in the situation. Modern science is grudgingly discovering what we believers have known for centuries. Modern human beings began as modern human beings. The Bible tells all: "Then God said, 'Let us make man in Our image, in Our likeness, and let them rule over the fish of the sea and the birds of the air, over the livestock, over all the earth, and over all the creatures that move along the ground.' So God created man in His own image, in the image of God He created him; male and female He created them" (Genesis 1:26–27).

Rather than revile scientists who postulate unbiblical ideas, we can pray for them. How sad to earn advanced degrees and sacrifice so much for the sake of understanding humankind. It's especially disheartening when all that's needed is what many of us already have—faith and Scripture.

Science would counter that faith and Scripture are mere beliefs, figments of human hope for comfort and immortality. Better we trust in some bones and mathematical projections! Tragically, scientists convince others that religion is impotent and foolish. Yet God gave us such power! Did you read how He created us in His own image? We have to admit, though, that human history clearly refutes this. Sin has so poisoned humanity that we bear little resemblance to God. But thanks to Jesus, our blemishes are only skin deep, and we remain God's creation. Someday the scientists will be right—we'll be billions of years old!

Jars

2 Corinthians 4:5–11

HAVE YOU NOTICED how some people collect jars? You'll find them (the jars and the collectors) in antique shops, skillfully buying and selling these precious collectibles. And why not? The ancestors of modern jars—urns and other vessels—festoon the shelves of many museums.

We collect jars at my house too. Most are on shelves in the cabinets or refrigerator. Some appear quite ancient, like that jar of Oil of Kumquat. Others contain happily reproducing bacteria and plant life (isolated as they are in the dark hinterland of the refrigerator's shelf). Hey! Close the door and turn off the lights. You want the kids to see?

God told the apostle Paul to call each believer a jar. We read in 2 Corinthians 4:7: "But we have this treasure in jars of clay to show that this all-surpassing power is from God and not from us."

Jars of clay weren't worth any more in Paul's time than jars of glass are today. They were simple containers. What was on the inside was far more valuable and important than the jar itself. That's good news for us Christian "jars."

Our bodies are worth little, subject as they are to chipping, cracking, and gradual deterioration. Someday they'll be so worthless that they will end up buried in landfills we politely call cemeteries. Yet the faith and power that lives and breathes inside us will live forever. We contain, as Paul calls it, a treasure within ourselves. That fabulous fortune is nothing less than Jesus Christ.

Like all jars, we get jostled, dropped, or simply develop loose covers. Sickness, family problems, accidents, and other tragedies dribble and spill us out of our bodies and senses. Even this can be a blessing! As our treasure escapes its boundaries, we have opportunity to witness our faith despite our frailties. In fact, it's during those troubled times that our testimony about God's love can have the greatest impact. Besides, our treasure will never leave us empty.

Undoubtedly, we want to retain this treasure forever. But we know our bodies will not last that long. Isn't it just like our loving God to recycle the old into something new? Although our old jars are crushed into dust by sin, God will make that dust into a better jar—one whose quality we can't begin to imagine. That makes us part of a priceless collection too.

17
Guide to Trees

Isaiah 65:17–25

W HEN IT COMES TO TREES, some people can't tell an oak from a northern pike—probably because pike are in the perch family and perches obviously come from trees. Having established my credibility as a tree expert, expect a meditational miniseries for the next several entries.

The Bible leaves us with the distinct impression that trees were one of God's favorite creations. Not only are trees mentioned often in a variety of contexts, but no fewer than 26 specific varieties made the pages of Scripture. Wood you believe it? (Okay—no more puns.)

We often marvel at the magnificence of trees, whether it's the age and height of colossal redwoods, the girth of stout oaks, or the colors of massive maples. Trees, whether brawny or scrawny, contribute to feelings of well-being too. Consider these encouraging words from Isaiah 65:22: "No longer will they build houses and others live in them, or plant and others eat. For as the days of a tree, so will be the days of My people; My chosen ones will long enjoy the works of their hands."

Long live the tree! Long live we! And it's all because of God's love. Though God certainly loved trees, He loves us more. He gave us trees for food, shade, construction, beauty, and forgiveness of sins. No, trees aren't some new sacrament. But one of God's superb creations figured prominently in the death of His Son. We behold the tree not only as a symbol of lengthy life, but also as a symbol of death. We can praise God that life and death are as intimately entwined as ivy on tree bark.

The prophet Isaiah addressed God's people during a terrible time in their history. Isaiah voiced mostly fearful and tragic words, but God also gave him words of comfort for the faithful few. Today's reading tells believers of all eras that their lives will be as the days of the tree—long and fruitful, though not devoid of weathering.

God made us strong enough to stand firm despite infestations of sin, as well as outright attacks by the vicious, voracious devil. He takes us through the seasons of life, pruning away those parts that threaten our existence. He nourishes us with Word and Sacrament and draws us upward to Himself. We have a long way to grow, but we have forever to get there. And that leaves Satan time to count our rings!

18

Apple Trees

Song of Songs 2:1–13

PEOPLE WHO DON'T GET into nature may picture apple trees differently than you and I do. Perhaps they've seen apples growing neatly in piles and rows about 18 inches wide by 36 inches high. This is perfect for picking, especially because the lighting is good, the fruit glossy, and the temperature carefully controlled. Better yet, this orchard has a forest of other fruits and vegetables nearby, just waiting to be gathered inside plastic bags.

You may recall an old song entitled "Don't Sit under the Apple Tree with Anyone Else but Me." The lyrics stem from wartime sentiment that craved romantic loyalties while lovers were separated. The Bible's Song of Songs speaks of apple trees and faithful love too: "Like an apple tree among the trees of the forest is my lover among the young men. I delight to sit in his shade, and his fruit is sweet to my taste" (Song of Songs 2:3).

Song of Songs compares the love between God and His people to the romantically poetic love between a man and a woman. Later, in the New Testament, the church is called the bride and Christ the bridegroom. How appropriate that we consider our relationship to Jesus in these terms!

We sit shaded by the One who loves us beyond any earthly love we can experience. As good as that shade is, we often wander away, seeking the shade of lesser gods who promise wealth, power, freedom, or other forms of self-fulfillment. When our hopes wither and die, Jesus remains, beckoning us to return to the shelter of His love and promise. When we return to His welcome shade, we wonder how we could have left Him in the first place. Until another temptation seduces us.

"Don't Sit under the Apple Tree with Anyone Else but Me" might be a good song for Christians. Jesus wants us to stay with Him, and the love He offers surpasses any offered elsewhere. But He also wants us to remain faithful to Him. He gives us power to resist sitting with anyone else. He feeds us with His sweet love, compassion, and care. Jesus listens to our most personal thoughts and innermost desires. Indeed, He knows them even if we don't speak them. His faithfulness to us through good times and bad assures us that we always can trust Him. So sit under an apple tree, and take a Friend.

Evergreen

Psalm 1:1–6

OFFERING MORE PROOF of my expertise in treeology, I can tell you that *evergreen* is the scientific name for a group of trees that are ever green. Even more important, rarely is science so clear on the meaning of a scientific name.

Of course, *evergreen* really isn't the name of a specific tree. Most evergreens are members of the pine family, and the most famous member of the pine family is the Christmas tree. Nothing beats the aroma—to say nothing of the aura—of a Christmas tree. While research in this area is somewhat suspect, many people like to think that Martin Luther was the first to drag a tree through the snowy fields of Germany and into his home. He had a good idea. What better tree to "plant" in your home than one that points toward heaven?

Evergreens are great symbols of faith. Their ability to remain green during cold winters and hot summers reminds us of the characteristics of enduring faith. Let's probe this idea more completely. A good place to begin research is with the Bible—Psalm 1:3 in particular: "He is like a tree planted by streams of water, which yields its fruit in season and whose leaf does not wither. Whatever he does prospers."

Psalm 1 comments on blessings that accompany those who "delight in the law of the LORD." Such people are compared to a healthy, happy, fruitful evergreen tree planted in the best possible location. The water flowing nearby provides the food and moisture necessary for a productive life. The meaning of the psalm is that when Jesus is in our lives, when the Holy Spirit is at work in us, we are fed with sufficient love and wisdom to support a productive faith.

Christians aren't, however, "ever green." The devil and our sinful desires make us brittle and dry, ready to snap or burn or drop our faith, leaving us naked to destruction. That's a good time to remember that Jesus is "ever green"—without exception. He remains faithful to us, and the proof is that He sacrificed Himself for us while we were still sinners.

What consolation we have because we know Christ's love and sacrifice! We can use it to needle the devil every time He tries to chop us down.

Climbing Trees

Luke 19:1–9

THE HUGE SYCAMORE in front of the house needed trimming, and the wedding reception at the home across the street needed cheap entertainment. The situation was custom-made for a warm, sunny Saturday.

Propping up the largest stepladder I could muster, I climbed to the top step, saw in hand. (Don't try this at home, especially within sight of a wedding reception.) I attacked a large limb, and my labored grunting arrested the wedding guests' attention. Only when the limb surrendered and fell did I realize my balance depended on a left hand clinging to the now-departed limb. The saw was in my right hand. Having quick reflexes, I dropped the saw and raised both hands to the limb above the stricken one, kicking away the ladder in the process. Good choice. The audience clapped and laughed as I dangled from the branch trying to plan my drop so I would descend between the sides of the ladder that was waiting on the ground to swallow me. But enough about sycamores and me.

Sycamores make good trees for climbing, despite their lack of cooperation for trimming. The Bible lends credence to that contention when Luke reports an incident involving a short man: "So he ran ahead and climbed a sycamore-fig tree to see Him, since Jesus was coming that way" (Luke 19:4).

Zacchaeus wanted to see Jesus. Nothing would stand in his way, including the crowds along the street, craning their necks for a closer look at the miracle worker. Short on stature, but long on problem solving, Zacchaeus ascended the now famous sycamore. He accomplished his goal. He even made eye contact with Jesus, who, to the amazement of the crowd, stopped and addressed the man infamous for his tax transgressions. The encounter was friendly. Jesus invited Himself to Zacchaeus' place.

Witnesses didn't like what they saw. No supposedly righteous, holy person would ever personally visit brazen sinners. But these witnesses didn't know what we know and what Zacchaeus hoped. Jesus came for sinners. He came into their homes, into their leper colonies, into their "red-light districts," not to join them in sin, but to save them from it.

Get a closer look at Jesus. He came for us, and He wants to stay at our homes. Better yet, He came into our hearts and made us believers just like Zacchaeus so we'll never have to take our lives out on a limb again.

Red Delicious or Red Deceptive?

Matthew 12:33–37

IN THIS LAST INSTALLMENT ON TREES, we'll consider fruit. Fresh pears or peaches recently plucked from heavy branches yield extraordinary flavor. Allow the fruit to linger on the tree and it will drop to the ground. Such fruit may be easy to pick, but the taste is mushy. Worse, you may find yourself munching on a den of insects bent on eating themselves out of house and home.

Jesus had something to say about choice and crummy fruit in Matthew 12:33. He said, "Make a tree good and its fruit will be good, or make a tree bad and its fruit will be bad, for a tree is recognized by its fruit." We know, of course, that Jesus wasn't lecturing about orchards. He was talking about people.

Imagine a vast forest, home to a sizable variety of trees. Each one is a person created by God to glorify Him and to serve others. Your fruit is whatever you produce to meet God's purpose for you. You don't have to think too hard to see where this is going, do you?

Obviously, trees—er, people—sometimes disappoint God by their words and actions. Less obviously, some inadequate trees produce what appear to be good works but their motivation is all wrong, and the fruit's appearance is deceptive. It's hard to condemn such fruit because by human standards it appears to do much good in the world. But any motivation less than love of and love for Jesus Christ is only so much wax.

What kind of fruit hangs from your branches? Are you laden with kindness, forgiveness, and compassion? Do you droop under a load of encouraging words and cheerful smiles? Are you chock full of deeds such as sending cards to shut-ins, calling sick neighbors, mowing a little extra grass on your neighbor's side of the property line, playing your TV a bit softer so the kids in the next apartment can do their homework, or working harder than the boss expects?

We can't produce even one fruit of faith by ourselves, much less an abundance. But God gives us the ability to produce because He has perfected us in the saving grace of Jesus. And the Holy Spirit keeps us well-rooted in Scripture so we can grow strong and fruitful. With help like that, we can produce enough fruit to open a branch office!

22

Fresh Fish

John 21:1–14

A CCORDING TO the *New England Journal of Medicine*, a 30-year study of nearly 2,000 people indicated that regularly eating fish cuts the risk of heart attack by 42 percent. Before you stuff yourself to the gills with sardines, note that similar studies showed no proof that eating lots of fish actually prevented heart attacks. So on a scale of one to 10, how do you rate fish?

Lacking research, people in Jesus' time appreciated the nutritional value of fish. So significant were fish that early Christians drew them in the sand to identify themselves as believers. That's not so strange when we remember how Jesus called His disciples "fishers of men" and showed them how much they could catch—with Him as their guide. The scene is described in John 21:5–6: "He called out to them, 'Friends, haven't you any fish?' 'No,' they answered. He said, 'Throw your net on the right side of the boat and you will find some.' When they did, they were unable to haul the net in because of the large number of fish."

Over the years, God has guided a whole fleet of "fishermen" in finding bigger and better catches. I'm not sure how the fish population compares with the human population, but we're talking a cavernous creel! Praise God that you're part of the catch.

Imagine that! God knew where you were, and He wanted you. Of course, God is good at that because He made you and cares for you, but it's mind-boggling nonetheless. God loved you so much that He chose you to be a prize catch—one that He could point to and say, "That one is Mine!" You're one that didn't get away only to face the snapping teeth of Satan. God caught you and you're a keeper.

Now you're a fisher too. You know that phrase "There's a lot of fish in the sea"? It's true. They might be hiding out in the home next door or huddled tightly in a school. You might find them lurking in shadows or openly sunning themselves. One thing is true: You have the right bait. Dangle the Gospel in front of them. Put some action into your faith. Lure them with love. Then draw a fish in the sand together. Or even in the dust on your desk!

No Thanks

Colossians 4:2–6

GRATITUDE IS RARE. This was proven recently by two medical emergencies witnessed on public transportation. The bus was crammed with people swaying chaotically in the aisle as the vehicle lurched to start or stop. A skinny, sick-looking man boarded the bus and slithered his way down the aisle. Suddenly, a middle-aged woman stood up and offered the man her seat. He fainted. When he regained consciousness, he said, "Thank you." Then she fainted!

Godly people know they have much for which to be thankful. But sometimes we forget. Some of us forget often. Like ill-mannered children, we offer no thanks—and perhaps feel no thankfulness—for the many blessings of God. When that happens, we confess our ungratefulness and receive God's forgiveness. (Then, at the very least, we can be thankful that only God knows everything about us!)

Whoever wrote to the New Testament Hebrew people had this to say about thanksgiving: "Through Jesus, therefore, let us continually offer to God a sacrifice of praise—the fruit of lips that confess His name" (Hebrews 13:15). Note the word *continually*. Our other Bible reading for today hinted at how to give thanks continually. While prayers of gratitude and praise always need to be in our hearts and on our tongues, another way to thank God is through our actions. Colossians tells us to be wise and keep our conversations "full of grace." The Holy Spirit gives us power—energized by Jesus' life and death and life again—to live our praise to God for His goodness.

Do you need a few solid reasons for gratitude? Dig out last year's tax return. Did you make enough money to pay taxes? There's a good reason right there. (Even if you owe lots of people lots of money, you can be thankful you're not them!) Now step right up to a mirror. Put your nose close to the glass and watch. See any condensation? Yep, there's another reason for gratitude.

As you search your daily life for reasons to be thankful, remember what Jesus did for you. Then it will be easier to do something for Him— to speak those graceful words to someone who doesn't deserve your grace or to skip the wisdom of this world in favor of wisdom that's out of this world.

Lost

Romans 3:1–12

YOU'VE HEARD THE TERM "necessary evil." It's how we describe an iniquity we like so well that we don't want to abandon it. When it comes to choosing between two necessary evils, it's easy to expand the choices. Christians, however, need not worry about such things, or do we?

How do you feel about yourself—as a Christian, that is? If someone were to ask how you support your claim to fame as a Christian, what evidence would you offer? Perhaps it's that you attend worship each week, or maybe you're a regular customer at the Christian bookstore. (Sounds good to me!) Maybe you could point to your Baptism or to the fact that you rarely swear.

Additional evidence could be the fish symbol stuck to your front door, family devotions around the dinner table, or your faithfulness in sending the pastor a Christmas card each year. If you can submit any of the above evidence, you must be … like the New Testament Jews who refused to believe in Jesus their Savior.

Ouch! You were having a decent devotion until that came along. See what Paul said in Romans 3:10–12: "There is no one righteous, not even one; there is no one who understands, no one who seeks God. All have turned away, they have together become worthless; there is no one who does good, not even one."

Paul described the condition of all people. He might have said they were lost. The naked truth is that we're more like dead—spiritually dead. Paul's point was that we can't claim evidence of knowing Christ based solely on things we do. That is nothing more than a recitation of the Law, and if we can't keep all parts of it—if we have necessary evils in our lives—we're guilty of disobeying the whole Law. According to Paul, we can't avoid lawlessness even through the technicality of saying we don't believe in God. When people set up their own system of laws and morality, they can't meet those demands either.

Talk about a bad hair day, now we're into a bad heir day! Our record of faithfulness is filled with all kinds of evil. Even as believers, we're powerless to "earn our keep" as Christians. Don't despair, though. Our "lost and found" hung on the cross. Be sure to read the next meditation tomorrow—if you can wait that long.

And Found

Philippians 3:7–14

A MONG ITEMS COMMONLY FOUND in a school's lost and found are some surprises. It's hard to imagine how students can lose one shoe, a leather coat, shoelaces, or eyeglasses. It's even harder to imagine not searching for the lost article. Then again, how many people look beyond themselves and their immediate surroundings to find what they don't have? That was yesterday's spiritual subject too.

After that last episode, let's get something clear right away. As masterfully as Paul exposed our sinful nature, he also proclaimed not merely good news, but the best news. "What is more, I consider everything a loss compared to the surpassing greatness of knowing Christ Jesus my Lord, for whose sake I have lost all things. I consider them rubbish, that I may gain Christ and be found in Him, not having a righteousness of my own that comes from the law, but that which is through faith in Christ—the righteousness that comes from God and is by faith" (Philippians 3:8–9).

Found in Christ! How does that happen? We are found in Christ when we are found by Christ. That's true evidence of our identity as a Christian. God found the lost, beginning with Adam and Eve and continuing through the ages. He not only found them lost, but also wanting—wanting someone to save them from their misery. The history of God's people clearly shows that human attempts at self-rescue didn't work—not that God didn't provide opportunities. Especially significant was the incident at Mt. Sinai when God told His people how they could be saved. "Obey the Law," He said. They said, "Okay. We'll try." We've been saying the same thing ever since!

God found every sin from the multitude of sinners and laid them on Jesus. Christ suffered and died for our sins and left them to decay as so much litter beneath the cross. The Holy Spirit found every sinner and offered the gift of salvation. Some of us, by His power in a most mysterious way, accepted the gift. The lost were found.

Recall times when you were lost—on a lonely road, at the airport, or in a windowless office building. Then think of your relief upon finding your way. (Unless you're still lost.) We have that sense of relief and more as we remember the difference between being spiritually lost—and found. May we always be among the found!

The Bosssssss

1 Peter 2:11–17

Don't you just love the boss? (Easy to say if you are the boss.) The term "boss" seems particularly appropriate—especially the way it hisses at the end. A neighbor moaned that his boss was so mean that she expected a receipt when she paid a compliment! No matter how you feel about bosses—and that probably includes you in some situations—it's good to treat them respectfully. For example, it's better to tell the boss he has an open mind rather than mumbling something about a hole in his head!

God is an expert on authority because He is King of kings, Lord of lords, and Boss of bosses. Unlike some of the earthly variety, God has real authority, and He uses it only for good. Wouldn't it make life more comfortable if all bosses looked for your mistakes so they could forget them? Wouldn't it be amazing if bosses placed responsibility for all your mistakes on one of their own family members? God did exactly that when He punished Jesus for the sins of the world. And this has implications for those of us who work under the, ahem, "guidance" of a boss.

God addresses the situation in 1 Peter and in Hebrews where He says, "Obey your leaders and submit to their authority. They keep watch over you as men who must give an account. Obey them so that their work will be a joy, not a burden, for that would be of no advantage to you" (Hebrews 13:17).

Aside from the practical disadvantages of becoming a boss' burden, we have more lofty reasons for avoiding this outcome. God invented leaders to prevent chaos. Back in the days of Moses and Aaron, God established lines of authority for His glory and the good of people—again, two characteristics of outstanding, godly leadership. The test, however, of being good employees, citizens, or family members is not the quality of the boss, but the quality of the follower.

The Hebrews heard of their responsibility to be good workers who brought joy to the boss. We hear it too. The love God has for us through His Son, and the love we feel toward Jesus, can be expressed through our daily family and career relationships. Showing this love probably will invite some derision and even hostility, just as it did in Bible days. But it also will provide a quiet witness to our relationship with the Big Boss.

27

Travel Guide

Genesis 3:17–24

HAVING RUN A SUCCESSFUL GUIDE concerning trees, it's time to embark on a new series—a guide to travel. Of the many difficulties faced and surmounted by intrepid astronauts, interstate highways were not among them. For example, had America's astronauts needed Interstate 80/90 south of Lake Michigan to reach their goal, TV viewers would have seen live shots of the Indiana Sand Dunes rather than the moon, and it would have been 1975 rather than 1969.

Like it or not, detours are designed for our good. Shake your road map at those signs once, and you'll find out why they're necessary. Those signs keep us from falling into rivers, plopping into wet cement, or running over sleeping highway department workers. (Okay—they're only on break.)

Among God's many activities during the early days of our universe was the development and design of the first detour sign. His sign was more impressive than our simple barricade topped by a battery-operated flashing light. Read about it: "After He drove the man out, He placed on the east side of the Garden of Eden cherubim and a flaming sword flashing back and forth to guard the way to the tree of life" (Genesis 3:24).

That's the passage that usually came to my mind when a Sunday school teacher talked about "fearing" the Lord. But like most disturbing verses (and distressing detours), God intends His words and deeds as blessings.

The angelic detour at the east gate of Eden saved Adam and Eve from a life of misery. Had they returned to the land from which they were evicted, they might have eaten from the tree that offered immortality—a guaranteed eternity of anguish on sinful earth. Instead, God sent Adam and Eve on a long detour that led them to an eternity like the one they had first enjoyed.

Has God placed some detours in your life? Thank Him. The devil slings obstacles and hazards onto the road to eternity. He wants us to lose faith in God's guidance to our final destination. But God is faithful to us. His Word leads us around desperate situations and past hopelessness and helplessness. So be sure to keep your travel guide handy. God will lead you to the finest million-star resort imaginable, even if it takes a few detours to get there.

28

Traveling Together

Exodus 13:14–22

I KNOW HOW TO GET THERE, but I can't explain it. Just follow me." Many adventures begin with those words. Traveling together is a common practice designed to drive otherwise close individuals or families apart while giving the deceptive impression of actually being close. Characteristics of such travel include bumper butting; adjusting the remote mirrors because the follower is, well, remote; playing the mechanical version of red light-green light; and sending coded messages via flashing turn signals.

Techniques of traveling together probably degenerated soon after the practice originated. The best method was introduced to the children of Israel by God. Exodus 13:21–22 reports: "By day the LORD went ahead of them in a pillar of cloud to guide them on their way and by night in a pillar of fire to give them light, so that they could travel by day or night. Neither the pillar of cloud by day nor the pillar of fire by night left its place in front of the people."

The children of Israel didn't know where they were going. Having just escaped 400 years of slavery, they simply were anxious to get away. Like young children, though, they became restless and asked the Hebrew form of the question, "Are we there yet?" Incidentally, they often complained about their food and lodging too. But God was a good leader. He knew they would never arrive at their destination unless He led them. So He did—in a most miraculous way!

We may speak philosophically about life's journey on the road to heaven, but that trip is far more than a heady topic of conversation. It's reality. And the stark reality is that we can't possibly reach our heavenly destination without divine leadership.

Today, pillars of cloud or fire are as uncommon as free road maps at gas stations. Yet God continues to lead us. He does it through His written Word in the Bible and through personal guidance by the Holy Spirit. The Bible tells us to follow Jesus. He slows down when we lag behind, and He even waits for us when we get separated or stopped by sin. The Holy Spirit travels with us, helping us focus on our Leader, filling us with vigilance for hazards, and keeping us in the right lane. If that sounds like a backseat driver, stop now. This one belongs in the front seat.

29
Asking Directions

John 14:1–7

FEW WORDS TURN TRAVEL to its dark side as easily as "Why don't you stop and ask directions?" With no chauvinism intended, the question is usually a "woman thing," and the answer is definitely a "man thing." Of course, at least 75 percent of you readers would argue that you can get lost just as easily when you're alone as when you have help.

Travelers may laugh retrospectively about episodes of being lost, but the condition also can be dangerous. Perhaps you've seen drivers, obviously confused and shaken, veer across several lanes of traffic to exit an expressway. Then there's the driver who drifts to the curb while hunting dim addresses. Worst of all, there's finding yourself lost in a hostile neighborhood.

Although Jesus' disciples shared a face-to-face relationship with their Savior, they sometimes felt lost. Thomas is a perfect example. "Thomas said to Him, 'Lord, we don't know where You are going, so how can we know the way?' Jesus answered, 'I am the way and the truth and the life. No one comes to the Father except through Me' " (John 14:5–6).

Thomas' statement is one that many people echo today. "We don't know how to get to heaven, so how can we ever hope to live there?" The answer remains the same as it was in Thomas' time. Jesus is the only way.

That doesn't stop some people from dispensing faulty directions. You know the kind. "Let's see, stay on this road for five or six miles—maybe more, maybe less—until you get to the public library. But you can't turn right there, so you have to go a couple blocks beyond that and make three right turns so when you go past the library, it's on your right. Then keep going until …" Helpful, right? To think—and tremble—that some would lead us to heaven with the same kind of "help"!

In spiritual language, such misdirection usually sounds like this: "Try hard not to sin. God will count that in your favor." Or "Volunteer lots of time at the hospital and be sure to attend worship every Sunday. God will see how good you are."

It's true that God sees how good we are, and it's not a scenic view. The only route to heaven begins beneath the cross as we confess our wretchedness and accept God's forgiveness in Christ. Then He leads us to the place we most want to be. Now those are some directions worth stopping to hear.

30

No Turns

Deuteronomy 28:1–14

RUSH HOUR IN A BIG CITY. Have you been there? If so, you have to wonder how anyone could call it a rush. Typical traffic jams have even changed the definition of "Sunday driver." Now it's one left over from Friday's "rush"!

One lament of rush-hour drivers is that no matter what lane you switch to, it will stop while the other lanes move. And just try to leave your lane! Too bad it's not that hard to stray from spiritual paths. God tells us to avoid lane changing—to make no turns on the road to salvation. Deuteronomy 28:14 says: "Do not turn aside from any of the commands I give you today, to the right or to the left, following other gods and serving them."

Next time you're in a traffic jam (and have plenty of time to think), try to enjoy it. That's right: Enjoy it. Envision yourself on the highway to eternal salvation. No wonder it's so crowded! Everyone is genuinely intent on getting home, and if others are a bit impatient, consider what awaits when they arrive safely. Oh, exit ramps slip off to the side here and there, beckoning weary travelers to greener pastures (or should we say blacker asphalt?). But those side trips, seductive as they are, only lead to delays, distractions, or dead ends. Stay on the highway. Make no turns.

That's how it is as we follow our Savior. In Deuteronomy days, the way to salvation was to obey God's commands. That was as difficult then as it is for today's drivers to obey speed limits. How can you go 60 m.p.h. when cars are bumper to bumper? How can you go only 65 m.p.h. when everyone is passing you? When it came to sins, God's people either went too slow or too fast. God knew the impossibility of obeying His Law so He sent Jesus to obey it for us.

God's new command is attainable because He sent the Holy Spirit to chauffeur us. He helps us believe in Jesus as our Savior. He helps us follow Jesus despite heavy traffic and tempting detours. He helps us accept God's forgiveness and His promise of eternal life despite temptations to follow the ways of human achievement, good works, and doctrines that fit popular lifestyles or attractive intellect. So make no turns.

Cater Walls

Psalm 95:1–11; Psalm 30:12

THE DIRECTOR SAID it was a special group created for singers like me who had, uh, similar vocal qualities—qualities that deserved to be distinct from the group known as A Capella Chorus. I overheard the director explaining this new group to the principal. He said it would be called the Cater Walls—probably a Latin word for something melodious.

One safe axiom is that singers like to sing, notes on the harmonic scale notwithstanding. Some singers hold membership in singing groups such as the Crows or the Grackles—certainly never attaining the height of a Cater Wall—and thus believe that because others think they are lousy singers, they are, indeed, lousy singers. But what they lack in quality, they compensate for in volume.

How do you sing? Whether lyrically or raucously, you have a right, maybe a responsibility, to sing. Perhaps Psalm 30:12 was written for the vocally challenged: "That my heart may sing to You and not be silent. O LORD my God, I will give You thanks forever." Singing hearts cause less aesthetic damage than twanging vocal chords, but as singers of every kind know, sincere singing rises from the heart.

Throughout the history of God's people, songs played an important role in praising Him. Some songs were so good that they were recorded—in the Bible, that is. The most popular songwriter was David, who rose from the rank of shepherd to fearless warrior and eventually to king. His songs reflected what was in his heart—sometimes anguish, sometimes fear, but mostly trust and praise. A little-known fact is that David probably created the first rock concert. After all, we hear in the words of Psalm 95:1: "Come, let us sing for joy to the LORD; let us shout aloud to the Rock of our salvation."

Sing a song today. Or at least whistle an original composition dedicated to Jesus. Our Lord isn't a music critic. He doesn't care how well or how loud we sing as long as the notes and lyrics spring from our heart. Despite circumstances, we have much for which to sing. Even if few on earth love us, One faithfully loves us from above. Even if employment, health, weather, or wealth abandon us, the treasure of salvation is always ours. So even if you're shy about singing, have a Rock concert in your heart. God will happily take note, even an off-key one.

32

Other Reasons

John 3:14–18

I<small>T'S NOT AN ENJOYABLE WAY</small> to begin a devotion, but recall some of the bad times in your life. Maybe you don't have to tax your memory, but perhaps you'll think back to a death, a serious illness or accident, a failed marriage, a rebellious child, or an economic calamity. Worse yet, perhaps you faced several of these difficulties at once. It's enough to make you wonder if God is mad at you, right?

The Old Testament reveals numerous occasions of God's anger. It was always just—just horrible! He destroyed whole cities or infested fields with grasshoppers or turned rivers into bloody baths. In every case, God was punishing the wickedness of unrepented sin. If God got mad back then, is it a sign of divine indignation when we suffer?

The answer is in the Bible. One of many places we can find an answer is John 3:17, which says, "For God did not send His Son into the world to condemn the world, but to save the world through Him." And the verse immediately before this is the famous one that tells how much God loves us. So when we suffer, it must not be God's fury that afflicts us. There must be other reasons.

Affliction and adversity are the result of sin, but not necessarily a one-to-one correspondence with personal sins. Risky behaviors certainly invite direct consequences, but anguish and hardship do not discriminate on the basis of personal saintliness. Worldly dilemmas might be traced to the first man and woman, whose foray into sin was so earthshaking that God called it original. Since then, humankind has introduced many new and improved, giant-sized varieties. The world is wracked—and wrecked—by the general nature of sin. Everyone becomes victims of it, from the most prurient pagan to the most chaste Christian.

Sin and its ugly, painful, and constrictive results were not introduced by God. Spiritual mutation results from the devil's deeds to alienate us from God. Sin is separation from God.

Thank God we suffer only a temporary taste of that separation. Isn't it true that we seek a closer relationship with God in times of trouble?

God is not mad at you. He spent His anger on Jesus. Now all is well, though we did nothing to deserve this treatment. There must be other reasons.

33

Did You Turn Off the Coffee?

Philippians 4:4–7

GETTING AWAY from the front door was always a bittersweet accomplishment when my family left for vacation (or even a Sunday drive). Dad would slide behind the wheel. Mom would slip into the passenger seat and slip right out again. Fumbling for the house key, she would say, "I don't know if I turned off the coffee." Dad would grunt, and I would groan. But it wasn't long before Mom was in the front seat again. And if Dad didn't screech away from the curb, Mom was back out again. "I don't remember locking the door after checking the coffee," she would say.

Stress and tension are nothing new. The disciples had plenty of it, which gave Jesus a chance to address the problem. He told His disciples (and that includes us) stories about birds and lilies and how they didn't need to worry about food, how they looked, or whether they left the coffee maker on. Later, Paul told the Philippians, "Do not be anxious about anything, but in everything, by prayer and petition, with thanksgiving, present your requests to God" (Philippians 4:6).

Paul wasn't talking about practical anxieties such as locked doors or brewing pots. Those are things we can and should do something about, even if it means shortening vacation by a week. His advice concerned worries about future events—the "what ifs" that keep us awake nights, as well as the realities of present stresses. "Take it to the Lord in prayer," was Paul's counsel.

But did you notice something else in Paul's words? Thanksgiving. How hard it is to feel thankful in bad times! How can you be thankful when you're worrying about your teenager, or about Uncle Harry's abusive alcoholism, or about tomorrow's edition of pink slips?

Paul knew that worries subside when you trust your life to God. God cares more for you than the birds and flowers that mindlessly exist with His blessings. Thank God for His care. He loves you in good times and bad and in sickness and health. Even death won't part you from Him. Little worries or big, give thanks that you can give them all to God.

With Paul, we exclaim, "And the peace of God, which transcends all understanding, will guard your hearts and your minds in Christ Jesus" (Philippians 4:7). But you probably should check the coffee maker anyway.

34

Locked in or Locked Out?

John 20:19–22

HAVE YOU HEARD of the satellite system that unlocks your car from outer space if your keys are trapped in inner space? It used to take a coat hanger and a little ingenuity to do the same thing. Of course, with some drivers, everyone is more secure when their keys are locked away!

Locks are flexible mechanisms. They can lock people in, and they can lock people out. Consider the disciples in this incident recorded in the Bible: "On the evening of that first day of the week, when the disciples were together, with the doors locked for fear of the Jews, Jesus came and stood among them and said, 'Peace be with you!' " (John 20:19).

The disciples feared their enemies. Even the lightest knock on the door or the faintest sound of approaching footsteps alarmed them. They felt much safer behind the sturdy door and the lock that separated them from their enemies. While the lock worked to protect them, it didn't keep out their best Friend, who greeted them with calming words. So shook up was that crowd that Jesus repeatedly said, "Peace be with you."

How often are we like those disciples—secure in our insecurity? We spend most of our lives locking out our fears. We want to keep the bad out, and at the very least, keep the status quo inside. So we lock the doors of our hearts, the windows of our minds, and the portals of our souls. Some good results. We may succeed in reducing the perils of evil and sin that lurk in the world's darkness. But wickedness is so powerful that it seeps in through cracks and crevices. It attacks our bodies with illness and injuries, infects our minds with doubts and despair, and seduces our souls with temptations. Our own defenses prove inadequate.

Just when we realize the weakness of our locks, Jesus breezes in to bring us peace. Through His forgiveness earned on the cross, Jesus broke Satan's bonds that so firmly locked us to sin. Jesus gave us power to resist sin and finally to escape its power to destroy us. We are locked inside His grace, and the devil is locked out in an eternity of darkness.

Each day when you lock your doors, remember that Jesus is with you to provide total security. Even if you misplace your keys, Jesus has a way to get inside.

35

Looking Up

Acts 1:1–11

WARNING: Don't try this at home. Do it where nobody will recognize you.

Practical jokes are sometimes dangerous, especially around humorless people. You might want to try this one when you're on a busy street corner or at the mall. Look up. That's right. Crane your neck and aim your eyes at the ceiling or the sky. Every once in a while, cast a shifty glance at the people around you (watch out for the ones sporting a badge). What are they doing? Probably the same thing you are—at least before they storm off in a huff or flee in terror.

The Bible tells about some men of Galilee who were staring at the sky. One minute Jesus was talking with them, and the next He was ascending into heaven. The disciples lost their good Friend once, and now it was happening again. As they gazed into the void, two angels addressed the group. " 'Men of Galilee,' they said, 'why do you stand here looking into the sky? This same Jesus, who has been taken from you into heaven, will come back in the same way you have seen Him go into heaven' " (Acts 1:11). It was just another way of saying that things were looking up—even if it didn't seem that way to Jesus' closest followers.

Like those early believers who witnessed the first Ascension Day, we might find ourselves looking up to heaven and feeling very much alone here on earth. Wouldn't it be good to see Jesus face to face, to hear His voice, to thrill to His blessed touch? Jesus would seem so much more real if only … If only we could avoid these dangerous thoughts. Like the disciples, we're not alone.

Just 10 days after the disciples lost sight of Jesus, God filled them with another Friend—the Holy Spirit. We have the Holy Spirit too. We no longer need to selfishly guard our friendship with God. Instead, God enables us to share His love and companionship with everyone we meet. Others won't always accept the way we look up to God—they might rush off in a huff or flee in terror. (Sound familiar?) But as our words and deeds point up to our Savior, others might want to know more. Then you can tell them about how God loves you—and them too. You can borrow the words of the angels and let people know that Jesus will come again.

Things are looking up, all right. No joking!

The Check, Please

Micah 6:1–8

COMMON SENSE SUGGESTS that when dining with others at the kind of restaurant where no prices appear on the menu, you probably should prepare to fight over the check. Or perhaps you should think about how to gracefully surrender. Or maybe you should suggest that fast food is fine with you.

Fighting for the check is acceptable if you can afford the consequences, including the unwanted attention you attract as other tables enjoy the entertainment. (The most exciting moment might be passing your sleeve over the candle as you tussle for the check.) On the other hand, only a fool (who is soon parted from his money anyway) would duel to pay for something he can't afford with something he doesn't have.

The same thing occurs in our relationship with the Savior. We have a plate full of sins. We've immensely enjoyed some; others have produced nothing but spiritual nausea and pain. We face the temptation of trying to pay the price of carnal gluttony on our own terms. The same was true in the prophet Micah's day. At the Lord's command, Micah confronted God's people with this rhetorical and divinely sarcastic statement: "With what shall I come before the LORD and bow down before the exalted God? Shall I come before Him with burnt offerings, with calves a year old? Will the LORD be pleased with thousands of rams, with ten thousand rivers of oil? Shall I offer my firstborn for my transgression, the fruit of my body for the sin of my soul?" (Micah 6:6–7).

Translated loosely, Micah was saying that no amount of money, barter, or bribes could pay the price of sin. It would cost our lives, and we would continue paying thereafter! The devil, like an indulgent but impatient waiter, gladly passes the check to the fastest hand.

No amount of good deeds, hours of prayer, hearty worship, or hefty contributions can pay for our sins. Only pride or deceit motivates sinners to attempt to liquidate sinfulness on their own terms, though sometimes we might try it in temporary ignorance. The only way to pay for sin is to hand over the check.

Next time you're involved in a table-side squabble over the check, you should accept gratefully the other person's generosity. Then breathe a word of thanks to Jesus too.

37
Life in the Big City

Joshua 6:1–21

L IFE IN BIG CITIES has an image problem. Some city dwellers are sensitive to that reputation and intentionally address it. When I moved from the south side of Chicago to a small college in a small town in a small state, I worried that my rural-raised peers might fear me. I gave up smoking because the cigarette hanging from my lip looked sinister. That didn't work because the nicotine withdrawal made me surly. The best I could do was hide the headlines of my Chicago newspapers and try to act like I knew something about wheat blight and cattle auctions.

It is ineffective to hide corruption or make believe it doesn't exist. But that's not the biggest problem of life in the big city. The problem that looms larger is tolerating, accepting, or even enjoying evil. That's what those who lived in that ancient, big city called Jericho discovered. Thick walls surrounded their bastion of wickedness—walls impenetrable by anything good. They even attempted to keep God out.

You know the story. Joshua reports: "When the trumpets sounded, the people shouted, and at the sound of the trumpet, when the people gave a loud shout, the wall collapsed; so every man charged straight in, and they took the city" (Joshua 6:20).

Sin attempts to erect a fortress around itself. Sometimes the walls surround the human mind, which invents so many ways to doubt God's Word and to challenge His promises. Sometimes it's the soul that surrounds itself with mounds of false teachings that make sin comfortably tolerable or entirely absent from life. One thing spiritual walls always separate is the sinner from the Savior. Until God crashes the party.

When Jericho's walls collapsed and crumbled, God's army marched in and destroyed everything evil. Then they dedicated the city to God. How similar to what Jesus did for us! He annihilated every barrier between us and God. He crushed the devil's violent bid to claim us. He ripped through the walls of evil and planted His peace and love. Then He built a truly impregnable wall around us—one fortified with His holy might and guarded by His Holy Spirit. Satan may sneak into our spiritual city to aid and abet our sinfulness, but he is powerless to win us over without our consent. God's walls will never tumble.

Life in the big city? Nothing could be safer.

Throw the Book at Him

Luke 4:1–13

N O MATTER HOW YOU FEEL about capital punishment, one thing is certain: It greatly reduces the number of repeat offenders. Sadly, our society witnesses many court cases that future historians are likely to label "bizarre." Criminals who are guilty based on evidence go free on technicalities. Judges must sentence criminals to hundreds of years in prison to assure the public that parole won't lead to freedom for felons who are still young enough to commit serious crimes. Some people are convicted based on the zealous ambitions of prosecutors when, in fact, they committed no crime. I rest my case. But this isn't a newspaper editorial, so perhaps we should move for a continuance.

The most famous criminal prosecutor in history will turn out to be the devil. He boasts a long history of delivering evidence of sin—even against the brightest and best people, including King David, Peter, Paul (a.k.a. Saul), and you. This legal slime ball gladly will promote and facilitate crimes against God and people so he can build a case. With malicious glee, he can prove each of us sinful before the God who judges us.

The devil's legal career would be completely successful except for one thing: He lost his most important case. In one unprecedented trial that lasted more than 30 years, the devil lost his bid to condemn God's Son—and all of us with Him. The trial included this incident: "Jesus, full of the Holy Spirit, returned from the Jordan and was led by the Spirit in the desert, where for forty days He was tempted by the devil" (Luke 4:1–2a).

As part of his strategy, the devil cleverly used passages from Scripture—out of context. He's good at that, and maybe he's done the same to you. But Jesus had the right defense, and it established a powerful precedent. He threw the book at the devil—the whole book, not just a few pages. That book was the Bible. He repeatedly answered the devil's loaded questions with the phrase, "It is written." Written where? In God's Word, the Holy Bible.

The only sure defense against the devil is God's Word—the one in actual words, as well as in the Word come to life, Jesus Christ. Though personally innocent, Jesus took the punishment reserved for us who would surely be convicted. Assured of this, we don't need to defend ourselves. We've got an "in" with the Judge. Just mention His Son's name.

Dream Come True

Psalm 139:1–18

Do you dream of a castle in the sky? Before you leap into a commitment to live there, it's good to list pluses and minuses. *Pluses:* Great view, good neighbors, and no flooding. *Minuses:* Watch the first step, unstable foundation, a bit drafty, and long-distance phone bills.

The trouble with most dreams is that eventually you have to wake up. However, one dream will come true. The psalmist identified it this way: "How precious to me are Your thoughts, O God! How vast is the sum of them! Were I to count them, they would outnumber the grains of sand. When I awake, I am still with You" (Psalm 139:17–18).

"When I awake, I am still with You." What loving words! Take a moment to think about someone—maybe someone who lives far away or seems to live far away; maybe it's a new love in your life or an old one; perhaps you haven't seen each other in years or it's been only minutes. What are you thinking? Are they fond memories or bitter disappointments, future hopes or past history, dreams or realities?

Enough dreaming for now! Has it changed anything? Some dreams come true; others don't. That's only half true with God. When He thinks of us, He isn't sleeping. Although we sleep and dream, when we awake, God is also in our company.

If God sent a "thinking of you" card, what do you suppose He would write? Realizing that He knows everything about us, we might hesitate to open the envelope. Don't fear, though. God thinks of us as redeemed, saved people—thanks to Jesus Christ. Here is what God might write:

> *Thinking of you? I always think of you! I know how hurt you are when others let you down. I knew you were in danger on your last trip to Wal-Mart, so I sent an angel to protect you. (Didn't know about that one, did you?) Oh yes, and I thought about what makes you laugh, so I'm planning to send more joy your way. Watch for it and think of Me next time you chuckle. There is so much more I'd like to tell you, but notes are just too short. I'll always remember you, and someday I want you to move in with Me. I've got a real castle in the sky.*

Three's a Crowd

John 1:1–3

OUR GOD IS TRIUNE—three in one in a way too divine for human comprehension. Human efforts have tried in vain to define or describe the Trinity, but one of the best illustrations comes from John Wesley. He said that the Holy Trinity is like three lighted candles in a dark room. Though each candle is a candle, they provide one light.

Scripture never uses the word *trinity*. It only implies this description of the true God, who introduced His three-some-ness in Genesis 1:26 when He spoke in the plural, saying, "Let Us make man in Our image."

Perhaps you took time to read the opening passages of John 1— that familiar and mysterious "In the beginning was the Word …" One of the clearest references to the Trinity appears in Matthew 3:16–17: "As soon as Jesus was baptized, He went up out of the water. At that moment heaven was opened, and He saw the Spirit of God descending like a dove and lighting on Him. And a voice from heaven said, 'This is My Son, whom I love; with Him I am well pleased.' " Do you see it there? Jesus … Spirit … Father.

It's unwise to dissect this doctrine because it remains central in the foundation of Christianity. We can, however, appreciate God's comprehensive nature. Three's a crowd—a powerful crowd that spreads unique love and abundant blessings to all creation. Think about it. God the Father not only created "the heavens and the earth," He continues to care for it. Everyone has air to breathe, water to drink, food to eat, and shelters to protect. And, of course, there's Jesus, whose single, unselfish, courageous act on the cross changed the course of eternal history. The Holy Spirit works for our benefit too. The Spirit carries God's merciful love to us now that Jesus finished the job of forgiveness. It's the Spirit who tapped you on the soul and brought you to meet your Savior. It's the Spirit who continually fans the flames of faith in you. What a God! What a God! What a God!

Have you heard the old adage, "What you don't know can't hurt you"? Sometimes it's true. We don't have a logical clue as to the concept of the Trinity, but we do have faith. You're here, aren't you? And you know where you're going, right? Someday, you'll join millions of other believers in praising a Triune God that you fully understand. You'll follow the crowd forever!

News Flash

Acts 22:1–16

WE INTERRUPT THIS BOOK to bring you a news flash. Dateline Florida, 1997: The world should know that an American president's knee is worth no more than any other knee. That's right. The White House issued a press release that revealed the surgical costs to repair a tendon torn during a presidential trip (forgive me) in Florida. The White House press secretary also reported that President Clinton's insurance plan required him to pay about $1,400 of the $7,000 bill. This presumably is good news because the costs seem in line with the price of knee surgery on average knees. It's also good news because most other government projects seem a bit pricey. Clinton's knee could have cost taxpayers the purchase price of Alaska.

What news is worth knowing? It had to be a slow news day when wire services foisted the preceding report on the public. Maybe they should have reprinted an old story—one reported by Luke: "Then [Paul] said: 'The God of our fathers has chosen you to know His will and to see the Righteous One and to hear words from His mouth. You will be His witness to all men of what you have seen and heard. And now what are you waiting for?' " (Acts 22:14–16a).

Paul's headlines are our headlines too. God knocked us down. He didn't need lightning or earthquakes or slippery stairs. Our sins were enough. In His holy presence, we can only fall on our face before God and plead our guilt. Yet He picked us up, and He continues to pick us up and brush us off each time we fall. If God kept a wallet in His back pocket, He probably would drag out a worn snapshot of His Son for us to appreciate. After all, it's for His Son's sake that He bothers with us at all. Then God steadies our steps and sends us on our way, whispering to the Holy Spirit to keep us faithful.

This is news worth knowing—even on a big news day. What other news could be more earthshaking? Knowing what we know, it's important to heed Paul's question, "What are you waiting for?" You have a scoop, and you need to report it. Tell it to anyone who will listen. And if you don't know what to say, hum or whistle it in the wordless tune of your favorite Gospel hymn. Maybe those around you will get the message and you all can enjoy some Good News today.

Now You See It—Now You Don't

2 Corinthians 4:13–18

WHO SAYS FAITH IS DEAD in modern society? Have you seen the lines of people waiting to play slot machines on gambling boats? There's a real case of "Now you see it—now you don't"! If people are so willing to give away their money, some entrepreneur should figure out a way to simply deposit cash at the bank—the riverbank—and skip the cost of building those fancy riverboats.

Real faith—the kind that people have in God—seems somewhat endangered. It's hard to believe in something you can't see, yet our entire faith is built on the unseen (as it should be). The Bible says: "So we fix our eyes not on what is seen, but on what is unseen. For what is seen is temporary, but what is unseen is eternal" (2 Corinthians 4:18).

Slot machines eventually break (but not before their users are broke). Everything humankind has made will disappear. Indeed, entire civilizations have vanished (probably because of some uncivilized acts!).

Evidence doesn't work well either. Consider the evidence viewed by a small crowd on Good Friday. What they saw was the cruel but typical execution of three men, including One who was not guilty. They saw the sky turn black, felt the earth shake, and gasped in horror as the sacred temple curtain ripped apart. There were even stories of people stepping from their graves! Was it convincing? For some, the wonder and the awe didn't last more than a few hours. Others who witnessed the event refused to believe that the Savior died to take away the sins of the world.

Faith cannot rest on what we see. What we see is made. Even God's magnificent earthly creations will disappear someday. Now you see it. Someday you won't. But faith, our individual faith that is given and maintained by the Holy Spirit, will reach its climax when everything else disappears. Then we will see God in person. Then our faith will be perfect. All those things that disappeared on Judgment Day will be replaced by things so much better—including our bodies. How do we know this? God promised. He promised to give us something we can't even begin to dream about. But don't bother dreaming. Just have a little faith. It's a case of now you don't see it. Now you will.

43
Parts of Speech

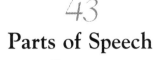

James 1:19–27

COLOR DRAINED FROM the teacher's face as he corrected my English test. Unfortunately, it drained all over my paper. Red ink nearly obliterated my response to the question "What are the parts of speech?" I still think I deserved partial credit for my answer: The parts of speech are nouns, verbs, adverbs, and expletives. Ha! Even grammatically challenged people can right books though. Write?

One part of speech that needs more teaching is the part called *listening*. The apostle James valued listening, though he was also a good writer. He said, "My dear brothers, take note of this: Everyone should be quick to listen, slow to speak and slow to become angry" (James 1:19).

Quick to listen. Listening—genuine listening—is such a lost art that students often practice specific exercises to build the skill. What they really learn are words such as what?, huh?, and … No, they really learn active and reflective listening strategies designed to help them understand what others say. Such exercises often include knowing nods, murmurs of affirmation, and repeating what others say. However, James probably was not talking about active listening. So how do you listen to God?

First, you tell God what you need and what you want. He already knows this information, but He invites you to make your requests known. God hears so many requests for personal, sometimes selfish, attention that He probably enjoys hearing what others need. (Words of thanks and praise are certainly in order too.) You can talk to God about anything.

The second step in listening to God is to quit talking. Do some reading instead. God told us everything we need to hear in the words of the Bible. Regular readers have discovered that God speaks to their needs, often before they even know their needs. In addition, a good topical or indexed Bible helps to pinpoint what God says about specific topics.

The third phase of listening is to sit still and let God talk to your soul. Quiet reflection on God's Word gives the Holy Spirit wonderful opportunities to help you. Try it now. Ask yourself these questions:

1. *What do I need help with now?*
    2. *What does the Bible say? (Take time to look.)*
        3. _____ *(That's you listening.)*

44

Something to Crow About

1 Kings 17:1–6

THE SIMILARITIES BETWEEN crows and ravens are such that only bird experts and the birds themselves know the differences. The only difference I can see is that crows live in my neighborhood and ravens don't. Human experience with crows is often unpleasant. The birds are brassy, noisy, and they eat disgusting things. On the positive side, though, crows remind us of ravens, and ravens remind us of God's love, which is something to crow about.

As reported in the Bible, God's perpetual care rode the wings of ravens several times. The first occurrence was when the floodwaters receded and Noah needed information about the risks of disembarking from the ark. We hear about ravens again in the story of a hungry Elijah. Listen to how God took care of His prophet: "The ravens brought him bread and meat in the morning and bread and meat in the evening, and he drank from the brook" (1 Kings 17:6). (Perhaps this is the thought behind the phrase "on a wing and a prayer.")

God has both normal and unusual ways of caring for people. Often, He mixes both the spectacular and the unremarkable. Consider how He feeds us. Seeds are deceptively simple. You can regain a sense of wonder and appreciation if you imagine yourself in the tiny shoes of a kindergarten child who wonders aloud how a plump radish can pop out of such a small seed. The only satisfactory explanation is God. Yes, God continues to provide for us with or without ravens, and that's something else to crow about.

The most important way God ever cared is through His Son—a curious mix of true God and true Man. God could have solved everyone's problems simply by uttering a creative word. Instead, He chose to use things to which we can relate—such as birds and people. Jesus, as true man, talked with people as He healed them, forgave them, and died for them. He was God in human flesh—quite demeaning for God when you think about it. Yet God sent Jesus to feed us with His Word, a diet that nourishes forever. That's even more to crow about. In fact, it's something you could go on ravin' about for a long time!

Mint Condition

1 Peter 1:17–21

THE SALESPERSON CLAIMED the car was in mint condition. She was right. It would have taken the entire Denver mint to pay for it. The term "mint condition" probably refers more to what the seller can receive than what the buyer can expect. Too bad the only mint to which most of us have access is the kind you savor after dinner.

Speaking of mint condition, what are you worth? Please don't run off for your calculator and investment portfolio (or your wallet and piggy bank!) Look in your Bible instead. A good place to start is 1 Peter 1:18–19: "For you know that it was not with perishable things such as silver or gold that you were redeemed from the empty way of life handed down to you from your forefathers, but with the precious blood of Christ, a lamb without blemish or defect."

There are two ways to think about that passage. First, we were worth so much to God that He spent His Son, Jesus, to buy us back from Satan. Second, it cost Jesus' life to fix us and make us presentable to our original Owner. Which thinking is correct?

Both answers are right. Let's examine them in reverse order. It's not pleasant to think of ourselves as worthless, yet our sins make us that way—at least in the eyes of Satan, who may be the universe's most renowned junk collector. He loves what he hates, namely, worthless, sinful, despairing humans—especially because they were created originally in God's image.

We are worthless. Worse, we might even be called a deathtrap for God's Son. Sadly, it took Jesus' life to remake us in God's image. Jesus' life was the only thing worth enough to make us worthy to be called the children of God.

Why did God expend the effort and sacrifice to save us? Certainly it was nothing He saw in us. He wasn't partial to blue eyes, dark skin, straight hair, or pointed noses. He didn't need us. We treated Him badly. He saved us because He loved us. That's it, and that's all.

Now go out and show everyone your shiny, restored self. Brag a little about the God who is powerful enough to save you, and be sure to stay close to your owner. He'll keep you in mint condition forever.

Original Sin

Romans 3:21–26

ORIGINAL SIN IS DEFINED most often by theologians. It's also defined, with a few flaws, by ordinary people interest in trying to excuse themselves from personal responsibility. The stories go something like this:

> *Officer:* Why were you speeding?
> *Speeder:* I was just keeping up with all the trucks.
> *Or:*
> *IRS Agent:* Explain this $92,000 deduction for hearing aids.
> *Taxpayer:* You do want me to hear you during the audit, don't you?
> *Or:*
> *God:* Adam, did you abandon your diet today?
> *Adam:* My wife made me do it!
> *Eve:* The devil made me do it!
> *Devil:* Gotcha!

Sinners like the above (who bear a striking resemblance to us) might describe original sin as sin that originally was caused by someone else. In fact, anyone with a two-week course in criminal justice easily could trace all sins back to the first sinners, Eve and Adam. Their lives were ruined, and the only one who really enjoyed their sin was Satan. God created humans with free will—free will to obey or disobey Him. The result? "All have sinned and fall short of the glory of God" (Romans 3:23).

Free will is not the freedom to blame others for personal sinfulness, though we come from a long line of sinners. We have freedom to choose right from wrong, and we usually know what we're doing. Pursuing God's will isn't always pleasant, but Christians have power to choose His holy will. We have that power because the Holy Spirit fuels us with God's Word and His will. We can fight sin. All who agree say, "Amen." (Warning: Don't try this when using public transportation!)

Before you get overconfident or too enthusiastic, reality suggests that you might lose the fight. Then what? Whistle a happy tune? Start again? Yes—after sincere confession to the One who already died for your sins and saved you. He knows all about sin, original and otherwise. He also knows all about forgiveness. He was the first to forgive. That makes Him an original too!

47
Doomed to Success

1 Chronicles 18:1–15

SOMETIMES SUCCESS is measured in dollars. If you make them faster than the government can take them away, you're successful. On the other hand, if you don't feel successful, there's probably lots of people who will gladly offer advice. Some of these individuals even do it in the name of religion. Perhaps you've read some success books: *How to Grow Perfect Bananas the Adam and Eve Way* or *37 Ways to Raise Children Who Honor Their Father and Mother* or perhaps *The Abraham Principle: How to Succeed in Business Even with a Large Family*. Well, maybe you won't find those exact titles, but you get the idea.

Some people consider success elusive. Is it? There seems to be a lot of it going around—even if it's going around you. As much as we seek success, we also must identify its origin. King David, successful by most standards, knew the truth about success. He identified the source in 1 Chronicles 18:13: "[David] put garrisons in Edom, and all the Edomites became subject to David. The LORD gave David victory everywhere he went." David's response? Many psalms proclaim his revelry.

Success comes from God. That means others' successes as well as our own. Sometimes the success of others may come at the expense of our own. Like rain and sunshine, God bestows success to many people. He doesn't discriminate on the basis of race, sex, or even religion.

Behind every successful person stands God. Believers know this, though sometimes success is accompanied by serious bouts of forgetfulness. At such times, successful people might become like the children of Israel. In their heady successes, they forgot their source of victory. As a result, God often caused other nations to succeed against Israel to bring His beloved people back to their senses.

Successful people need not be doomed to success, though. Not if they're as conscious of the Power behind the success as David was. Not if they refuse to use God and His people as stepping stones to ungodly success. Not if they remember Jesus, who succeeded in history's most important venture.

True success does not lie in accomplishments, wealth, or status. True success lies in knowing who succeeded beyond a sinner's wildest dreams and who is willing to share that success with His friends. But you already know that, don't you? Ah! The sweet taste of success. His success.

48

Too Many Pots Spoil the Cook

Zechariah 14:16–21

SOME COOKS FIND IT EASY. Most amateurs, however, would struggle to manage four pots on a cook top, especially if all of them needed constant attention to prevent the contents from congealing, boiling over, or becoming welded to the bottom of the pot. Attempting too much at one time easily leads to dinner out.

Pots, however, can remind us of an interesting Bible passage and at least one lesson to learn from it. The prophet Zechariah said, "Every pot in Jerusalem and Judah will be holy to the LORD Almighty, and all who come to sacrifice will take some of the pots and cook in them. And on that day there will no longer be a Canaanite in the house of the LORD Almighty" (Zechariah 14:21).

About the closest thing to "holy pots" today is when the contents resemble a burnt sacrifice. Not surprisingly, sacrifices were exactly what Zechariah was talking about. In his day, many people couldn't make it to Jerusalem, the location of the temple, to offer sacrifices at the Feast of the Tabernacles. Zechariah, speaking for God, assured them that they could make a sacrifice anyplace they found themselves. They didn't have to use the special pots for sacrifices located exclusively in the temple. They could use the ones in their kitchens. This was good news for everyone who wanted to observe this holy day. But what does this mean for us?

Next time you see a pot, think of how you honor God—the modern equivalent of the Old Testament sacrifice. Do you contribute generously to the Lord's work? Do you tell God how thankful you are and how much you love Him? Have you applied your skills by serving others to His glory? Your pot of sacrifices may be brimming over or the contents may barely cover the bottom, but you surely honor God in some ways.

One danger, however, is keeping other "pots" cooking in addition to the one dedicated to God. Those other "pots" are anything that distracts us from love of and obedience to God. So much of life needs attention to keep it from boiling over, blazing up, or becoming a mess. At those times, we're tempted to forget our Lord—to try to manage without Him. That's a mistake. Our Lord invites us to worship Him not only with thanksgiving, but with trust. Honor God by trusting Him with everything you've got cooking. He'll make your life "done to perfection."

No Minors

Psalm 5:1–8

YOU DON'T ALWAYS see the sign, but the rule exists anyway. *No minors.* The rule applies in bars and cigarette shops and that steamy corner of the video store. Then there's all the hoopla surrounding the Internet and television and ways to prevent sensitive young eyes from scenes and words that threaten indelible damage on fragile values. The judicial system sometimes singles out minors too. What do you think of laws that carry more severe penalties for minors when the same acts bring only a slap on the hand to adults—drunken driving laws, for example. It seems unfair, but would God agree?

"You are not a God who takes pleasure in evil; with You the wicked cannot dwell. The arrogant cannot stand in Your presence; You hate all who do wrong" (Psalm 5:4–5). Note the phrase "hate all who do wrong." Not those under 21 or 18, but *ALL*. If you find yourself squirming like an adolescent caught with an "adult" magazine, you're probably not alone. If you're not taunted by some degree of discomfort, you're probably not—excuse me—honest with yourself or with God.

We are all sinners. We tend to group sins into categories such as "not too bad," "everybody does it," "I would never get caught doing such a thing," or "Why would anyone want to do that?" Sins in the last two categories are those from which we most want to shield children—though those "of age" don't mind dabbling in them at the movies, in the tavern, or on the mattress.

When it comes to spiritual life, all humans are minors—spiritually immature, feeble, and all too susceptible to temptation. We shouldn't be exposed to "certain things," but there they are. The devil dangles them in front of us. Good thing Someone is out there to help us minors.

Confess and pray this: "But I, by Your great mercy, will come into Your house; in reverence will I bow down toward Your holy temple. Lead me, O LORD, in Your righteousness because of my enemies—make straight Your way before me" (Psalm 5:7–8).

Because Jesus took away our sins on that best of days, God welcomes us into His presence. When temptation wins over us, the victory is only temporary. God's forgiveness is permanent. And that's no minor accomplishment.

50

You Do the Math

Matthew 18:1–35

IF FORGIVENESS WERE AN ANIMAL, it would be an endangered species. (It has, however, been replaced by a wanton mutant identified as "sue.") Have you noticed that to err is human, but to forgive is about as common as a porpoise in Nevada? Of course, when discussing forgiveness, it's easier to receive it enthusiastically, but more difficult to give it. When forced to think about it, our personal archive of forgiveness surfaces from beneath the dust once in a while as we recall how so-and-so did such-and-such to us (approximately 13 years, two months, six days, eight hours, and 27 minutes ago). And now they did it again!

The apostle Peter, being flagrantly human, once questioned Jesus about forgiveness. The scene went like this: "Then Peter came to Jesus and asked, 'Lord, how many times shall I forgive my brother when he sins against me? Up to seven times?' Jesus answered, 'I tell you, not seven times, but seventy-seven times' " (Matthew 18:21–22).

You do the math. Perhaps that is 483 times more than reason dictates. Yet even that's not enough. Before we're tempted to hire the accounting firm of Sinbad and Slink to monitor the additional 483 misdeeds, we need to remember that Jesus spoke figuratively. Very figuratively! The Savior meant that forgiveness is never an option. His proclamation of symbolic sevens indicated that forgiveness should be comprehensive and complete. Well He should know. Forgiveness cost Jesus His earthly life.

Our 490 and then-some sins were forgiven completely. Completely. Gone and forgotten. That forgiveness gives us power to forgive others as we have been forgiven—in both quantity and quality. That's not to say that the quality of our forgiveness is the same as the quality of God's forgiveness. If only we could forget what we've forgiven as easily as we forget where we left our car keys! Good thing God forgives both our efficient and deficient memory.

Memory, teamed with guilt, is another plague on forgiven sinners. Have you forgiven yourself as often as God has forgiven you? Next time you remember your own sinfulness, think about Peter's question. And remember Jesus' answer.

Marriage Vows

Hosea 1:1–11

ONE WIT (well, maybe he was only a half-wit!) defined marriage as a situation in which two people agree to change each other's habits. This might have been the case with the prophet Hosea and his unusual, albeit God-given, wife, Gomer.

Scripture reports: "When the LORD began to speak through Hosea, the LORD said to him, 'Go, take to yourself an adulterous wife and children of unfaithfulness, because the land is guilty of the vilest adultery in departing from the LORD' " (Hosea 1:2).

Hosea's marriage to Gomer was ordained as a living parallel to the believers' unfaithfulness to God. (*Note:* I said "believers.") Can you imagine Hosea's feelings as he embarked on this sea of God-ordained matrimony in a leaky boat? Yet Hosea obeyed, and there was good reason for his obedience.

Believers are God's Gomers. (This includes us, as well as those early believers known as the children of Israel.) Our relationship with God is decidedly one-sided, and the better half is undisputedly God. From the very beginning of humanity, God promised to love and care for His people—in good times and bad, in sickness and health, and in trips to craft shows or auto dealers. We humans, sincerely believing in the powers of spiritual passion, agreed to treat our beloved Creator and Companion in the same way. Both of us knew the predictable results, though we humans tend to be a bit more optimistic (or naive). In reality, believers are constantly unfaithful to God.

The problem is that temptation flirts with us all day and all night. We often succumb to immediate pleasures, temporarily losing memory of our faithful God or brazenly chasing some fleeting joy. We can't help but confess what God already knows. Believers are sinners. Frequent sinners. Sinners who often stray from the One who loves them most. It's an age-old story of unrequited love.

Yet there is hope—hope that doesn't rely on our attempts to improve the relationship. Our only hope for a lasting relationship is grounded in God's commitment to each of us. Ours was a marriage to die for. And He did.

Silly Question

Matthew 22:24–32

T HERE ARE MANY GOOD QUESTIONS. The best questions are those that are better than the answer you'll probably get. Of course, being open-minded individuals, we acknowledge at least two answers to every question: ours and the mistaken or uninformed. Therefore, it shouldn't surprise us that a crowd asked Jesus some loaded questions that they hoped would lead Him to answer with toes protruding from His mouth. One of the most ridiculous queries went like this:

> *"Teacher," they said, "Moses told us that if a man dies without having children, his brother must marry the widow and have children for him. Now there were seven brothers among us. The first one married and died, and since he had no children, he left his wife to his brother. The same thing happened to the second and third brother, right on down to the seventh. Finally, the woman died. Now then, at the resurrection, whose wife will she be of the seven, since all of them were married to her?" Matthew 22:24–28*

Be sure to read Jesus' answer in verses 29–32, but that's really not the point of this meditation. Silly questions are. How often don't we like to speculate about insignificant spiritual matters and avoid the really important issues?

One example might be the engrossing interest some have in predicting the end of the world. They cite with great expertise how prophecies of THE END have been fulfilled through historic events in Russia, Israel, and in global economic matters. This wouldn't be idle conjecture except that Jesus clearly taught that His return would be a complete surprise—in fact, He will arrive when we least expect Him.

Other silly questions come from an unexpected source—educated scholars who have studied the Bible and other writings so extensively that the academic abbreviations behind their names would fill a can of alphabet soup. These are the most dangerous inquirers. They carry credentials that lend (and I do mean *lend*) credibility. These are the people who question the truth of burning bushes, parting waters, pillars of fire, virgin birth, and resurrection. They profess to know the answers too.

Considering the abundance of silly questions, remember one thing: *Keep it simple.* The most important answer is Jesus Christ.

53

Spell Check

Romans 10:1–13

HERE IS A DIVERSION that will provide you with many hours (well, many minutes) of delightful entertainment. All you need is a computer with the ability to check spelling. Type in your last name or your first name, if it's the least bit unusual. Use your friends' names too. Then let the spelling program loose. It's funny what it does to … Hey! Look what it did to my last name! It's bad enough that most people don't pronounce the *e*, but for my personal computer to call me a garden insect. Well!

Spelling programs, useful as they are, recognize only the most common names. It's the cyberworld's way of telling us that it really doesn't know us. In that way, computers are like much of the world. Few of us are well-known. But what about Jesus Christ?

Even the computer recognizes that name. It is ironic that much of the world doesn't! You and I are probably in the minority when it comes to identifying the name of Jesus with our personal Savior. It certainly is a good name to know, and here is the reason why: "For, 'Everyone who calls on the name of the Lord will be saved' " (Romans 10:13).

Many have called on that name. Some have called it without even knowing it. Think of Adam and Eve in those terrifying, guilt-laden moments immediately after they sinned. They were scared speechless, but the Lord God comforted them by predicting the future when one whose name was a mystery would come to crush the evil serpent's head. Then there was David who through both perils and victories envisioned a Messiah. Did he ever call Jesus *Jesus*? Probably not, but he knew what God planned to do for him and others like him who believed.

Eventually, people learned the Savior's identity. There was that band of 12 famous men and other unidentified ones who knew Jesus by name and face. They called on Him for healing and forgiveness. He did so freely, encouraging them to abandon sin and welcoming them back when they couldn't.

How often do you call on Jesus' name? Too often we do it only when we're sick or troubled or as the finishing touch on a formal prayer just before we say *Amen*. Yet we remain free to call on Jesus at any time. He loves us and wants us to be His own. His whole life clearly spelled that out!

Gate-Crashers

Mark 2:1–12

THERE ARE TWO THINGS to think about as you look at the neighbor's light in the window late at night. Either someone is sick or they're giving a party and you're not invited. If the latter is true, comfort yourself, if you want, by thinking of your neighbors as naturalists—heavily involved in wildlife! Of course, you always could invite yourself. Gate-crashing isn't uncommon.

The Bible tells about some gate-crashers, or should we say roof-rippers? Mark recounts the circumstances. "Some men came, bringing to [Jesus] a paralytic, carried by four of them. Since they could not get him to Jesus because of the crowd, they made an opening in the roof above Jesus and, after digging through it, lowered the mat the paralyzed man was lying on" (Mark 2:3–4).

Some in the crowd undoubtedly thought this a most rude intrusion. How dare this rabble drop in unannounced! After all, they had assembled to hear Jesus divulge His shocking and exciting message. Perhaps He would say something that contradicted Scripture—something to put a little deadly excitement in their by-the-book lives.

Jesus disappointed nobody. Those who gathered to learn about Jesus witnessed the object lesson of their lives. The four faithful men who lowered their friend to Jesus' feet heard the Savior proclaim healing—both of body and soul. And if those who observed the day's miraculous event were pleasantly astonished, just think how that man felt when he rose to his feet, free from his horizontal prison!

Of course, there are a few at every party and in every crowd. The scoffers. The legalists. The troublemakers. Mark tells us they conspired among themselves, criticizing Jesus for forgiving sins! Apparently, they weren't in the crowd to learn or to enjoy Jesus' message. They wanted to find something wrong with it. They weren't disappointed.

Today, Jesus holds a huge and happy crowd adoringly spellbound in heaven. Imagine the angels singing and the souls of saints laughing loudly in unrestrained glee as they dance in God's dazzling glory. But you're not there. Yet. Meanwhile, don't be afraid to do some gate-crashing at that heavenly festival. Send your prayers up to God. It gives Jesus another chance to heal another sinner. Drop in anytime!

Easy Mark

Acts 4:8–12

MOST FISHERPERSONS ARE easy marks for advertisers. As a boy, I remember responding to an ad for a lure that guaranteed I would catch fish. Forgetting that every lure I ever purchased was similarly destined for success, I bought this marvelous gadget. When it came, I discovered the lure held a battery (not included), a buzzer, and a tiny propeller motor. It was supposed to call fish. It must have called them something offensive because not one fin rippled the water the day I used it.

Which personal weaknesses do advertisers exploit? Perhaps it's new cars, the latest computer, a particular toothpaste, or a favorite fast food. Advertising is successful because it tells us what we want to hear. It offers answers and hope to all we question or desire. It makes everything sound sooooo good.

The devil would have been a successful advertising tycoon. Can't you see his agency? Satan and Sons, Supreme Sellers of Sin. He could boast a long history of fruitful campaigns, starting with the very first consumers, who eagerly believed his fraudulent claims of glory. Like any effective advertiser, he remains persistent, slinging one angle after another to hook us. One of his largest modern advertising challenges parades itself before our hearts and souls. It might be called "Ways to Get to Heaven."

Admittedly, that doesn't sound like something the devil really wants to sell. It's against his religion. Or is it? How often have you tried to do good things because God requires such behavior to enter heaven? Or maybe money is your downfall. Large contributions make God happy, don't they? And a happy God will surely notice my generosity, won't He? Or perhaps someone you know assures you that he has plenty of time to become faithful because God is a sucker for deathbed avowals of faith. We're all suckers for some pitch that the devil broadcasts. Like the worst of advertising, however, his sales pitches are all lies.

Jesus did some advertising of His own. You'll find it in a book that adorns the shelves and coffee tables of many homes. Page through it and you'll see this catchy phrase: "Salvation is found in no one else, for there is no other name under heaven given to men by which we must be saved" (Acts 4:12).

You know the name. You know how much it costs. Surely this is the best buy ever.

Declared Incompetent

Mark 3:20–35

Y OU MAY NOT KNOW any fanatics personally, but they aren't difficult to identify. They're the people who stick to their guns, whether or not they're loaded.

Two thousand years ago, a well-known figure roamed the regions of Israel. Many thought Him a fanatic. Even His family had doubts, as we hear in Mark 3:20–21: "Then Jesus entered a house, and again a crowd gathered, so that He and His disciples were not even able to eat. When His family heard about this, they went to take charge of Him, for they said, 'He is out of His mind.' "

Forget the label "fanatic." His family figured Jesus was a lunatic, and they declared Him incompetent. After all, with all His fame, He should have sought His fortune. His entourage should be keeping His name in front of supportive crowds. Instead, He often ordered His followers to keep quiet. Now He was so busy with His job that He couldn't find time to eat!

This section of Mark might be considered hard on families. Later in the reading, we hear Jesus rebuke His family—almost repudiate them—by announcing that His "real" family consisted of those who listened, learned, and believed in Him. Think of how this must have stung Mary and Jesus' brothers—how others must have whispered their opinions about His gruff talk. This was not a rebellious or disobedient son talking. Jesus told the divine truth, and at least some of Jesus' family later believed "their" Jesus was God's Son, the Savior.

As the world, both ancient and modern, views heroes, Jesus certainly was incompetent. His humility and honesty, combined with compelling authority and an unrelenting work ethic, made Him a target for those who view such qualities as characteristics of fanaticism.

Not much has changed. Christians, as you may have experienced, might be accused of incompetency when it comes to dealing with worldly issues and problems. Critics scoff when Christians say they have to pray about something. Then there's the way you spend your time and money. And there's this forgiveness thing. Revenge satisfies more!

Crazy Christians. That's what we are. But we have a great example to follow. So stay with the crowd—the crowd that gathers to learn and listen and believe in Jesus.

57
Lopsided Odds

1 Kings 18:16–39

THE ONLY WAY to make a small fortune in gambling is to start with a large one! It's best to view gambling ventures with a little horse sense. You've never seen a horse betting on himself, have you? Most gamblers are out to get something for nothing; in truth, they get the opposite. Odds always seem stacked against those least able to lose.

The prophet Elijah understood odds, especially because they were frequently against him. Here's one example: "Then Elijah said to them, 'I am the only one of the LORD's prophets left, but Baal has four hundred and fifty prophets. Get two bulls for us. Let them choose one for themselves, and let them cut it into pieces and put it on the wood but not set fire to it. I will prepare the other bull and put it on the wood but not set fire to it. Then you call on the name of your god, and I will call on the name of the LORD. The god who answers by fire—he is God.' Then all the people said, 'What you say is good' " (1 Kings 18:22–24).

The odds were 450 to 1. In fact, they were worse because an additional 400 false prophets threw their support to the prophets of Baal. How could Elijah face such a disadvantage? What was he thinking to blurt out such a defiant bet in the face of such overwhelming odds? He wasn't thinking, though. He knew what would happen.

God won the contest; Elijah was just the dealer. In reality, no odds were involved. God revealed His power that day as He won the battle of sacrifices. His opponents perished trying to beat Him.

Perhaps you're a gamer of sorts—the kind who plays a friendly game of canasta, four corners, or even poker. Those games involve odds. Even solitaire has odds stacked against a lone player. Your chances of winning are just that—a chance. Good thing it's not that way with God.

Winning with God is a certainty. He passed the winnings along to you when Jesus died for your sins and, against all odds, came to life again, inviting you to share His victory. Next time you play cards, take a moment to savor your losses. Let them remind you that you're never a loser with your Savior. Odd, isn't it?

58

Extra Ordinary

Acts 4:13–20

HOW DO WE DESCRIBE average Americans? We might surmise they have an average of three televisions, three cars, three telephones, and three credit card payments they can't meet even with three jobs. An average American takes more than 19,000 steps each day—not necessarily in the right direction. The average American has more food to eat than the average citizen anywhere else in the world. Also more diets. Finally, average Americans might have made Jesus' short list of potential disciples.

One striking feature of Jesus' followers was their lack of striking features. They boasted minimal social or employment status. Most of His followers held jobs that didn't require much education. (Don't tell an experienced fisherman that!) Tax collectors, disabled people, and women formed a large contingent of His followers—and those people often were classified as less than ordinary. In deference to political correctness, we might euphemistically identify them as extra ordinary. Critics of Jesus noted this as well. Acts 4:13 says: "When they saw the courage of Peter and John and realized that they were unschooled, ordinary men, they were astonished and they took note that these men had been with Jesus."

The average reader of this book probably considers himself or herself ordinary. Few among us have accomplished great things for which we'll be remembered for, say, more than 12 minutes. Yet we're in excellent company when you consider the likes of Peter and John. How have these ordinary people attained a place in history so lofty that we remember them 2,000 years later?

Behind every successful person is God. God takes common people and empowers us to do uncommon things. You say you don't do anything out of the ordinary? Pig cleanser! (Hogwash.)

You and every other Christian have faith. That's not ordinary. It's miraculous. The Holy Spirit chose you to believe in Jesus as your Savior, and you do. Not enough evidence? You put that faith to work too. You're reading a devotional book. You forgive others too. Right? Ordinary people like us forgive others for only one reason: God forgave us first.

Like the astonished disbelievers in today's Bible reading, there is one thing others may notice about us. It's the "secret" of our uniqueness. We have been with Jesus! Only He can make the extra ordinary extraordinary.

59

News Flash

Matthew 7:24–27

IF TODAY'S TITLE SOUNDS FAMILIAR, it should. Every so often, news so compelling, so momentous, so so-so erupts and begs for worldwide proclamation. *Dateline:* Notre Dame University, June 1997. Research scientists determined that playground sand builds better sand castles than beach sand.

You have to hand it to eminent scientists employed by major universities. This is cutting-edge stuff. Had modern science discovered this phenomenon 20 centuries ago, it might have influenced one of Jesus' most memorable parables. One verse sums up the Savior's story quite well: "Everyone who hears these words of Mine and does not put them into practice is like a foolish man who built his house on sand" (Matthew 7:26).

You know the result of such folly. Houses built on sand collapse with the first wind and rainstorm. (Maybe they fall apart more slowly if built on a playground.) Of course, Jesus wasn't lecturing on architecture. He was talking about hearing and learning. He talked about faith, growth, and strength.

Jesus talked and talked. Some listened and listened. Others even digested His message. But words mean nothing unless hearers believe and respond to them. In Jesus' day, it seemed that everyone wanted to know more about God—except, of course, those who thought they already knew enough. Questions surfaced constantly: How can we be saved? How can we be healed? How can we find true happiness?

Do you have similar questions? Many people offer advice; some even make a good living doing it. But their advice often is limited to human wisdom. Only one resource forms the foundation for true help—secular or spiritual. Look for answers from heaven.

Jesus provided clear answers. Those who listened heard solid truth in a message that delivered salvation, healing, and joy. That truth—and hope—can weather any storm of adversity, temptation, and attack. Believe on the Lord Jesus Christ and you will be saved, healed from sin, and live in bliss forever. Plug your ears (or bury your head in the sand) when others suggest that you must do anything to be saved in addition to believing in Jesus. Trust the message our Savior left behind. Anything else you hear will give you only a sinking feeling.

60
The Means Justify the Ends

Titus 3:1–8

ACCOMPLISHMENTS. What role do they play for you? A wise man said you really don't know what you can do until you've undone what you did. Personal experience confirms that philosophy. I once tried to replace the fuel filter in my dad's Oldsmobile. The filter screwed into the carburetor. However, I cinched it in at an angle and found myself needing to undo something I did. I had to undo my wallet, perform a painful extraction, and hope the new carburetor fit!

We seem to live with a philosophy that the ends justify the means. If we accomplish what we set out to do, the only thing that matters is how we finished it. This ideology, however, leads to things like the Watergate burglary or the bombing of the federal building in Oklahoma City.

Had Jesus chosen to let the ends justify the means, He may have zapped the evil Pharisees into smoldering cinders or leaped off the cross and vaporized His antagonists. Instead, Jesus did things the way God intended simply because God intended Jesus to do it that way. Part of our Lord's holy work was to obey, even when it meant suffering and death, which He didn't deserve. Because Jesus lived and died according to God's will, we can turn around that faulty philosophy and say, "The means justify the ends." Well, perhaps it sounds better in Titus 3:7: "So that, having been justified by His grace, we might become heirs having the hope of eternal life."

The end is coming. That news would have us cowering in a dark corner were it not for the life, death, and resurrection of Jesus. As we look forward to The End, we can, indeed, look forward to it in bold, fearless, capital letters. We head for that new beginning thoroughly armed with the means that justify the end—what some call the means of grace.

Our Father who waits for us in heaven left us with the Bible—a book understood only through the eyes and mind and soul of faith. We understand it. Well, at least the most important parts! The means of grace that justify our end also include two holy acts—Baptism and the Lord's Supper. God left us with those simple but powerful gifts—all because we have been justified by Jesus! Now we can count on a happy ending to our brief chapter on earth!

61

New Punctuation

Psalm 13:1–6

HAVE YOU EVER WONDERED who invented punctuation marks? I haven't either, and it's probably good that we don't know. Can you imagine what it would cost if the inventor of the comma had patented the device and we had to pay to use it? Then again, many modern students wouldn't spend much according to current assessments.

After ages of commas, question marks, periods, and exclamation marks, the time might be right to invent a new mark. The mark would represent a question to which no current or complete answer exists. The new mark would be useful for spiritual people like us. The psalmist David might have appreciated it too. He could have used it in passages such as: "How long, O LORD? Will You forget me forever? How long will You hide Your face from me? How long must I wrestle with my thoughts and every day have sorrow in my heart?" (Psalm 13:1–2a).

Let's examine each of David's questions. "Will You forget me forever?" Those separated from loved ones might relate to David's anguish. Perhaps you've even felt the ultimate loneliness—separation from God. Although people may be gone, they're often not forgotten. And we don't want them to forget us, either, though it sometimes seems that way. Perhaps it's a time when our fervent prayers seem to go unnoticed. Has God forgotten us?

"How long will You hide Your face from me?" We might reason that our perfect God cannot forget, so if He doesn't appear to hear our prayers, maybe He is hiding from us. Have we done something unforgivable? Have we exceeded our sin quota? Why don't You look at me when I'm talking, God?

"How long must I wrestle with my thoughts?" I read the Bible, but it doesn't have the answers I want. Why don't You tell me more, Lord? I want to know.

These questions shouldn't end with question marks. I'd like to suggest a new mark that is actually an old symbol. It's a ✝. How do you like it? When prayers don't get answered according to our schedule and when our curiosity isn't satisfied by the Bible, we can look to the cross and end our questions there. The one-and-only most-important answer was given at the cross. Wait patiently. Someday we'll have all the answers. When God is ready.

62

A Little Culture

1 Corinthians 5:1–8

SOME SOCIAL SCIENTISTS predict that our culture will last another 200 years. Maybe they can tell us when it will start too! American culture may suggest that we shouldn't get too much of a good thing; therefore, we have a convenient excuse for not having much—culture, that is.

Before we hop on the culture bandwagon, we need to define the term. Culture can refer to the finer things of civilization and society— music, literature, arts, technology, and yes, even religion. Culture also may be defined less nobly—as in yogurt or yeast. Then there's the bottom stratus of culture—mold and other oddities that frolic in petri dishes. In human form, sinners match the last definition! Clearly, then, the word *culture* is used in different ways. Perhaps we can use it several ways at once.

Paul warns Christians about "culture" in 1 Corinthians 5:6–8: "Your boasting is not good. Don't you know that a little yeast works through the whole batch of dough? Get rid of the old yeast that you may be a new batch without yeast—as you really are. For Christ, our Passover Lamb, has been sacrificed. Therefore let us keep the Festival, not with the old yeast, the yeast of malice and wickedness, but with bread without yeast, the bread of sincerity and truth."

Jesus used a similar example of yeast's power to permeate when He described how the worst features of society—even religious society—can spread and negatively influence spiritual life. In less "politically correct" terms, sinful society has the same effect on spiritual nourishment that yeast would have if you swallowed it raw. Lots of gas. Bad gas.

Much sinfulness has seeped into religious life in the form of faulty doctrine, pride, self-sufficiency, and an emphasis on success rather than Scripture.

There's the other side of yeast too. It produces great bread when it's allowed to work with good ingredients. Christian spiritual culture doesn't have to be victimized by society. Christians can turn the tables and influence society and its culture. We can share the Gospel along with the Law. The sincerity and truth to which Paul refers is the truth about Jesus. He came to save all sinners, whether or not they have culture.

Grave Dangers

Ecclesiastes 7:1–4

OKAY, SO IT'S NOT A GOOD WAY to start a devotion, but today's title begs the question. For what kind of death do you hope? Most people hope to die of natural causes—you know, that's when you die naturally. There are some things worse than death, however. For some, it's life.

The wise writer of Ecclesiastes had an intriguing outlook on death. He talks about funerals in this passage: "It is better to go to a house of mourning than to go to a house of feasting, for death is the destiny of every man; the living should take this to heart" (Ecclesiastes 7:2).

That might seem morbid, especially coming from someone like Solomon, who had every reason to live festively. But Solomon understood that all people die. It's a natural consequence of living—with or without doctors. He advises us to anticipate our own passing—in a healthy way, of course.

Why think about death? One good reason is life. For example, how do you feel today? Have you been sick recently? What do you fear most in life—storms, loneliness, family crises, neighborhood violence, demonic drivers, cancer, your next dental visit? The list probably could go on, but suffice it to say that life isn't always what we would like it to be. Suffering is common. What do we say when someone dies after a particularly agonizing illness? "Well, at least she's at peace now."

Solomon warns of grave danger in loving life too much, probably because it can be so disappointing. But we also can experience peace alongside reality. We know death is temporary. But that suggests another grave danger—belief in reincarnation. (Who would want to come back as Aunt Delia's canary?)

Christ's reality, which He so graciously shares, is that death is just another stage of life. Moreover, it's the last unpleasant stage! We know that because Jesus returned to life, we also will live again. Which brings us to one last misconception about death—that we'll return as angels.

Not so. The Bible tells us that we'll have brand-new bodies and that we'll be ourselves. So don't worry about how you'll keep your halo straight or your wings strong. Don't avoid funerals because they're surrounded by sadness. In death's grief, we find the reality of the resurrection. Don't be so grave!

Don't Tell a Soul

Mark 7:31–37

DON'T YOU LOVE SECRETS? A secret makes you feel so important when you tell it to friends! Keeping secrets is difficult because you must forget the secret. Sometimes secrets are important for national or personal security—or reputation. At the same time, everyone wants inside information, especially the secret to success.

Several times during Jesus' ministry, He gave what seems a strange command. He wanted His work kept secret. Mark reports one such incident: "Jesus commanded them not to tell anyone. But the more He did so, the more they kept talking about it. People were overwhelmed with amazement. 'He has done everything well,' they said. 'He even makes the deaf hear and the mute speak' " (Mark 7:36–37).

Sometime after seeking to surround His ministry with secrecy, Jesus told His disciples to do just the opposite. He wanted them to tell the world about Him. So why the initial secrecy?

Perhaps Jesus didn't want to focus exclusive attention on His miracles. Crowds followed Him, hounded Him, for healing from all types of sickness—physical and demonic. His great compassion never failed, but He probably worried that the crowds would miss His message about faith, forgiveness, and forever. That happens today, too, as people look for miracles to solve their problems. Faith healers and other miracle workers still ply the crowds, but how often is the message of salvation by grace alone hidden behind the mystery and marvel of miracles?

Jesus was more than just a miracle worker. Well, maybe not. What miracle was greater than God loving sinners so much that He sent His Son to take the form of a human and suffer and die for them? What a magnificent miracle was Christ's coming back to life, defeating death and the devil for us! Yet another miracle, one we personally have experienced—the miracle of faith! We have it not by our learning or goodness. (Thank God!) The Holy Spirit gave it to us. Not only that, but He nourishes us each day and keeps us close to Jesus.

Maybe the Holy Spirit wants you to share some "secrets" today. Go ahead, but just share your faith. Leave the miracles to Him.

65

Good Intentions

Luke 18:18–23

M Y MOTHER HAD A SAYING. Actually, she had many sayings and exercised little restraint in saying them. Anyway, when I offered excuses about my work in school or my chores around the house or getting up before 11:30 on Saturday morning, she would say, "You'll never get anywhere on good intentions."

Jesus said something similar in Luke 18:22. "When Jesus heard this, He said to him, 'You still lack one thing. Sell everything you have and give to the poor, and you will have treasure in heaven. Then come, follow Me.' "

Placing Jesus' words in context, we hear a young man with good intentions ask how he could earn eternal life. The young man claimed to have a head start on everlasting life because he obeyed the commandments. How sad when this "achiever" learned that his efforts were inadequate! He couldn't muster the faith to do what Jesus required—sacrifice every earthly thing and become a disciple.

Was it too much for Jesus to ask? His closest disciples gave up all they owned, though it probably wasn't too hard to leave behind empty nets, fishy fragrances, tax ledgers, and stiff competition. But in their own uniquely humble ways, Jesus' disciples surrendered everything to learn from Him and spread the Gospel. Many of them even gave their earthly life. Does our Savior ask the same of us?

He does. It might be hard at times, and we may be wishy-washy about it. Nevertheless, all believers are expected to give up everything and follow Jesus. As difficult as it is, it's also surprisingly simple. Jesus gives us so much more than we give up.

Our Lord probably hasn't asked you to sell your home and leave your family so you can follow Him. More important, Jesus doesn't ask you to earn salvation. He wants you to desert every temptation that seduces you into thinking you've obeyed the commandments and are good enough to be considered successful in God's eyes. In place of all that, He wants you simply to follow Him.

To follow Jesus means to trust Him for everything, whether you have much or little. Following Jesus means wanting to live by His rules—not to earn His favor, but to show your love and gratitude. Following Jesus is more than good intentions. It's a way of life. Eternal life.

66
Misery Loves Company

Hebrews 2:14–18

DON'T SAY YOU HAVEN'T BEEN TOLD! Flee from temptation. Run from it! Needless to say, speed records aren't endangered by people racing from temptation. In fact, most who run from temptation leave an obvious trail for new temptations to follow. Then there are those who are ever vigilant for temptation. The more they see, the better it looks!

Temptation is an ever-present fact of life. While sinful enticements change specifications with each passing stage of life, their basic allure and potential destructiveness remain the same. For example, children seem beset by temptations to challenge authority. Not coincidentally, their decisions often conflict with what their parents would decide.

Next, we have young adult temptations so frequently associated with sexual matters and justified by claims of personal freedom. Middle-age temptations continue with much of the same and add financial discontent, career pressures to succeed at any cost, and anxieties associated with both. Then comes old age. It seems that in old age, hope sags along with everything else.

Those outside Christian circles, as well as those within, sometimes think that Christians should somehow be devoid of temptation. But listen to what the book of Hebrews has to say: "Because He Himself suffered when He was tempted, He is able to help those who are being tempted" (2:18).

The "He Himself" is Jesus. He suffered human temptations during childhood, adolescence, and young adulthood. In fact, He probably suffered more. The Bible relates how the devil gave Jesus personal attention! If misery loves company, Jesus is right there with us. But don't despair.

One resource Jesus provides to fight temptation is communication. He willingly listens when we share what tempts us most. Perhaps He'll remove that temptation from the devil's repertoire; perhaps He'll strengthen us by letting us struggle more with it.

Another "temptation tool" is what Jesus used in His personal battle with Satan—God's Word. When we know what the Scriptures say, we're able to fling those words at the devil just as Jesus did. The catch, of course, is that we need to know what the Bible says. You're working on that now as you meditate, but get involved in Bible classes and daily Bible reading too. Misery doesn't really love company, but Jesus does.

Bravado

Nehemiah 4:1–9

WE MIGHT SUBTITLE the following three-part series "Life on the Farm." Being a city dweller, I consider rural life unique and suited for some scriptural parallels. Having spent approximately three days on a farm in southern Indiana at 9 years of age, I consider myself an expert. My first topic is chickens and what I learned from them.

Visitors on a farm should be useful. I certainly wanted to help, so I didn't hesitate when asked to feed the chickens. It didn't appear overly challenging, especially since I saw only three or four chickens wandering around the fenced-in yard surrounding the coop. I strode into the compound with a bucket of feed. The chickens strode too. Only they were fast and appeared menacing, so I banged on the bucket in an effort to discourage their aggressiveness. They kept coming, and they were joined by a herd of others who apparently mistook my banging for the dinner bell. Soon I was engulfed in chickens, so I banged harder. Even more chickens responded. I think some came from neighboring farms. I learned that bravado doesn't work with chickens.

Yesterday, we read about temptations and how to face them, and because assaults from Satan remain prevalent, we'll spend more time on the topic today. Bravado doesn't work with attacks by the devil. In fact, nothing we do alone will diminish Satan's fierce diligence as he persistently tries to win us. (And lose us!) Nehemiah, of Old Testament fame, shared his method of dealing with satanic trouble: "But we prayed to our God and posted a guard day and night to meet this threat" (Nehemiah 4:9).

That's the answer. Pray and post a guard. We thought about prayer yesterday, now we can think about the guard. The Holy Spirit is the only guard with adequate vigilance and power. The Spirit warns us when temptation is present. That might sound useless to Christians like us who can recognize temptation, but temptation can be subtle at times. For example, do we identify temptation when we think of ourselves as "good" Christians who don't sin like others in the world? Or in the church? Or in our family? The Spirit reveals temptations that are so tempting we don't even realize we're being tempted!

Don't delay. Post the Guard today. And don't bang any pots at the devil. He might think it's a come-on.

Different Dogs

1 Corinthians 12:27–31

Here's another true-life episode from "Life on the Farm." Did you know that farm dogs and city dogs don't have much in common? Sport was a farm dog. He disappeared for hours, returning to the farmyard encrusted with burrs, thistles, and something he rolled in. Chief, on the other hand, was a city dog. He felt secure confined to a fenced front porch and going into the house at night to sleep. Chief loved dog biscuits; Sport didn't know what they were. Neither did Sport's master.

I brought Sport some very special biscuits. They were small and dark brown and smelled like beef soup. I placed one on the back steps for Sport—a treat for when he returned from his day's pilgrimage. Sport's master saw the biscuit and thought the beast had committed an atrocity on the steps. Poor Sport.

Christians differ from each other too. Aside from their common faith in Jesus, they share some wonderful differences. Paul recounted them this way: "In the church God has appointed first of all apostles, second prophets, third teachers, then workers of miracles, also those having gifts of healing, those able to help others, those with gifts of administration, and those speaking in different kinds of tongues. Are all apostles? Are all prophets? Are all teachers? Do all work miracles? Do all have gifts of healing? Do all speak in tongues? Do all interpret?" (1 Corinthians 12:28–30).

Think of yourself. When we examine ourselves for gifts, we may conclude that we don't have (m)any. Maybe that's because we look for those that garner lots of notice. Not many of us have those gifts, but we all offer something. Maybe God gave you the ability to help others. That might mean driving someone to church, baby-sitting, gathering the neighbor's mail, and … let your imagination go wild.

There were all those other gifts too. If you're good at administration, serve on a church or social service board. You may have healing powers in the art of soothing broken hearts or listening to breaking ones. Miracles? Probably not, but who knows what good the Holy Spirit works through you? Perhaps someone's faith was strengthened as you shared your faith and God's Word.

Christians may be as different as city dogs and farm dogs, but they share one thing. And that's enough to make your tail wag for hours.

69

Picking Pickles

Philippians 1:27–30

Here's another lesson from "Life on the Farm": You pick pickles off grocery store shelves. You pick cucumbers from vines.

I saw them growing—no, sprawling—in the field. I asked if could pick the pickles. My farm hosts were kind enough not to laugh. Instead, they gave me a basket and set me loose. The first one I picked pricked me. Another lesson: Pickles are prickly when you pick them. Perhaps it's their defense against getting pickled. So much for Peter Piper. I bet he didn't emigrate from the city. One thing can be said about the experience though: The taste of homemade pickles surely justifies the scratches.

Harvesting bristly cucumbers is like life as a Christian. Paul put it more soberly: "For it has been granted to you on behalf of Christ not only to believe on Him, but also to suffer for Him" (Philippians 1:29).

Some Christians suffer under the misconception that faith in Jesus results in nothing but merriment and tranquility. There does exist a deeply rooted, unfailing contentment and serenity in the lives of Christians. It comes from trusting God through every moment of life, both good and bad. But Christians need not be giddy. What they are is realistic; otherwise, they face some brutally harsh disappointments.

Like Jesus, most of His immediate followers suffered for their faith in ways that horrify us. Christians in many parts of the world still suffer torture and fatal persecution because of their faith. Persecution is less physical for most of us. But suffering wears different masks, all hiding the devil's hideous face. Our suffering may come from the snickers of coworkers as we meditate on God's Word during break instead of sharing juicy jokes. Or suffering may result from our repeated practice of forgiving those who continue to take evil advantage of us because we seem "good natured." Our menu of suffering may include loneliness because, as much as we would like fun with friends, we don't drink ourselves silly or sit and swear at the local sports team. Perhaps our career suffers because we refuse to succeed at any cost.

Suffering accompanies the faith given by God. It's a small price to pay—even a blessing to pay—for the sake of faith. So don't let suffering get you down. Next time you eat a pickle, remember that it came at a cost. And the scratches eventually go away!

Branch Office

Zechariah 3:6–10

YOU'VE HEARD THE ONE ABOUT the forestry company that opened a branch office reserved for small jobs only? Alas, there was so little business that most employees packed their trunks and took leave. (It's knot polite to groan!)

Now might be a good time to introduce the first of today's Bible passages. "Listen, O high priest Joshua and your associates seated before you, who are men symbolic of things to come: I am going to bring My servant, the Branch" (Zechariah 3:8).

Many years later, Jesus revealed Himself as that branch. From Him would grow and prosper a new way of thinking and living. In Zechariah's years and through the ages (including the present time), people knew much more about sin than about mercy and forgiveness. They especially knew about sins committed by others, and they freely unveiled these for all to see. The Branch tried to change all this and ended up nailed to a tree. This didn't stop Him from opening global Branch offices.

It began with His closest friends and spread to many more disciples and on to anyone who would listen. Branch offices sprung up anywhere Christians witnessed their faith. It's like Zechariah reported: " 'In that day each of you will invite his neighbor to sit under his vine and fig tree,' declares the LORD Almighty" (Zechariah 3:10).

Reposed in the shade of God's love through Jesus Christ, Christians can spread the Good News of eternal life wherever they are. That's how faith spreads, with the Holy Spirit's help. Each of us is a branch office for Christ. We're part of a vast network of disciples with a long history and a bright future.

You know what sin did to you and what it would still like to do. Everything bad in life is a result of sinfulness. It leaves a huge blemish on life. It's a terminal disease. You also know what Jesus did for you when He died and rose to break the bonds of sin. You have the hope—the sure hope—of eternal life in the presence of Jesus, who loves you more than anyone can imagine.

Find a way to branch out and tell how you feel and what you know about the Branch Manager. You may find yourself out on a limb, but He's sure to keep you from falling.

Fruit Market

Galatians 5:22–23

For the next several days, we'll sample zesty goodies from the fruit market. You may be familiar with the passage from Galatians listed above. It's the one about fruit of the Spirit, and we're about to taste each. The first is love.

Love is a popular fruit. We use the word in many ways. You may love your spouse, children, a certain TV show, your parents, job, car, and sleeping late. As the song says, "Love makes the world go 'round." Of course, so does high blood pressure. You've also heard of love at first sight. (Don't knock it. Some of us might not make it past a second look!)

Jesus believed in love. We might go so far as to say that He believed in love at first slight. Luke 6:32 and 35a say: "If you love those who love you, what credit is that to you? Even sinners love those who love them. … But love your enemies, do good to them, and lend to them without expecting to get anything back." Jesus didn't mince any valentines; instead, He cut straight to the heart.

Love is easy if the object of one's affection is lovable. Think for a moment of those you love most. What is it about them that makes them lovable? They probably aren't perfect, but love has a blind side—a forgiving side that might be called the "commitment component" of love.

Now think of someone you don't love. In fact, think of someone you positively dislike—perhaps someone who recently "slighted" you. However, you don't need to know someone not to love them. What dastardly criminals are in the news? Which world leaders plunder their own people? Have you heard stories of Christian persecution? There's more today than there was in Jesus' time! These questions should help you list real people. Unlovables. Now put this book down. Pray for the people on your list.

For what did you pray? Perhaps the most important thing you can ask is that these people would come to faith; however, some already may claim to be Christians. Yes, "bad" people might believe in Jesus, but they also may bear bruised fruit. Pray that they recognize their sinfulness and repent. Your enemies may never realize that you're really their lover. You may find yourself singing a song of unrequited love. "What a Friend We Have in Jesus" is a good song.

Fuzzy Fruit

Psalm 4:1–8

SOME PEOPLE SHIVER at the fuzz, but they do enjoy what's beneath it. Peaches are my selection for the fruit closest to the spiritual fruit of joy. Ah, what juicy joy awaits those who slurp their way through a ripe peach! As my mother used to say at least once each summer, "How did you get peach juice on your undershirt?"

Life can be fuzzy on the outside, but a Christian's joy lies ripe beneath the surface of all worldly experiences. David the psalmist said, "You have filled my heart with greater joy than when the grain and new wine abound" (Psalm 4:7). God not only made David happy, He also implanted a wealth of indelible joy in the psalmist's heart and soul. God gave us the same gift.

Joy is a permanent condition. Laughter and mirth usually are temporary. They depend on a set of conditions that exist at any given time. Often they're random, enjoyable events. When the "event" is over, we stop laughing, and we don't feel particularly happy. For example, a family gathering at Christmas may bring delight and laughter. Then the family returns to its normal routines, and the happiness remains as only a warm memory.

Joy is different. Joy is like that contentment deep inside that says the family that gathers at Christmas is still a family though many miles (or other obstacles) separate it. Joy is happiness well beyond any smile or sense of humor. It doesn't come or go, nor does it depend on any specific circumstances.

How often Christians forget their gift of joy! Sometimes we're like the peach eater whose errant bite squirts peach juice up his nose (or down his undershirt!). He finishes the peach but won't admit to liking it! The Spirit's gift of joy wants us to splash around in its juices and share its succulence.

At times it's formidable to find the joy the Spirit placed within us. If you have trouble digging it up, just think about who you are. You are a sinner. (Not much joy there.) You are forgiven. (Whew!) It won't be long and you'll live with Jesus in perfect joy—a joy we can't begin to imagine now. (Hooray!) That's the gift of joy that lives inside us. Isn't that peachy?

73

Olive Alive

1 Peter 3:8–12

PEACE IS THE TIME between two wars during which nations find new ways to goad each other into armed conflict. It's ironic that we often fight to preserve peace. Perhaps the world should diet on the fruit of peace—olives. Of course, we probably would end up arguing over black or green, with pits or pitless, or …

Another fruit of the Spirit is peace, but it's unlike the human variety. When nations negotiate peace, they convene military officers, diplomats, and other experts. The reason their treaties don't last, however, is that they usually don't invite the Savior to the peace table. While they might argue that He lives too far beyond their boundaries, consultation by prayer remains a practical and speedy alternative.

Jesus had extensive experience in the peace process. People declared war on God. They rebelled often, and they still do, never having learned their lesson. Jesus did everything necessary to negotiate a lasting peace. He stepped between humans and God and sacrificed His life for the sake of sinners. God accepted that sacrifice and declared eternal peace between Himself and the redeemed saints.

Peace takes work, as Jesus proved. And the peace He sends our way through the Holy Spirit isn't the kind where we can sit back and relax. In 1 Peter 3:11, we read, "He must turn from evil and do good; he must seek peace and pursue it." The pursuit of spiritual peace requires us to make peace with God every day. We do that when we identify our personal declarations of war on God and confess our sin. God then forges the peace process with forgiveness, and He arms us to fight all that seeks to destroy our relationship with Him. We do it all again the next time.

We strive for peace with others because the Spirit makes peace an integral part of spiritual life. That takes work, too, as you know if you've ever tried to keep peace with family, neighbors, or members of your church.

An effective way to offer the olive branch of peace is to be like Jesus. It might take some personal sacrifice, and it certainly will take effort that is guided by the Spirit. Unlimited forgiveness is essential, and you won't get much rest. So always be ready to pass the olive branch. Anything else is the pits.

Watermelons

Romans 8:18–25

WATERMELONS ARE THE FRUIT of patience. You have to have lots of it as you separate the seeds from the good stuff. In fact, I think the first watermelon seed-spitting contest started because of frustration. Maybe not. It probably originated with some seedy characters.

I'm quite a patient person, but only when it involves doing jobs around the house. I can wait patiently all day to accomplish those tasks. If you want to test your patience, you might be surprised how much you have, especially while listening to the boss argue with you. The truest test of patience, however, comes when you must listen to someone telling you what you already know. Patience is a virtue. So hurry up and get some!

Patience is also a fruit of the Spirit mentioned by Paul. He comments on it in Romans 8:24–25: "For in this hope we were saved. But hope that is seen is no hope at all. Who hopes for what he already has? But if we hope for what we do not yet have, we wait for it patiently."

To paraphrase Paul, if you hope for a watermelon and you already have one, it's really not a hope. However, if you hope for a seedless watermelon, you may have to practice some patience. Okay, that's not exactly what he had in mind, but you get the idea.

Patience usually involves waiting. Because God's plan for us is something only He understands and because He carries it out according to His divine time line, the Holy Spirit gives us patience. We wait confidently for God to do His will.

We practice patience when we pray. God promises to answer prayer, and He always does. Conflict arises when we want God to answer prayers in ways that seem logical and timely according to human standards. Patience involves trusting God to answer prayer in ways best for us, even if it doesn't meet our specifications.

We practice patience as we wait for Jesus to return. Thousands of years passed between the time God first promised a Savior to Adam and Eve and the time the angels sang the birth announcement to scruffy shepherds. When Christ's work on earth ended, He promised to return and take us to heaven. How many days do you become impatient with that promise? Of course, when He shows up unexpectedly, someone probably will ask if He couldn't wait a little longer!

The Kind Kind

Ephesians 4:20–32

I HOPE YOU'RE NOT TIRING of this fruit diet—fruit of the Spirit, that is. We have several more varieties to go. Perhaps you'll exercise some patience and love, and with joy and peace in your heart, you'll be kind enough to read on.

The milk of human kindness is always a bit curdled. Someone always tries to skim a little cream off the top. But milk serves as an object lesson if we pour it over some sugared strawberries. Consider this as an example of the fruit of kindness—a smooth dessert, tame on the taste buds.

Kindness is a fruit of the Holy Spirit. The apostle Paul says, "Be kind and compassionate to one another, forgiving each other, just as in Christ God forgave you" (Ephesians 4:32).

A wise person once defined kindness as loving someone who doesn't deserve it. Wow! That fits you perfectly! Don't get defensive. That statement fits every one of us. Because it does, we begin to comprehend how much God loves us. His kindness exceeds absolutely anything we ever could expect. But there is a catch. Paul tells us to be as kind toward others just as God is kind toward us.

You'll discover your personal share of kindness as you go about daily routines with heightened awareness. Some examples? If you drive, you'll have numerous opportunities for kindness—and remember our definition. There's that guy who waited until the last minute to merge away from the lane closure and that woman strolling leisurely down the lane—in the parking lot! What kindness can you express toward that store clerk who drops your change or to the person stocking shelves who doesn't know where to find the bread? Then there's that crabby, next-door neighbor who complains that your heart beats too loudly and keeps him awake at night. Finally, there's that person who keeps doing the same aggravating things over and over. He usually expresses contrition, then he's back to his old tricks. (If you look in a mirror, he might look like you!)

God gave Jesus a special measure of kindness, and the Holy Spirit has heaped some on us too. Thank God for His unwavering kindness. Ask Him to kindly give you some extra, especially for sharing with people just like you. Tell Him you want to be the kind kind.

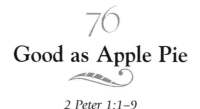

Good as Apple Pie

2 Peter 1:1–9

Y OU REALLY NEED ICE CREAM to top it off. Apple pie is good, but with ice cream, it's great. Speaking of goodness, it's mentioned by Paul as a fruit of the Spirit.

It's said that there is a little goodness in everyone. We must admit, however, that it's hard to find in some people. And for others, it's so far inside that it never gets out!

Not so with Christians who have this good gift from the Holy Spirit! Goodness is an essential ingredient in the Christian lifestyle. The Bible says this: "His divine power has given us everything we need for life and godliness through our knowledge of Him who called us by His own glory and goodness. Through these He has given us His very great and precious promises, so that through them you may participate in the divine nature and escape the corruption in the world caused by evil desires" (2 Peter 1:3–4).

God's goodness—through Jesus Christ—made possible our goodness. Just being good, however, isn't good enough. We must be good for something. Passive goodness is like the air bag in your car. It's good, but it does nothing unless you're in serious trouble. God's goodness is more active. It consciously attaches itself to everything we do and remains vigilant in pursuing the course of godly behavior.

Translated into action, human goodness tries to copy God's goodness. God always makes the correct choices, which, you'll have to admit, is a bit beyond our grasp. We probably best approach God's type of goodness by hating evil and loving good. This means we avoid certain things in our vocabulary—phrases such as "Goody Two-shoes" used to describe people who obviously try to make good choices or avoid immoral behavior.

On the positive side, our intentional goodness helps us evade corruption. That's good for something. It helps us bypass situations that might weaken our faith or our relationship with Jesus.

Goodness speaks volumes to those around us. Onlookers may even wonder why we're so good, which provides an opportunity to witness about the One who bought our goodness on the cross. Jesus Christ is like the ice cream on a warm slice of apple pie!

Too Much of a Good Thing

2 Chronicles 18:1–34

PICK ANY FRUIT, eat lots of it, and the results are predictable. The same might be said of our next fruit of the Spirit—faithfulness.

Understand that abundant faithfulness is excellent; it also can get you into trouble, just as it did for a not-so-memorable man in the Bible named Micaiah. He was one of God's prophets. He thought it more important to offer truthful prophecies than to say what people wanted to hear. That got him in trouble. "The king of Israel then ordered, 'Take Micaiah and send him back to Amon the ruler of the city and to Joash the king's son, and say, "This is what the king says: Put this fellow in prison and give him nothing but bread and water until I return safely" ' " (2 Chronicles 18:25–26).

Micaiah warned Israel's king to avoid war despite the fact that the king's bevy of yes-prophets assured him of victory. The king believed the yes-men. He never returned alive.

We might point to others whose faithfulness got them into trouble—Joseph, John the Baptist, Stephen, and Paul among them. We can't let this "fact of faith" discourage us. All who have suffered for their faithfulness found the condition temporary, and some went to their "reward" sooner than others.

Faithfulness is a gift of the Spirit. Just as Christians possess different degrees of the Spirit's blessings, they also have various degrees of faith. The Holy Spirit started us with the right amount of faith. Through the years, we may have lost some of that faith as we wandered away from Bible study, the Sacrament, worship, and prayer. Or perhaps we've been blessed with a stronger faith. Strong faith becomes even more potent as we weather crises, trusting that God always brings good from bad. Stronger faith results from Bible study, our presence at the Lord's table, and through worship where we hear God's Word of promise.

When called on to express our faith, trouble may accompany the experience. We would do well to expect it because then we won't be shattered by criticism or other persecution. Faithfulness is a benchmark of believers through the ages. The bench may be nicked, burned, and sat on regularly; nevertheless, it persists and even prospers. Better yet, faithfulness keeps us in touch with our loving, forgiving Savior. When it comes to faithfulness, there's never too much of a good thing.

Gentle Fruit

1 Thessalonians 2:1–9

CONSIDER THE APRICOT a nominee for the title of gentle fruit. It's neither too juicy nor too dry; not excessively sweet yet pleasingly mellow; tasty without sending taste buds into shock. That's how gentleness is—wonderful but not spectacular.

Among the many attributes of our Savior, gentleness would rate a strong second to love. In fact, gentleness may be generally defined as love in action. All Christians have a measure of this quality as a gift from the Holy Spirit. Paul mentions gentleness in 1 Thessalonians 2:7, which says: "But we were gentle among you, like a mother caring for her little children." Gentleness characterizes the way God wants us to treat others.

God has been generously gentle with us. We deserve His wrath, but He softly sprinkles blessings on us. The world should end because of its wickedness, but God maintains it, giving more time for others to be saved. When we confess our sins, God would be justified in slapping us down and making us grovel; instead, He extends His merciful hand to forgive us and to bless and strengthen us. God is an excellent role model for gentleness.

Consider what it means to be gentle. Being considerate may be another way of stating it. Jesus always was considerate; He did what He knew people needed. He didn't set up conditions, for example, when He healed others. He simply did it, healing their physical afflictions along with their spiritual maladies. He met the needs of hurting people, often neglecting His own human needs.

Another manifestation of gentleness is a willingness to listen. Do we listen beyond words to hear the heart speak? People may offer a variety of explanations to describe what they think and feel, but beneath their words, they reveal unmet needs or aches. A good listener might determine that "what goes around, comes around" or that suffering is sometimes a direct consequence of behavior. It might be easier to bluntly tell others why they feel the way they do. It's better to listen sympathetically, perhaps offering to pray with someone for healing of mind, body, and spirit.

As with all gifts of the Spirit, if we want to learn more, we can study God's Word. We can hear it straight from the mouth of the world's foremost gentleMan.

Enough

Matthew 27:1–14

R AY WAS THE WISE MAN of the produce department. With only the mere trace of a benign snicker, he helped young, ignorant customers tell the difference between lettuce and cabbage. (Try bringing home lettuce when the menu calls for sauerkraut!) When a dozen bunches of grapes seemed good judgment because the grocery list stated "grapes," Ray would spot the bulging bag and urge a little self-control. Ray probably saved a lot of young lives!

Self-control is the last of the fruit of the Spirit. You've probably had your fill of "fruit," this being the ninth day of this miniseries. Perhaps it's fitting that the last installment is self-control, the motto of which is "Enough!"

An old proverb suggests that the emptier the pot, the quicker it is to boil. Translated loosely, it means watch your temper. Exercise self-control. Again, Jesus provided an excellent example. His trial was a sham, and both He and His enemies knew it. At the very least, we might expect Jesus to let fly a tongue-lashing befitting the situation. Instead, the Bible reports this response: "When He was accused by the chief priests and the elders, He gave no answer. Then Pilate asked Him, 'Don't you hear the testimony they are bringing against You?' But Jesus made no reply, not even to a single charge—to the great amazement of the governor" (Matthew 27:12–14).

We all admit the necessity of self-control under stress, especially if the stress happens to outweigh or outrank us. Good advice, not of biblical origin, suggests that we count to 10 when we're angry. When we're livid, it's best to count at least 10 times further—then shut up anyway. Self-control can be a challenge in good times as well.

You've probably noticed that those who have much want more. This may be evident especially at the Thanksgiving table where the turkey isn't the only thing that gets stuffed. Or how about the generous credit limit that gets stretched beyond its already bountiful boundaries?

Self-control is a gift of the Spirit because it encourages us to be content with what we have. It keeps our life in perspective. It's God's way of confining us to that which makes us truly happy and satisfied. It also comes in handy when eating salted peanuts.

Cheap Gifts

Ephesians 2:6–10

MOST CHILDREN are haunted by pet fears. For some it's thunderstorms; others dread darkness. Mine was sparrows. They were a special menace during November and December. They perched on my neighbor's gutter—a scant three feet from our kitchen window—and watched me during breakfast. They watched me during lunch and supper too. They had only one motive. My mother said they were watching me eat. If I didn't clean my plate, they would report the matter to Santa Claus. With every tweet, the gift list grew smaller!

How good to hear the news that probably appears in every worthwhile devotional book ever written: "For it is by grace you have been saved, through faith—and this not from yourselves, it is the gift of God" (Ephesians 2:8).

God's gift is a true present. We do nothing to earn it. It's not that He doesn't know about us just like that imaginary guy at the North Pole. God has plenty of informers who roost on the gutter of life and report our sins. No, these informers aren't God's angels. They wouldn't think of doing such things because they know about His grace. The informers are employed by jolly old Satan whose happiest moments occur when he exploits our faults or divulges them to higher authorities.

God's gift of salvation doesn't depend on us. God sent Jesus because He already knew how rotten we were. He knew our destiny as sinners even before we were born! He gave us a gift that lasts forever. Despite the dossiers laid before Him, God looks past our sins to the life, death, and resurrection of Jesus.

While gifts are always welcome, they're more desirable when you don't have to qualify for them. What genuine gratitude we have when we receive something completely undeserved! What an opportunity to show our thankfulness! Like a box of candy passed around the room, we can share the gift of salvation. We share when we forgive as freely as God forgives us. We share when we're generous with our blessings, trusting that no matter how much we share, we'll never run out of what we need. We share when we pray for others and when we comfort them with the confidence we have in Jesus Christ.

Enjoy the best gift you've ever received. Open the shade so the sparrows can see.

Siren's Song

Nehemiah 2:1–5

FOREIGN AID seems the solution to so many world problems. This suggests that more localized problems would benefit from foreign aid too—the kind we get from God. It's easy to apply for help. Prayers need not be long or well planned to reach our Lord. Consider Nehemiah, a prime example of one who seemed to pray spontaneously. "The king said to me, 'What is it you want?' Then I prayed to the God of heaven" (Nehemiah 2:4).

Nehemiah prayed "on his feet." It didn't matter what else was going on. Even in the middle of a conversation, he could think a prayer and confidently await God's answer. The whole situation resembles an "instant mix" formula. Take a given situation, add prayer, and wait for God's blessings.

We probably experience more calls to prayer than we realize. The most familiar call may be church bells, though there seem fewer of these today. Here are some examples of other calls to prayer:

1. **Sirens.** They usually signal trouble. Moaning from a passing ambulance, they wail about someone in pain or close to death. When sirens howl beneath storm clouds, they warn of impending danger and possible destruction. The siren's song signals a good time to pray, both for ourselves and for others, even as we're taking cover or pulling to the side of the road. We don't need to know who occupies the ambulance or what path the storm will take. We can pray that victims are comforted and saved and that they become more aware of Jesus their Savior in the process.

2. **Anger.** It's hard to remain angry when you're praying. When that speeding driver zigs and zags between lanes, cutting you and others off with complete disregard, pray. Pray for your safety, but also pray for the safety of others—including the reckless driver.

3. **News broadcasts.** Prayer is a good alternative to clucking tongues and useless complaints about the world's depravity. Enough calls to prayer cry out in one news broadcast to keep you busy all day.

Like Nehemiah, we can pray anytime, anyplace, doing anything. God hears and answers. And it's a whole lot more productive than talking to yourself.

Great Expectations

Matthew 12:14–24

ONE OF HIGH SCHOOL'S great expectations was that we would enjoy reading Charles Dickens' book of the same title. The first several chapters didn't meet my expectations, so I never finished the book.

Great Expectations also might be a good title for anyone writing a history of Christians. The story could begin with Jesus Himself. The Messiah's people expected Him to wield earthly power, unassailable by any other king or nation. They expected someone who could crush opponents and lead them to a dynasty of wealth and military might. Here's what they got:

> *This was to fulfill what was spoken through the prophet Isaiah: "Here is My servant whom I have chosen, the one I love, in whom I delight; I will put My Spirit on Him and He will proclaim justice to the nations. He will not quarrel or cry out; no one will hear His voice in the streets. A bruised reed He will not break, and a smoldering wick He will not snuff out, till He leads justice to victory. In His name the nations will put their hope."*
> *Matthew 12:17–21*

Jesus clearly failed the expectations of His countrymen. We may find ourselves in a similar situation as people try to define Christianity by their own standards. So how might we measure up in society's expectations of Christians?

Those outside Christianity expect great things of Christians. They presume high moral standards and anticipate a certain aloofness from worldly pleasures. Of course, when Christians fail to meet those standards, critics enjoy a good spell of derision.

Christians expect much of other Christians too. We tend to define Christianity by personal standards—and most other Christians either don't measure up or, if they're really good, they're probably hypocrites.

What's really important is what God expects of Christians. The key to Christianity is faith in Jesus as our Savior. If we have nothing else, we're saved anyway. Beyond that, God sends His Holy Spirit to move us to respond to His love with godly lives and good deeds. When we recognize our flawed attempts to respond, God invites us to repent and receive forgiveness. Talk about forgiveness—now that's an expectation that makes Christians truly great!

Wild Roses

Matthew 21:18–22

THE BATTLE WAS FIERCE and the warfare long. When it was over, 40,000 enemy aphids lay dead and their domain lay withering and wasted. This was the war of wild roses, and what thorny problems they present-ed! What scratching and clipping! But now the hybrid roses could bloom in peace, safe from alien aphids that lived so smugly on unwel-come neighbors.

The duel with the wild plants and their inhabitants reminds me of Jesus' encounter with a fig tree. You might remember it from Matthew 21:19: "Seeing a fig tree by the road, He went up to it but found noth-ing on it except leaves. Then He said to it, 'May you never bear fruit again!' Immediately the tree withered."

I know the disruptive roses will return to compete with the real beauties, and Jesus probably could have withered any number of unpro-ductive fig trees. This meditation really isn't about plants. It's about peo-ple—believers and those who claim to believe.

Religious people are of two varieties. There are those who resem-ble hybrid roses or fruitful fig trees. They bear the name *Christian* on strong, straight stems. They bloom energetically and saturate their envi-rons with fragrance. These are the people who practice what they preach. Not that they're perfect. Like the misshapen roses that appear even on the finest bushes, Christians are damaged by sin. They contin-ue blooming, however, knowing that what beauty they demonstrate is really a reflection of their maker and caretaker.

It's different with the wild roses of religious people. They like to bolt up and show off, hoping to take control of the garden. They are pretty in their own way, but only on the outside. Inwardly, they are bent on destruction—usually, someone else's. They might imitate a hybrid well, but inside they're unchanged and remain wild.

Watch out for wild roses. They want to mislead us. Their human counterparts are those who talk like Christians sometimes but refuse to acknowledge that salvation comes only through faith in Jesus our Savior. They may blossom with beliefs that all religions lead to the same end. Although a tolerant attitude, it's most dangerous for those seduced by its shades of humanitarianism. Pray that they learn the truth.

An Easier Way

Matthew 4:1–10

IT'S THE DEVIL'S burning ambition to help people find an easy way to heaven. His hungry clientele is the whole world as it seeks the way to be saved. Strange, isn't it, that Satan would employ himself this way? Stranger still is that so many people believe him.

Never a slouch, the devil even approached Jesus in hopes of converting Him. Matthew tells the story: "Again, the devil took Him to a very high mountain and showed Him all the kingdoms of the world and their splendor. 'All this I will give You,' he said, 'if You will bow down and worship me' " (Matthew 4:8–9).

The devil had a real case with Jesus. The Savior knew what His ministry would involve, including a gruesome, excruciating death. He realized that His sacrifice would involve anguish of soul and pain of body. Therefore, the devil's offer probably didn't sound half-bad. Imagine, for a moment, how you would feel faced with the same future.

People face similar situations today. Perhaps the most noteworthy example surrounds the issue of assisted death for those who are terminally ill or for those who will suffer throughout their lifetime. Racked by pain and hoping for a death that just refuses to rush, sick people are prime targets for the smooth-talking devil. "Whose life is it, anyway?" he reasons. "If you can die in dignity, why not speed up the process? God won't mind." It's easy to believe.

The devil proposes other angles in his "easy-does-it" scheme. Weak faith invites him to introduce doubts about God's existence. "Why believe this phony business? Churches are just out to get money from naive people who need something to believe in," he complains. Sounds logical. If you can't see it, why believe it?

Another scam involves the popular do-it-yourself syndrome. Here Satan convinces us of what we want to believe—that with persistence, *we can* be gods just like the real thing. (This was Satan's first successful fraud!) He encourages us that *we can* be good enough or work hard enough to earn God's favor. Just try it and see …

Experience suggests that the easiest way to get something done is to let someone else do it. While Satan sizzles around trying to convince us that something else is actually easier, we relax and rely totally on Jesus for eternal life. What could be easier?

News Flash

Hebrews 10:19–25

W E INTERRUPT this devotional message to bring you yet another momentous news bulletin. This item was released in late June 1997: Misery does not love company, especially the misery of colds. Researchers revealed that social interaction reduces the number of common colds. The study involved volunteers who were given cold viruses, probably from small children who sneezed on them. Volunteers with three or fewer types of social interactions had a higher incidence of cold symptoms than did people with four or more types of social interactions.

If it works for colds, it works for Christians too. Consider Hebrews 10:25, which says: "Let us not give up meeting together, as some are in the habit of doing, but let us encourage one another—and all the more as you see the Day approaching."

Christians need to swarm together like busy bees. It's good to have both social and spiritual interactions with other believers. In fact, can we really separate social and spiritual interaction? Probably not. The Bible says that when even as few as two believers get together, Jesus is with them.

Interacting with others like us is good for spiritual health. Devilish viruses such as doubt, self-pity, self-centeredness, and worldliness prey on those who are isolated from other Christians. When we're in the habit of gathering together, the unity we experience with one another and with Jesus bolsters our spiritual immune system to fight sin-filled infections.

We participate in fellowship in several different ways. One way available to most people occurs in weekly church services. Together we listen, confess, receive forgiveness, pray, and sing. We might think of it as a party without the hats, streamers, and designated drivers!

Christian fellowship also takes place in less-organized ways when we join others for shopping or recreation, during coffee breaks at work, or in a neighborly chat. During times such as these, we have opportunity to flex our faith and strut our salvation. We're also available to encourage and comfort others.

A great thing about Christian fellowship is that it often includes many happy returns. Showing love, compassion, and friendliness somehow gets back to us when we need it. So why are you sitting here reading this book? Get out there and join the party.

Hang On

Zechariah 8:14–23

IF YOU WANT TO GO FAR, you have to stay close. Sorry if that sounds like some inscrutable, ancient, Asian philosophy. It's true. Look at this terrific Old Testament verse: "This is what the LORD Almighty says: 'In those days ten men from all languages and nations will take firm hold of one Jew by the hem of His robe and say, 'Let us go with You, because we have heard that God is with You' " (Zechariah 8:23).

We have the advantage of reading these words in a different context from that in which they were first spoken. In Zechariah's day, the world felt contempt for the Hebrew nation. So often it claimed to be God's chosen! So often it defied God or even forgot Him! The prophecy of Zechariah predicted that all this would change. And was he right!

Today, we can name the "Jew" whose hem people clung to. Jesus was the ultimate Jew, both in ancestry and history. He was so holy that merely touching His robe brought healing, as with the woman who had bleeding problems (Matthew 9:20–22). But Jesus brought healing not only from physical affliction, but also from spiritual illness.

Going back in time, imagine yourself grasping Jesus' robe as He gently nudges His way through the crowds seeking His help. Do you hear His impassioned voice encouraging individuals away from their sin and into His realm of forgiveness? Do you see Him smiling, touching, hugging, and making eye contact with the disheveled, disabled, brokenhearted rabble? The people knew they had a good thing going, and they didn't let go.

Let's not dwell only on history, as awesome as it is. We have a part in this story that transcends imagination. In a way, we are the Jew mentioned by Zechariah too. We know God. Do others know we know God? If they don't, we've got some witnessing to do. If they do, get ready for them to hang on to your hem. As you share your love in actions and words, they'll want to be with you because you're something special. Let them hang on. You have more strength and power than you realize. After all, you're hanging on, too, and God will pull you through anything.

The Snub

Matthew 10:32–33

IT LEAVES EMOTIONAL bruises that sometimes last for years. Perhaps you've experienced it yourself. Maybe it was the time you were with several acquaintances. They agreed to meet for lunch next Tuesday, but they didn't say, "See you then." Or it could be that child who is just too grown-up to associate with you anymore. He doesn't want you to park too close when you pick him up after school; his friends might see you. Or it might be during that dinner at church when the pastor recognizes several volunteers for their generous service. You've done more but don't get even a smile.

Snubs aren't just emotional dings; they're serious business, especially when applied to our Savior. Jesus said, "Whoever acknowledges Me before men, I will also acknowledge him before My Father in heaven. But whoever disowns Me before men, I will disown him before My Father in heaven" (Matthew 10:32–33).

Snubs may seem to be innocent mistakes, but sometimes they are expressions of conceit. Even conceited people don't like conceited people; of course, they're too conceited to know that they're conceited. Right? You may know several conceited individuals, but do you know anyone so conceited that she sends her parents a "congratulations" card on *her* birthday? (I don't either, but we need a little humor to break the tension.) Conceit is when people are all wrapped up in themselves. Not only are such people overdressed, they're often muffled from reality.

So far, today's message has been about other people, right? It's been about the conceited ones who wouldn't give Jesus an invitation to dinner because He dressed oddly, right? We wouldn't be that way ... or would we?

Most of us could confess that we occasionally snub our Savior. We might do it when we ignore His holy presence during a crude conversation with our friends. Our snub might come when we discuss our problems with everyone but Him. Or perhaps we go out of our way to visit friends and relatives and neglect a short trip to church or the family altar.

Despite our guilt and our shabby treatment of Jesus, He doesn't snub us. He's like that friendly puppy that wags its tail in our direction though we shout and swing newspapers at it. He loves us, and He will to the end. That's nothing to snub our nose at.

88

Tell a Vision

Luke 1:8–17

*Early to be bed and early to rise
Means the TV won't televise!*

Most TV programs at the time of this writing (compare it with current shows) involve holdups. Either criminals are holding up victims or doctors are holding up x-rays. (Too bad the doctors can't surgically remove commercials and implant good taste!)

If you're an avid television fan, perhaps you've wondered what people did in the BC (before channels) era. How could anyone be happy without this technology that transforms invisible signals into visions of things such as millionaire sports heroes dribbling tobacco down their chins? You may be happy to know that some of our biblical brothers and sisters had visions without the benefit of cable or satellite. Here is an account from Luke 1:10–13a:

> When the time for the burning of incense came, all the assembled worshipers were praying outside. Then, an angel of the Lord appeared to him, standing at the right side of the altar of incense. When Zechariah saw him, he was startled and was gripped with fear. But the angel said to him: "Do not be afraid, Zechariah; your prayer has been heard."

Prayers are almost like a television experience. The TV set loiters in the room. When you turn it on, picture and sound appear. It's almost like a vision is just waiting to be used. In a similar way, God waits around heaven (rather than Hollywood), waiting for you to contact Him.

Zechariah actually saw the messenger who reported God's answer to his prayer. So frightening was it for Zechariah, and so incredible, that he was speechless for nine months afterward! We might not want to see the messenger who reports answers to our prayers, but Zechariah's experience assures us that God is real and that He does respond to prayer.

It's no less miraculous when God answers our prayers, even if it is less dramatic. Like Zechariah, we might hesitate to believe our ears—rather our hearts—when God says that He's taken action on our behalf. But God loves us for the sake of Jesus, who died and rose to take away our sins. God will give you vision for the future as He answers your prayers. When He does, don't keep the news to yourself. Tell a vision to friends and give the Sponsor all the credit He deserves.

Justin Time

Esther 4:1–17

A RE YOU UP FOR A LITTLE QUIZ? Select the correct answer to this question: Who is Justin Time?

A. The inventor of the wristwatch
B. A songwriter
C. A spelling mistake
D. A recent concept of warehousing and inventory

If you answered A or B, you're an incurable victim of puns. Of course, the answer is C! If you read the chapter from Esther, you know that she was just in time. Remember this excerpt in which Mordecai speaks to Esther? "Do not think that because you are in the king's house you alone of all the Jews will escape. For if you remain silent at this time, relief and deliverance for the Jews will arise from another place, but you and your father's family will perish. And who knows but that you have come to royal position for such a time as this?" (Esther 4:13–14). Esther's timeliness saved the whole Jewish population!

The answer to our quiz is also D. Manufacturers have discovered that supplying items "just in time" to meet demand, saves money on storage and inventory.

Just in time. That's part of God's efficiency too. He acts for people exactly when they need Him. The Old Testament reports many "just in times": Abraham about to sacrifice his son; Moses and the Israelites standing before the Red Sea; and David confronted by a king bent on murder. We hear of it in the New Testament, too, especially when "just in time" refers to Jesus, who came at precisely the right time to save us.

The "just-in-time" concept continues with us. As with Esther, God placed us on earth for a reason—a reason that includes sharing the Good News with family, friends, strangers, and even those whom we dislike. Maybe we're here for an even more sensational reason, such as saving someone's life or serving the Savior under difficult circumstances.

When Jesus returns for the world's end, it will be just in time too. No one, not even the angels, know when that time is. Time will tell, and by the time you read this, time may already have told! One thing is certain: Jesus will come just in time. Just in time for the end—of time, that is.

Wearing a Cap

Psalm 96:1–13

POSSIBLY YOU'VE NOTICED the subtle change that's taken place in the way we read references to God. You may have to be over 40 to recognize this change, but that's okay—you can still see well enough to read no matter what your kids say. Before we proceed, let's examine a verse from a psalm: "For great is the LORD and most worthy of praise; He is to be feared above all gods" (Psalm 96:4).

If you contrast Scripture quotations in most books you read with the wording in this book, you'll notice a difference in the appearance of personal pronouns referring to God. Even your Bible probably uses a small *h* when *him* or *he* refer to God. The publisher of this book follows the traditional practice of using a capital *H* for these words and has permission from the publishers of various Bible translations to do so even in the Scripture references.

I'm uncertain why the pronouns no longer wear caps in the New International Version Bible. They probably had a good reason for eliminating them—maybe so I would have a topic for this devotional or to provide stimulating conversation or to make me feel guilty for not researching the reason. Perhaps it's because capital letters in the middle of sentences completely frustrate computerized grammar checkers. The fact remains, despite mandates from the publishing world, God deserves praise and honor. One small way to show we revere Him is by putting on our caps.

One might contend that this is a minor issue. Other more significant ways exist to worship and exalt our Lord. But whenever we have opportunity, shouldn't we show our love and respect for Him? God appreciates the little ways as well as the huge ways. Capital letters are one small way to demonstrate respect. Others may include the Christian fish symbol stuck to your car or the cross that we wear in our ears, around our neck, or on our finger. Maybe it's only the twinkle in our eye when we talk about our loving God, His Savior-Son, and the mysterious Holy Spirit.

God appreciates our praise. It's not that He needs it. Instead, when we praise Him, He hears our gratitude for forgiving our sins through the suffering and victory of Jesus. So next time you write about God, be sure He's wearing a cap.

Crowds

Mark 6:41–55

How do you feel about crowds? If you like them, you would have floated on savory air at the 1997 Taste of Chicago on the city's scenic Lake Front. The first three days drew crowds of more than 250,000 people. Now, let's see, 250,000 divided by six portable outhouses equals ... Oh, never mind what it equals. (In fairness to the fair city, there were more portable toilets than food booths!) Can you image a quarter million people shuffling from sizzling ribs to stuffed potatoes to Washington Monument-sized ice-cream cones to antacid tablets as big as sewer covers?

Jesus drew large crowds as He roamed the countryside teaching famished hearts what they needed to know about forgiveness and eternal life. At times, He personally supervised food preparation for thousands of people. And if you think your doctor's office is busy, listen to this: "As soon as they got out of the boat, people recognized Jesus. They ran throughout that whole region and carried the sick on mats to wherever they heard He was" (Mark 6:54–55).

Mark's words create an image of hundreds of people scrambling from small villages, some even hustled off by ancient ambulance, to the man Luke calls the Great Physician. They came with skin diseases, stomach disorders, disabilities, and perplexed psyches. No talk of HMOs or limited services or masks and rubber gloves! Jesus healed bodies as freely as He saved souls.

We might imagine similar scenes today when we think about the millions of people bringing their sin-sickness to the only one able to cure them. Can you see them charging in from North America (who else but North Americans would think of charging?), rushing from Russia, dashing from Europe, hurrying from South America, and racing from Africa? We can't forget the Australians either, hopping in by the hundreds for an appointment with the Great Physician.

Sometimes it's good to be part of a colossal crowd, especially when it's a crowd of sinners who lay claim to the healing Jesus earned on the cross. But only about 30 percent of the world's population know that Jesus is their lifesaving doctor. Next time you hear complaints about the miseries of life, be ready to make a referral. You've been treated by the best doctor in the universe. And He makes house calls.

92

The Case of the Avenging God

Nahum 1:1–15

W E CHRISTIANS PROBABLY would agree that the Bible offers comfort as we read the history of salvation—including ours—earned by Jesus Christ on the cross of Calvary. We're pleased to hear how Jesus restored our relationship with God after we both inherited and actively achieved separation from our Father. There's comfort in knowing that God loved us so much, even while we were sinners, that He spared nothing to save us. Then there's Nahum—and perhaps we sense some cold beads of sweat.

> *The LORD is a jealous and avenging God; the LORD takes vengeance and is filled with wrath. The LORD takes vengeance on His foes and maintains His wrath against His enemies. The LORD is slow to anger and great in power; the LORD will not leave the guilty unpunished. His way is in the whirlwind and the storm, and clouds are the dust of His feet. Nahum 1:2–3*

Nahum offers fearsome meaning to the phrase "We should fear and love God." Is God really like us, with emotions that smolder and explode into an inferno of revenge?

The difference between God and humans is that nothing He does is polluted by sin. He is perfectly just in all He does. That should comfort us, and not because we are sinless or marvelous in His sight. Because we aren't, we're tempted to fear the worst because sinners and God result in a volatile mixture—from God's standpoint. Our comfort comes because we know that God is a jealous lover. He loves us so much that He wants nothing to vie for our attention. He wants us to remain with Him, so He threatens all that seduces us.

While it's wonderful to be popular, the attraction fades when we think of how much the devil wants us and what he's willing to dangle in front of us to win our affection. It's good to know that God will end this someday. He is slow to anger at everyone and everything that jeopardizes our relationship, but those enemies should be forewarned. He will aim His holy vengeance their way and destroy them. Then we'll be out of danger for good.

As you can see, the Case of the Avenging God has a happy ending, depending on whose side you're on.

93
Guide to Hair Care

Acts 8:26–40

THE NEXT SEVERAL DEVOTIONS will present a unique guide to hair care, in addition to the usual meditation. Be assured that I'm an expert in this field, My credentials include adolescent years spent drenching my scalp with several gallons of Vitalis.

The first piece of advice is this: Don't let your hair go to your head. If you do, you'll be devastated when it forsakes you. No amount of combing, brushing, stroking, or encouraging will help if your hair follicles are determined to drop out. This attitude toward hair might be extended to every other item of vanity—or, for that matter, anything at all.

Vanity is costly in many ways. Generally, others don't enjoy the company of haughty people, and pride also can have spiritual consequences. Taken to extremes, vanity results in self-righteousness, and self-righteousness leads to hell. Pride convinces us that either we don't need a Savior because we're not really all that bad or that we can earn our own salvation.

Today's reading from Acts, upon closer examination, offers a prime example of the opposite of pride and vanity. Acts 8:30–31 says: "Then Philip ran up to the chariot and heard the man reading Isaiah the prophet. 'Do you understand what you are reading?' Philip asked. 'How can I,' he said, 'unless someone explains it to me?' So he invited Philip to come up and sit with him."

Each man mentioned could have allowed pride to prevent him from doing God's will. First, Philip could have reasoned, "Run to catch up with a speeding chariot? Why? If he wants to know about God, let him come to me." Second, the Ethiopian was an official of considerable status in his country. He could have tossed the book aside in frustration, writing it off as trite hogwash. Instead, he asked for help. The results? God's will was done. Philip served God, and the Ethiopian was saved.

Guard against pride, both spiritual and otherwise. It obstructs God's will and can cost lives. As you go about your business, ask the Holy Spirit to open your mind and heart to those in need of hearing some Good News. Also ask that the Spirit make you willing to learn from others more about God's love. After all, we don't want our faith to go where our hair should be.

Splitting Hairs

1 John 5:16–21

I THOUGHT SPLIT ENDS were positions on the football field until television commercials enlightened me. Split ends seem to be a major plague, especially for models, who react to this condition in the privacy of a TV commercial. For others, this isn't a problem. For example, my hair doesn't have split ends; it just split. Hair today; gone tomorrow.

Splitting hairs isn't confined to a physical condition. It's also a pastime of people who like to draw the finest of lines between questionable elements of behavior. They categorize faulty behavior into big sins and little sins. It's all splitting hairs to God. Note 1 John 5:17: "All wrongdoing is sin, and there is sin that does not lead to death."

No excuses for splitting hairs—I mean sins—here. It's all wrong. Every sin has consequences. Some consequences are more serious, both in how they affect the sinner as well as the victim of the sin. For example, it's easy to rationalize that lustful thoughts aren't nearly as serious as outright adultery. And hating that person who broke into your house isn't as bad as murdering her. In the same way, those caught stealing cars receive much harsher sentences than those nabbed for shoplifting groceries.

Place all our sins on a heap, both the ones we consider minuscule and the ones that amass to several tons, and the pile reaches mountain-size nonetheless. As sinners go, we've all gone a long way. Sins normally kill people, as today's Bible passage implies. The death is eternal. The passage also indicates that sin isn't always a terminal situation.

The only deadly sin occurs when we abandon our faith completely. You might say that's when people split from God for good, or rather, bad. All other sins are forgiven forever. This time we might say that the sins split, which is only because Jesus took them away. He brushed aside the devil and combed our souls clean and neat.

As you confess your sins to Jesus this day, repent of all of them—even those you might have forgotten because they seemed so small. Don't be afraid to confess the ones that loom large either. When it comes to forgiveness, Jesus doesn't split hairs.

95
Hair Raising

Jude 1–25

Ａ FRIEND TRIED that hair-growing formula called Rogaine. One night he left the bottle in the shower stall. The next morning, his wife mistook it for body gel. Too bad the stuff works as advertised.

The specter of such a hair-raising experience might leave us smiling and shuddering. I wish the prospect of all frightening experiences would offer such a humorous image! The truth, as you know it, isn't funny at all. Sin has so spoiled the world that dangers lurk within seemingly benign situations. For example, a Christian school may assemble a playground, which must be surrounded with a fence to protect the equipment from vandals and lopsided lawsuits.

Every day is fraught with threats. Occasionally, we read of "freak" accidents—when something with paltry predictability of ever happening happens. Drive-by shootings or death by drunk driver provide other examples of random threats. And there are those with high-risk jobs, such as firefighters, police officers, military personnel, and dentists. (How many people do you know who actually love their dentist?)

Life would be gloomy, apprehensive, and unbearably anxious—a truly hair-raising experience—were it not for God's loving protection. It probably hasn't escaped your attention, however, that believers and unbelievers seem equally susceptible to danger. Sometimes it's hard to believe that God promises to protect us when we see what happens to faithful people around the globe. We need to understand what God's protection is all about.

Don't be discouraged from praying for daily protection or for safety during special situations. God watches over us during those incidents. He always cares for us despite outward circumstances. God won't let sin take us to hell. Even if we lose our earthly life, God won't let us remain dead. Like Jesus Christ before us, we will rise to live with our heavenly Father, never to die again. It's like Jude says:

> *To Him who is able to keep you from falling and to present you*
> *before His glorious presence without fault and with great joy—to the*
> *only God our Savior be glory, majesty, power and authority, through*
> *Jesus Christ our Lord, before all ages, now and forevermore! Amen.*
> *Jude 1:24–25*

96
Hair Trigger

Proverbs 15:1–4

A s you read this, maybe you're upset that here's another takeoff on hair. If you've liked the hair series, perhaps you'll be angry to know this is the last installment. If you read the devotions out of sequence, you're unhappy because none of this makes sense. If you're annoyed at all, this meditation is for you. The topic is hair-trigger tempers.

Just about the time I get my temper under control, I go fishing again. My rod, reel, and bait fail to produce the desired results, and that sets me off. Can you cite some of your own eruptions caused by a hair-trigger temper?

The book of Proverbs is a good place to look for scriptural commentary on temper. Proverbs 15:1 says: "A gentle answer turns away wrath, but a harsh word stirs up anger." Diplomats subscribe to this proverb as do successful salespeople, counselors, and anyone else who deals regularly with the public. Like most proverbs, the greater its truth, the harder it is to follow consistently. We need a good role model—someone with lots of experience—someone like Jesus Himself.

The gospels record many gentle words from our gracious Savior. They also report a few instances of holy and righteous frustration when kind words fell only on deaf ears. There was the "den of thieves" incident in the temple and the "brood of vipers" label pasted on those determined to destroy the Messiah. But note that Jesus' justifiable anger was aimed not at those who loved Him, but at those who attempted to arrest the Gospel's progress.

Jesus also would be excused if He did some sanctified screaming at us. Every sin we have ever committed and will ever commit caused Jesus to wince in pain as His executioners slammed the nails through His hands. We brought Him nothing but misery, and we certainly deserve His anger. What do we get instead? The most gentle words ever uttered: I forgive you.

Forgiveness is the gentle glue that cements relationships. Hair-trigger tempers are easy to set off, but repairing damage they cause may be impossible. Angry words hurled at those we love—or at those we don't love—usually fracture relationships. Pray for the kind of "temper management" our Savior practiced even in His most painful moments. Is it okay to lose your temper? Sure. Permanently.

97
Unfinished Business

Haggai 1:1–15

MANY STRATEGIES EXIST to combat procrastination, but we'll address that later. Procrastination isn't a recent phenomenon. God moved the prophet Haggai to shake up some lazy people with these words: "This is what the LORD Almighty says: 'These people say, "The time has not yet come for the LORD's house to be built." ' Then the word of the LORD came through the prophet Haggai: 'Is it a time for you yourselves to be living in your paneled houses, while this house remains a ruin?' "(Haggai 1:2–4).

While the circumstances surrounding Haggai's proclamation are evident from the context, we might wonder how we could fall prey to spiritual procrastination. Like other forms of procrastination, it comes naturally. Here are some examples:

1. *Younger people, in particular, sometimes feel they will have plenty of time to exercise their faith when they grow older. The obvious flaw in this reasoning focuses on one four-letter word: when. A more accurate choice of words, one which a procrastinator ignores, is if.*

2. *Christians and Christian-tolerant people procrastinate on behalf of their kids. Their favorite statement is "I'll let them decide what they want to believe when they get older." Viewed from a spiritual perspective, it boycotts God's concept of parental responsibility.*

3. *Regular worship habits are easy victims of procrastination. "It's been a rough week. I'll sleep in this month—er, Sunday."*

4. *Prayer habits may be postponed for any number of logical excuses, such as "Dinner is getting cold," "It's past my bedtime," or "I've got to get this work done first."*

5. *Service, motivated by Christian love, may seem inconvenient. "I promised to drive Mr. Garcia to the grocery store today, but I'll miss my favorite TV show if I do."*

Most of us plead guilty to procrastination. We praise God, however, that He didn't delay sending His Son to take away our sins. Jesus came right on time according to God's planned schedule. And Jesus doesn't procrastinate in forgiving us each day. He immediately dispenses pardon on request. May the Holy Spirit enable us to do likewise and place procrastination on hold.

Lease on Life

1 Corinthians 6:15–20

IF YOU'VE PRICED NEW CARS LATELY, you have to agree that prices are eye-popping—or perhaps we should say bank-busting. In fact, a good way to keep your old car running for a few more years is to check the prices of new ones! The popularity of leasing new cars testifies to high sticker prices. In 1997, for example, 30 percent of all new cars were leased rather than bought through credit, cash, or loan.

One so-called advantage to the lease is an individual with an average income can drive a well-equipped car for about half the cost of purchasing it (as if you could afford to purchase it). During the lease, you must take good care of the car because the lease company that owns it wants it back. At the end of the lease, you have no obligations toward the lease company and vice versa. So you start all over again.

Christians have a lease too—a lease on life. How expensive is life? Listen: "You were bought at a price. Therefore honor God with your body" (1 Corinthians 6:20). If you want sticker shock, look at the price tag plastered on each of us. Jesus worked to purchase us throughout His entire life. He made the final payment when He died.

We can't purchase ourselves. Nothing we could do would ever meet God's requirements for salvation, but Jesus gave us a lease on life. He put us on earth to glorify Him just as a shiny, new car glorifies its owner. He wants us to serve others and take care of ourselves so when our lease expires, we will come before Him with only the normal wear and tear of life in a sinful world.

Taking care of ourselves is the subject of today's Bible reading. Not that we require any pampering! Because we belong to the Savior, we avoid behavior and lifestyles that harm us. God wants us as good as we were at the moment we were baptized. If we abuse our bodies, the very things we consider pleasures may wreck our lives. Wrecked lives all too easily end in the devil's junkyard.

We're never so dented, scratched, or sputtering that Jesus doesn't want us. He shines us up so we truly do look just like the day we were baptized. And when our lease ends, we'll remain with the same, benevolent owner. Only this time we'll remain gleaming and new forever.

99
Gridlock

Proverbs 5:15–23

CLAIMS OF PROGRESS in transportation are of dubious accuracy. Early settlers traveled in crude, bumpy wagons that leaked when it rained and provided little warmth in the cold. It took months to cross the country. Today, travelers ride in comfortable automobiles on smooth roads. But, depending on construction zones and local traffic volume, it still can take months to cross the country. When you try to avoid those traffic jams by using alternate routes, you discover the meaning of a word Henry Ford would have considered vulgar: gridlock.

We can draw from the book of Proverbs to confirm the condition of gridlock for sinners. Proverbs 5:22 indicates: "The evil deeds of a wicked man ensnare him; the cords of his sin hold him fast."

It's simple to cope with snarled traffic compared to the smothering gridlock of evil. Next time you're in a traffic jam, think of each surrounding vehicle as some type of sin. There's that belching, battered hunk of junk in front of you. The smoke gags you and makes your eyes water. It's like sins of slop that pollute life with sexual filth and immorality. Alongside you is that dazzling, luxury car. It's like sin encased in a lustrous shell of respectability. Beneath its facade is a hot, greasy, churning engine just like all the other cars. Society considers some sinners and their sins acceptable because of personal reputation. But God sees beneath the hood nonetheless.

See that mammoth truck in your review mirror. It represents those terrifying sins that constantly threaten to run over you. Will you be the next innocent victim of random violence, or will you unwittingly provoke someone into crushing your life? Will credit card debt overrun you, or will someone smash the love of your life?

The wise writer of Proverbs knew what he was talking about when he used words such as *ensnare* and *hold.* That's exactly what sin does. It keeps wicked, unrepentant sinners imprisoned in the jam. Good thing we've got a handy off-ramp at our disposal. Jesus freed us from sin's gridlock. His forgiveness enables us to race up and away from sin's route and toward our final destination.

Still in that traffic jam? You can stop imagining now. After that experience, you might even enjoy the real traffic jam you're in. It could be worse.

Collector's Edition

2 Timothy 3:12–17

YOU SEE THE ADVERTISEMENTS in magazines. Yes, you, Annie Average and Ozzie Ordinary, can own a collector's edition plate, suitable for display, commemorating the very first bottle of dishwashing liquid. (Future editions are planned depicting the entire history of dish detergent—so start your collection now!) It's all yours for only four installments of $39.95 each. Or maybe the collector's edition books attract you. For a small mortgage, you can own gold-edged volumes by famous writers. These books come complete with yellowed pages and musty odor.

Seriously, you probably own the best of any collector's edition. Between its covers you'll find the immortal words of blessed heroes, including Jacob, Ruth, Daniel, Jeremiah, Peter, Paul, and Mary. (Not to be confused with the singers.) You'll read what writers such as Matthew, Mark, Luke, and John say about the life and times of the God-Man, Jesus Christ. You can even read the words of our great Hero (printed in red for your convenience).

Here is what one fan of God had to say about the collector's edition: "All Scripture is God-breathed and is useful for teaching, rebuking, correcting and training in righteousness, so that the man of God may be thoroughly equipped for every good work" (2 Timothy 3:16–17).

The Bible offers instructional reading, but it's intended for more than that. In addition to teaching about and strengthening faith, it prepares us to demonstrate our faith. Once read, we put God's words into our actions.

Within the welcome and comforting Gospel passages, we hear the Holy Spirit whispering, "Get busy. Because God loved the world so much that He sent His Son to pay for your sins, get out there and tell the world His story. Because Jesus loves you so much that He suffered on your behalf, get out there and share that unconditional love with others. Because you are forgiven, act like it. I will help you abandon sinful ways and use My power to change your life."

Difficult tasks? Yes, indeed. But like old age, it's something into which we gradually grow as we study God's Word and participate in His Sacrament. We can see our faith in its resulting deeds. Someday, we'll be part of an amazing collection too.

Role Model

Ephesians 5:1–7

ROLE MODELS ARE vitally important for children. My high school role model was senior Kip Matts. He could do 87 forward rolls without throwing up. Now there's a real roll model!

Much has been made of role models, especially in the sports realm. Decent folk decry the loathsome examples set by some big-name stars whose life both on and off the field, if imitated by young people, would result in criminal records. Kids don't find better individuals to imitate in other high-profile arenas such as entertainment or politics either. Perhaps most difficult to accept are those people whose lives apparently reflect wholesome and decent values. Then we discover that they aren't Christians and so are doomed to an eternity in hell.

As with everything else in life, bona fide role models meet scriptural criteria. Active, faithful Christians best fit the role. Paul says in Ephesians 5:1–2: "Be imitators of God, therefore, as dearly loved children and live a life of love, just as Christ loved us and gave Himself up for us as a fragrant offering and sacrifice to God."

Michael Jordan, Ken Griffey Jr., Jimmy Stewart, or Abe Lincoln notwithstanding, God is the perfect role model. We can watch God as our role model in the person of Jesus Christ. If we imitate anyone, it should be Jesus. We could argue that His standards are too high, that they're unattainable by common people. That doesn't stop basketball players from imitating Michael or baseball players from trying to swing the bat like Griffey. People don't give up attempting to achieve the reputation and accomplishments of actors such as Stewart or statesmen such as Abe. We certainly can imitate them to some degree less than perfection.

Jesus set the standards for the way we treat God and people. He obeyed His Father, even when that obedience meant suffering undeserved horrors, even death for our cause. He treated people with compassion and affection, especially those who didn't receive compassion or mercy from others.

As we search for role models, we need not look far. Jesus is a role model for all ages and all eras. As the Spirit enables us to imitate Him, we live out the faith He has placed in our hearts. No other role demands quite so much nor is it as rewarding. You might even call it a sweet role!

B-o-r-i-n-g

Philippians 3:12–21

YOU HEAR IT MOST from adolescents and children: "Boring!" stretched out in twanging, nasally melodic tones with heavy emphasis on the first syllable. The derisive chant is directed most often toward things that adults enjoy. Thus offended adults usually counter with something clever, such as "You're boring!" with stout emphasis on *you're*.

At times, worship or anything religious becomes vulnerable to that word. Certainly, worship doesn't need to be entertaining to be worthwhile. If a few people nod their heads during a sermon, it doesn't affect the sermon's validity. Hymns may not be upbeat enough for some, and liturgy is, by its nature, rather set in its ways. Even this doesn't qualify as boring. But some hazards jeopardize religion when it's institutionalized at the expense of personalization.

Institutionalized religion takes place in church and other formal gatherings of Christians. Sadly, spirituality often begins and ends in the pews or in the hymnal pages or on the kneeling cushions. Church stays in church rather than going home with the people. That's when religion gets b-o-r-i-n-g. Religion gets boring when it's confined to a limited or specific time and location.

Paul described Christian life and its implied worship qualities as possessing great energy. He compared it to the quest for a prize. He says in Philippians 3:13–14: "Brothers, I do not consider myself yet to have taken hold of it. But one thing I do: Forgetting what is behind and straining toward what is ahead, I press on toward the goal to win the prize for which God has called me heavenward in Christ Jesus."

Words like *straining* and *press* and *win* fly in the face of boredom. They describe energized, lively, excited—and, therefore, exciting—Christians who worship regularly in fellowship and formality, then take what they've learned into the workplace, to the dinner table, to the bowling alley, to the mall, and on the road.

May we be exciting Christians! May the Holy Spirit saturate our existence with joy, hope, and power! May we consider heavenly life our goal, and as we strain in that direction, may we drag along by our Spirit-filled enthusiasm and our godly love all whom we have met. And don't let anybody see you yawning!

The Compass

Hebrews 11:8–16

Long ago, before cars had satellite navigation systems, people who wanted to know what direction they were headed bought compasses. These devices protruded condescendingly from the dashboard and swiveled merrily every time the car turned a corner. The major advantage of the compass was that at least you knew which direction you were headed when you were lost. Of course, there were always those confident individuals who knew their directions no matter what the compass indicated. ("The compass is wrong. The sun sets over there somewhere, so we must be going north-by-northwest—about 83 degrees I would guess.")

Imagine times much more ancient than the era of auto compasses. Going back to Abraham should be far enough. Listen to his travel dilemma: "By faith Abraham, when called to go to a place he would later receive as his inheritance, obeyed and went, even though he did not know where he was going" (Hebrews 11:8).

Can you imagine the conversation between Abraham and Sarah?

Abraham: God wants to relocate us to a better place. Get packing. We leave right away.

Sarah: Okay, dear. Where are we going?

Abraham: God didn't say, but we'll know when we get there.

Sarah: Oh, I love surprises!

Abraham's compass was faith. He packed his belongings and departed for the destination God intended. The Bible doesn't say if Abraham had any reservations, but that's not important (hotel chains didn't have worldwide reservation systems in those days). Concerns or doubts may riddle even strong faith, but strong faith perseveres despite incredulity and misgivings that infiltrate mind and heart.

We may think we know where we're going when we get up each day. But you know how easily plans are interrupted—sometimes pleasantly, but more often in the opposite way. We also face days when we're aware of the many variables that influence us. Plan as we may to provide alternatives, we never can replace Jesus as the supreme leader of life. He points us in the right direction. He takes us around obstacles and keeps us focused during times of uncertainty when we're unsure of the future course of life.

Keeping Cool

Psalm 119:145–160

BEFORE THERE WERE REFRIGERATORS, there were iceboxes. Our ancestors would marvel at how iceboxes now make their own ice! Of course, today's refrigerators have other advantages. Because they are metal, they're great devices for attracting magnets. Thereby they are effectively camouflaged beneath notes, pictures, school papers, calendars, coupons, and the like. This might be good news for dieters. However, smart—or desperate—dieters soon can see behind the ruse. This also might account for reports of people attempting to pry open bulletin boards for a snack!

The main purpose of refrigerators is to use cool temperatures to preserve food. Next time you open your refrigerator to see which left-overs will remain leftovers, think of the Gospel. It preserves us from the heat of sin with cool, refreshing waves of God's love. And do we ever need preserving!

David, the psalmist, said, "Defend my cause and redeem me; preserve my life according to Your promise" (Psalm 119:154). David had lots of problems with enemies. First, King Saul tried to kill him. Later, even his own son strayed toward murderous intentions. David faithfully laid his problems on God, and God faithfully kept David alive and victorious.

While we ask God to preserve our health and life from physical threats and afflictions, we have a more sinister enemy whose foremost goal is to spoil our relationship with the Lord. For this, we rest in a cool nook of the Gospel. Our only *sure* hope for preservation lies in the power of God through Jesus Christ.

Sin and its prime perpetrator blast away at us with torrid sheets of hot temptations, blazing walls of guilt, and fiery outbursts of rebellion against God. The Gospel extinguishes these fires because Jesus smothered the flames when He died on the cross and rose from the cool depths of the grave. He adopts and supports us, accepting us even though we still smolder with sin. He encases us in the delightfully frosty confines of forgiveness, reconciliation, and preservation. Sin no longer has power to cover us with fetid mold and bacteria that devour us from the inside out.

As we enjoy the comfort of Jesus' love and mercy, pray that we will end up at the back of His Gospel refrigerator where we can remain left-overs forever. Now that's the best way to remain well-preserved!

Sitting out the Dance

Matthew 11:16–24

FOR MANY YEARS, the faith tradition to which I belong frowned on dancing, so I was safe. It's not that I couldn't dance. I just couldn't master an approach to ask a female to dance. I stumbled just walking, which frightened prospective partners who feared the consequences of moving in specifically prescribed steps (or twists or jerks or wiggles). Finally, I gave up trying to dance when I couldn't master the newest dance craze called the Politician. No way could I handle all the backsliding and sidestepping!

Peers rarely taunted me for not dancing. They figured it was a public safety issue. But we read in the Bible about what apparently was a common gibe jeered by children in Jesus' day. Matthew 11:17 records it:

> We played the flute for you, and you did not dance;
> we sang a dirge, and you did not mourn.

In these verses, Jesus compared His antagonists to whining children who heckled other kids because they refused to play the whiners' games. Jesus refused to "dance" with the ideas and schemes and foregone conclusions of His detractors; therefore, they belittled and discredited Him as the genuine Messiah.

The devil would love to dance with you. He truly would enjoy gliding through life in a passionate embrace, keeping you oblivious to better suitors who might catch your eye. He could keep you carefree (or is it *careless*?) and laughing through a Polish hop or a German polka. The devil might even swath you in elegance as you circled the floor to a Strauss waltz. And if the tempo increased, he could fling and flail his arms and legs in a wild frenzy to the grinding beat and vulgar lyrics, all the while holding your gaze so you wouldn't realize what you were doing. Of course, there's always the chance that you would enjoy it too. That's how sin is sometimes.

However the devil and his allies mock you, sit out the dance. Don't participate in sin's folly no matter how attractive it might seem. (You'll know it's sinful if you will remember God's Word.) It's okay to be a wallflower in Satan's garden. Someday you'll bloom with God's splendor. You might even dance on the clouds.

106

What a Sight

1 Corinthians 13:8–12

IF YOU WEAR GLASSES OR CONTACTS, you'll identify closely with this meditation. (If you don't, borrow someone's glasses, wear them for a few minutes, then remove them. You'll get a similar effect.) The first time a poor-sighted person brings glasses or contacts to his or her eyes, it's like becoming aware of a new world. What was once a distant blur becomes startlingly clear. Everything becomes lighter and brighter. You probably would exclaim, "What a sight!" if it wouldn't draw curious stares—that you could see!

Experience with corrective lenses is much like our relationship with God. In the dim world of unbelief, sinful ignorance keeps us content with what little we do see. After all, we don't really know what we're missing. Then Someone quietly suggests that we don't know what's out there. That's the Holy Spirit, examining our eyes of faith and concluding that we're all but blind.

We can't see the Savior except through faith. Only the Holy Spirit delivers that faith. Once we have it, we might exclaim, "What a sight!" We see Jesus as true God and true Man. He's off in the distance, hanging on a cross, dying to take away our sins. We see clearly inside an empty tomb—nothing there but some folded burial clothes. Then we look up, farther than we've ever looked before, into heaven and see Jesus waiting for us. What a sight, indeed!

Faith enables us to see what those without faith cannot, but our sight remains a bit imperfect. In 1 Corinthians 13:12, Paul says: "Now we see but a poor reflection as in a mirror; then we shall see face to face. Now I know in part. Then I shall know fully, even as I am fully known."

We may wish to see better right now, but the view is already good. One heavenly delight we look forward to is perfect faith-sight (as well as 20/20 vision or better!). As wonderful as our Savior seems to us now, He'll be even better when we live together in the presence of God the Father.

Meanwhile, keep your sight as sharp as possible through Bible study, worship, and the Lord's Supper. When the Savior comes again, He'll surely be a sight for sore faiths.

No Crosses to Bare

John 20:1–8

WHAT WOULD YOU THINK if the government banned all symbols of violence? At first glance, it sounds mighty appealing. Violence pervades our society. Then reality sinks in. The government might prohibit the cross that we cherish as a symbol of salvation. Perhaps we've lost touch with the realities of this gruesome instrument of torture and execution.

What would you have in your house to symbolize Christ even if religious symbols were forbidden? What would you keep as a visual reminder of Jesus? Today's Bible reading hints at a replacement: "He bent over and looked in at the strips of linen lying there but did not go in. Then Simon Peter, who was behind him, arrived and went into the tomb. He saw the strips of linen lying there, as well as the burial cloth that had been around Jesus' head. The cloth was folded up by itself, separate from the linen" (John 20:5–7).

Bed sheets! You can think of Jesus every time you see bed sheets. (Just think how blessed those housekeepers in large hotels would be!) Come to think of it, crosses don't need to be barred for us to use other things to remind us of Jesus. (That's the point of this book. Anything and everything can help us keep Jesus in our thoughts.)

When the disciples saw those strips of linen and the burial cloth, they were stunned—with surprise and joy. Their friend wasn't dead after all. What He had said was true, unbelievably true! How foolish they were to doubt the Messiah's claims that He would come return to life after dying. Sin certainly plays havoc with faith, even the faith of those who lived and ate with the Savior for three years. It can do the same to us. That's a good reason to surround ourselves with symbols of our Savior.

Do you find it difficult to believe that you will experience what Jesus did? It's natural for doubts to tarnish our faith, especially if the news seems too good to be true. Does heaven seem far from reality? Oh, those qualms make us queasy. But look at the bed sheets. As sure as they are real, the linen strips and burial cloth, neatly folded after only brief use, were real. So is the risen Savior.

Even if someone takes away your cross, cling to your bed sheets. You're sure to have a restful sleep—and a great awakening.

Willpower

Colossians 1:9–14

GOD WORKS IN AND THROUGH US when we do His will. Of course, some people are so contrary that His will becomes their won't! Yet to those whose faith makes them open to God's intentions and desires, He gives willpower.

Colossians 1:9 says: "For this reason, since the day we heard about you, we have not stopped praying for you and asking God to fill you with the knowledge of His will through all spiritual wisdom and understanding." This was Paul's prayer for the Colossians, a prayer that God is happy to answer according to His will.

One important phrase in that passage contains the words "spiritual wisdom and understanding." What is the source of this component of faith? Can we equate it with human or secular wisdom and understanding? If so, we might be tempted to think that our own wealth of experience and dedication to study makes us wise and knowledgeable. But we can't obtain or attain spiritual wisdom and understanding through our own will or efforts. God reveals His will in the Bible. Anyone can read it. But it's the faith we received from the Holy Spirit that makes God's revelation meaningful. It's the Holy Spirit who gives us power to actually do God's revealed will.

We truly do God's will when we apply to daily life what He has revealed. That gives us experience that contributes to wisdom and understanding. Translated into practical terms, applying God's will to daily life means that we persist in doing good. Christian do-gooders have the advantage of knowing and experiencing God's goodness to them. In fact, God made us good through Jesus; therefore, good people like us do good things for others.

As we do God's will, we find ourselves extending forgiveness (even when it's not asked for), showing compassion (What can I do for that homeless guy on the corner?), generously supporting God's work in mission fields and in the local congregation (What can I sacrifice this week?), and smiling through it all (It's not like we were asked to sacrifice our son or anything!). As we continue to practice God's will, we realize that it isn't some parenthetical expression appended to our lives. It's the main idea.

Tit for Tat

Luke 6:35–41

REVENGE ISN'T SWEET. It's downright stupid when you think about it. Well, maybe it approaches acceptability if you do something such as fill out the check to pay your doctor in writing that looks like hers! No, don't do that. The truth about revenge is that while trying to get even, you never get ahead.

The Bible puts an unusual twist on revenge. Luke recorded Jesus' words on the issue: "Do not judge, and you will not be judged. Do not condemn, and you will not be condemned. Forgive, and you will be forgiven. Give, and it will be given to you. A good measure, pressed down, shaken together and running over, will be poured into your lap. For with the measure you use, it will be measured to you" (Luke 6:37–38). This is a refreshing way to reexamine the old phrase, "What goes around, comes around."

You only need to review the "casting the first stone" passage in Scripture to determine Jesus' attitude toward judging others. He stopped the stoning by asking sinners to examine their own condition before they condemned the sin of another. It's hard to toss even pebbles when we ourselves lie crushed beneath chunks of rubble. It's also good for us to know that the sentence that follows Christ's rebuke addresses forgiveness. The tit for tat with forgiveness is that it returns the divine favor. And isn't that what we pray in the Lord's Prayer? Of course, if you need a dose of fear in your life, there is the consequence of not forgiving.

Jesus also tells us to give and in return much will be given. The truth of the statement is evident to everyone except to those too selfish or too timid to give. Think for a moment what you have given and what has been returned. What were the consequences of giving love? Your love doesn't have to be returned by the object of your affection; you know God gives His approval and that satisfies you. What were the results when that financial appeal from the Cancer Society tugged at your heart? You gave, and God blessed you with enough money to live.

Ask God to give you more. Then you can give some of that away too. As the Bible says, you have a full measure overflowing into your lap. That gives you a lap of luxury.

Go Away

Mark 5:1–20

Place yourself in this situation. You haven't had a moment's peace for as long as you can remember. Most of the time you feel guilty—ashamed, even—of your thoughts and certainly damned by your acts. You know right from wrong, but most of the time you choose wrong because you seem driven to it. You find your whole life reprehensible and worthless, like serving a life sentence shackled to some demon.

Then a new person comes into your life. His soothing voice speaks words of consolation, but you're not quite sure you have the peace He offers. Something inside you seems to resist. But the man persists, makes some powerful commands that shake you to your soul. Suddenly, peace that you've never experienced brings a calm that settles you at His feet. Wouldn't you want to stay with this person forever?

You might not feel like part of this story, but it really happened. The story ends this way: "Jesus did not let him, but said, 'Go home to your family and tell them how much the Lord has done for you, and how He has had mercy on you.' So the man went away and began to tell in the Decapolis how much Jesus had done for him. And all the people were amazed" (Mark 5:19–20).

Though we may not be possessed by demons, we have demons in our lives. Those demons are our sins, and they don't allow us much peace. If we ignore them, they increase and become worse. Eventually gnawing guilt settles in, or worse, our demons become so much a part of life that we don't realize how disturbed we are. We may think that we're in control of our lives, but we're actually slaves to sin.

Jesus casts out our demons. He forgives us and brings us peace that passes human understanding. Wouldn't it be good to be with Jesus forever? Oh, that day is coming, but for now He wants us to go away. He wants us to take the peace that comes from healing and salvation and tell others about it. We do this with our words and with acts of kindness, generosity, grace, and mercy.

You're free from guilt, so avoid heaping it on others. Sweeten past bitterness. Get closer to your Healer through Scripture and at His Table. To borrow an old rhyme, "Go away, have your say, and He'll come back another day."

InDEPENDENCE Day

Psalm 62:5–8

OUR COUNTRY IS AS FREE today as it ever was. (Well, maybe taxpayers wouldn't agree.) We are free to speak, even if what we say offends both God and decent people. We are free to pursue happiness, which is good because it rarely chases us. We're free to bear arms, though it seems the bears might object. And we're free to participate in public gatherings, if we don't do anything dastardly such as pray. We have so many freedoms that few compare to us.

God probably wants us to celebrate our political independence. After all, it includes guaranteed freedom to worship Him. Along with that political freedom, we are responsible for being productive, active citizens who serve both the state and others, as well as satisfying ourselves. Throughout our history, many have died either to win or to protect that freedom. We're right to celebrate our costly independence.

The situation is different when it comes to our relationship with God. Here's what the psalmist says: "My salvation and my honor depend on God; He is my mighty rock, my refuge" (Psalm 62:7).

We depend on God for everything that matters. First, we depend on God to free us from sin. He fought that battle and won single-handedly. Prior to our dependence on Him, we were captives of Satan. The devil imprisoned us, and such was our lost condition that we were all too happy to labor in his work gang. When God sent Jesus to take away our sins, He freed us to choose salvation and eternal bliss or to return to the devil and an eternity of hell.

Second, we depend on God to keep us faithful. He sends the Holy Spirit to us so we may believe His Good News message and live as one of His dependents. (This probably doesn't qualify Him for any tax breaks, though.) When we exercise the freedom to wander, He remains willing to forgive (again).

Celebrate Independence Day. Celebrate Dependence Day too. It was the day the Holy Spirit brought you to faith.

Tabloid Targets

Psalm 109:21–25; 1 Peter 5:8–11

I HOPE THIS doesn't ruin your mood. It's time to pretend again. You're probably familiar with supermarket tabloids that beckon to you at the checkout counter. They usually have outrageous headlines such as "Pet Canary Swallows a Cat" or "Hero Brings Down Purse Snatcher with False Teeth." (No, the purse snatcher didn't have false teeth, but that's the kind of writing we can expect from putrid pulp.)

Now back to your imagination. Imagine that a reporter from the *Globe Enquiring Star* is assigned to watch you. He has access to all your financial, tax, and legal records. You can't escape his observation. He follows you everywhere, noting everything you do and don't do.

He heard you swear when you read today's weather report and curse when you saw what the puppy did on the floor. He read your lips when you mocked your best friend. He saw the lusty look in your eyes when the neighbor pranced around in a skimpy bathing suit. The reporter's stopwatch tattled on how much extra time you took for breaks and lunches. What was that you shouted when the rude driver slipped into the last parking space? Then there were those three martinis to calm your nerves. The reporter wanted to quit, but that movie you rented contained scenes that could illustrate his copy. Next, …

If you made the headlines, you probably wouldn't want to read farther. Perhaps you would feel like the psalmist, who said, "I am an object of scorn to my accusers; when they see me, they shake their heads" (Psalm 109:25).

Our accusers have good reason to shake their heads, don't they? We're lion food. Peter writes: "Be self-controlled and alert. Your enemy the devil prowls around like a roaring lion looking for someone to devour" (1 Peter 5:8). The reporter has all the evidence he needs to make us lion food, except for one thing.

Jesus edits our life. He takes out all the bad stuff, which leaves the devil with exactly nothing to report. As we stand before God our judge, the accusing (and accurate!) reporter is dumbfounded. Pages of the tabloid are blank, except for a short article. It describes how Jesus took away the sins of the world—including yours and mine. Oh yes, the devil knows that story. He just doesn't devote much space to it.

Reason to Live

2 Thessalonians 1:1–12

GOD PUT US ON EARTH for a reason. He wants to accomplish something through us while we're here. Some of us are already so far behind that we might live through the 21st century.

Social science suggests that people are only genuinely fulfilled when they have purpose in life. For some people, that purpose is a life spent teaching or in public service; for others, purpose is achieving some significant scientific breakthrough such as Teflon or the polio vaccine. Some create majestic works of art to be admired through the ages. Others take piles of notes and arrange them into unforgettable melodies. Of course, there are those whose purpose seems dedicated to useless and sometimes malignant endeavors in those same fields.

Through Paul, God revealed our purpose: "With this in mind, we constantly pray for you, that our God may count you worthy of His calling, and that by His power He may fulfill every good purpose of yours and every act prompted by your faith. We pray this so that the name of our Lord Jesus may be glorified in you, and you in Him, according to the grace of our God and the Lord Jesus Christ" (2 Thessalonians 1:11–12).

God created people for many different purposes. Note that He didn't want all of us to be preachers or construction workers or librarians or computer programmers or even Sunday school teachers. He gives purpose to our lives whatever we do, putting numerous blessings at our disposal. He gives purpose to our lives not because of what we are or what we have, but for the sake of Jesus and by the power of the Holy Spirit.

What tremendous reason we have to live! From the time we're old enough to realize that we're not here only for horseyback rides and talking cereal, we have opportunity to respond to God's love

Stop and consider the ways in which you might respond. Oh, there's the usual "go to church and pray before meals" answer. But what about integrating your response to God's love into your normal activities? Bring closure to this devotional on your own. Decide right now what you'll ask the Holy Spirit to help you do because of all that God has done for you. Don't put if off. Living to 1,000 probably isn't all that it's cracked up to be.

What a Deal!

Luke 16:1–12

SOME SURVEYS REQUEST the number of workers in a company. They probably should ask how many people actually work! Along those same lines, you probably know several individuals who don't work. Some of them even have jobs! (No, don't glare at any suspicious-looking coworkers or family members. They'll suspect you're reading about them.)

Jesus addressed a similar thought in Luke 16 when He told the story of a dishonest worker about to be fired. The guilty worker fears that loss of income will drive him to harsh physical labor or begging—and he isn't favorably disposed to either. But to take the curse—er, course—of least resistance, he decides to make lots of friends by altering their record of debts owed the boss. Surely, they will provide a handout if …

At the end of this story, Jesus says, "The master commended the dishonest manager because he had acted shrewdly. For the people of this world are more shrewd in dealing with their own kind than are the people of the light." And Jesus continued, "I tell you, use worldly wealth to gain friends for yourselves, so that when it is gone, you will be welcomed into eternal dwellings" (Luke 16:8–9).

What? Does Jesus really suggest that we make devious deals with people to gain their favor? Not at all. His story intends a practical spiritual message, as usual, and here it comes.

God entrusted us with many blessings, both spiritual and earthly. Forget the earthly gifts. (No, don't!) Jesus tells us in today's reading to use spiritual gifts as wisely as astute managers of money use their physical resources. Apply your spiritual gifts to others, making friends with them so you'll have someone to sit next to at His banquet table. Okay, it's really to give God glory and make new friends for Him.

As we manage our spiritual resources, we're faced with many choices. Then again, maybe they're not choices. Do we take God's gifts and store them in a "safe" place (only to find them moldy and rotten later)? Or do we improve on them by regular use and by growing in God's Word? Do we amass His blessings for ourselves, using them selfishly, or do we deal out those blessings to others?

Take Jesus' advice. Dole out the blessings He gave you. You've got plenty to give—and you'll make some new friends.

That Bugs Me

Romans 7:4–12

Arthropodiatrists (scientists who specialize in bugs with lots of feet) recognize about 425,000 species of beetles. (Whoops, make that 424,999. I think my wife squished the last one of a kind in the kitchen sink!) That's more than half the species of insects, spiders, and crustaceans put together. A famous bug biologist was once asked what theological ramifications this might have. He theorized that God just had a special fondness for beetles!

So how do we turn beetles into something that reminds us of our own spirituality? My theological theory is that a beetle is like guilt. It's meant to bug us. (If you're fond of beetles, bugs in general, or Volkswagens, you probably won't like this meditation.)

God put beetles and other arthropods on earth so we could call common things by names that defy pronunciation. No, that's not right. Even beetles have a God-given role in our complex ecosystem (or is it eek-o-system?). They annoy some and benefit others. It's the same with guilt.

Hear what Paul says in Romans 7:7: "What shall we say, then? Is the law sin? Certainly not! Indeed I would not have known what sin was except through the law. For I would not have known what coveting really was if the law had not said, 'Do not covet.' "

Guilt may bug us, but its God-given purpose is to reveal our sins. We need not worry about divulging our sins to others. (They probably are well aware of them already!) But we need to personally know about and admit our sins, otherwise we would continue living in ways that angered God and fractured our relationship with His creations—human and otherwise. We wouldn't know what we've done to earn eternal destruction. Without that knowledge, we would go about our normal routines completely ignorant of God's willingness to forgive for Christ's sake. We'd be unaware of the majesty of God's mercy and the generosity of His grace. And to make matters worse, guilt would still bug us!

Like prolific beetles, just as one episode of guilt gets extinguished, another appears. Thank God for guilt anyway! Thank God for His opulent opportunities to repent and receive forgiveness. Thank Him for His lavish love. And thank Him that we can bug Him about our guilt and His forgiveness anytime.

Back from the Dead

Luke 16:19–31

THE FUNERAL INDUSTRY enjoys downward trends in business. Okay, the humor is morbid, but it's here to suggest something that certainly isn't a new idea to believers. For faithful people, death is the only currently available portal to that immortal, glorious life in God's presence—a place where all jokes are actually funny. Death does bring grief to loved ones, but bereavement is easier to bear knowing it's not permanent. Our comfort—and even joy—is absent in the lives of some, though.

Did you read today's Bible passage? It's the sad and frightening story of a man who had opportunity to be saved but didn't take it. He pleaded for help to Abraham from hell—someone to warn his family to accept the faith offered them. But here is the tragic finale: "He said to him, 'If they do not listen to Moses and the Prophets, they will not be convinced even if someone rises from the dead' " (Luke 16:31).

Father Abraham's words ring true today. Unbelievers often are skeptical, seeking proof of God's almighty existence. Believers may wish for the same in hopes of convincing unbelieving loved ones before it's too late. Sadly, father Abraham was and remains right. No proof is solid enough to those bent on unbelief, disbelief, or nonbelief. But don't give up trying. We have an advantage. Someone we know came back from the dead.

You probably wouldn't be reading this book if you didn't know and believe that our Savior Jesus Christ defeated sin, death, and the devil. He died. He came back to life because He's more powerful than death and the devil. We've read about it and trust that it is accurate history. As we share that history, we pray the Holy Spirit's power that others may believe. And there ends our responsibility.

Be sure to share what you know about coming back from the dead. Remember that every believer was once dead in sins and has come back to life through the gift of faith. Look forward to that day when the many people you've known and loved will return from the dead to live forever. For now, you are a living link between heaven and earth. You bring truth to people while time remains. You've come back from the dead once. You'll do it again. Things are looking up!

Christians, Go Home!

Amos 7:1–15

IT MIGHT HAVE APPEARED on a sign at the city limits. Bethel: Population 378. Home of the Golden Calf Crusaders and the Shrine of Jacob's Ladder. Prophets Not Welcome.

Amos, God's draftee for prophet, entered town anyway. And did he get an earful: "Then Amaziah said to Amos, 'Get out, you seer! Go back to the land of Judah. Earn your bread there and do your prophesying there. Don't prophesy anymore at Bethel, because this is the king's sanctuary and the temple of the kingdom' " (Amos 7:12–13).

Amos faced the same problem that many people face today. People of faith aren't always welcome, especially when they speak boldly for God. Most Christians—even outspoken ones—haven't been called seers, but they've probably been called worse. Life in the world sometimes seems like it's fenced and posted "Christians, Go Home!"

Perhaps you haven't suffered prejudice or inhospitality, but our society has gradually, subtly, posted the land with signs of intolerance. When Christians complain about immorality, unbelievers respond that everyone has a right to decide what to do as long as it doesn't impinge on anyone else's right. (Except God's!) Abortion is a good example—er, bad example—isn't it? Humans must have options, even if options mean death for the innocent and helpless. (Humans explain it away with pseudoscience—idolatry in big words.) Then there's the debate about sexual preferences. Christians cite the Bible, and disbelievers claim exclusive ownership of their bodies. Need we pursue the matter? Government isn't too friendly to the one true God either. Though we dare not impose a national religion, we risk alienating the one true God by granting sterile status to any and all gods. Were Amos to stumble into town and address the issues, he would think he was back in Bethel.

Christians should go home. Maybe we should mumble God's will to more receptive ears. Our own! It's easy to speak against the big, overt, defiant sins of the world. But we need to address our own sinfulness too. We can examine ourselves to see where pride, greed, selfishness, prejudice, hate, or self-righteousness hold God in contempt. Then we can do something about it. Repenting and accepting God's forgiveness are in order. One day, when our last confession is over, we'll hear the now welcome words of Jesus as He says, "Christian, come home."

Christians Revolt!

John 15:18–25; 2 Corinthians 10:3–4

As you read in the previous devotional, Christians aren't always welcome. That we should expect such treatment is confirmed by Jesus, who said, "If you belonged to the world, it would love you as its own. As it is, you do not belong to the world, but I have chosen you out of the world. That is why the world hates you" (John 15:19).

Does this sound like a call to revolt? After all, we don't belong to the world and the world often reminds us of that reality. In fact, the world already thinks we're pretty revolting!

Now the question is, "What do we do about it?" The answer would be simple were it not so difficult or drastic to emigrate to a more God-friendly location. So how do Christians revolt? The answer, as we might expect, appears in these words of Scripture: "For though we live in the world, we do not wage war as the world does. The weapons we fight with are not the weapons of the world. On the contrary, they have divine power to demolish strongholds" (2 Corinthians 10:3–4).

Sounds like the ultimate terrorist weapon! Yessiree. Step right up and grab a God grenade. We'll wipe out those sniveling unbelievers and decimate the pagan population. One pop of God's awesome wrath and it'll be all over. Wait. Though God certainly possesses atomic capabilities, His way is different.

Revolutionary Christians rebel against the world by boldly proclaiming and living the Gospel. We dissidents don't seek revenge for wrongs done. We forgive them. How revolting—especially to those who neither want nor accept our forgiveness. We mutiny against the world by refusing to live according to its flimsy standards and adopting God's standards instead. We flout the world system of self-reliance in favor of complete dependence on God. We rebel against the world goal of mastery and freedom to win the right to become servants—even slaves—to our God. And all the while we look to our revolutionary leader, Jesus Christ, who won the right to live by dying on the cross. In disdain of everything for which the sinful world stands, He rose from the dead and leads us yet today.

Christians revolt. We'll soon be at peace.

119
Getting a Second Job

1 Thessalonians 4:1–12

How often has someone said to you, "Don't work too hard"? The thought expresses kind intentions, but perhaps it's not the wisest advice. (The best way to avoid being fired by the boss is to be fired by energy.) The Bible contains vastly better advice in 1 Thessalonians 4:11–12: "Make it your ambition to lead a quiet life, to mind your own business and to work with your hands, just as we told you, so that your daily life may win the respect of outsiders and so that you will not be dependent on anybody."

That's laudable counsel, especially as it applies to a second job. You know, the one you take on so you can afford some of the little pleasures—or the big necessities—of daily life. Perhaps you find your secondary employment as a banker, government official, checkout clerk at the grocery story, bus driver, homemaker, welder, secretary, or maintenance worker. Of course, you can never allow your second job to interfere with your primary occupation.

Your foremost calling is to serve God. No, we don't leave that task to preachers or other professional church workers. It's the vocation of each Christian. To understand this important position, we can examine a job description.

The job falls under the category of service profession and requires dedication and perseverance. Servants are willing to study the finer details of their duties through Bible study. Mistakes are expected, but the Employer offers a generous plan of forgiveness and retraining. Workers receive a generous benefit package through which all their daily needs are supplied, and the Employer provides a retirement plan that's out of this world! Because the work is so vital, workers cannot expect vacations and must sometimes serve in unanticipated ways at the will of their Employer.

Christians who hold two jobs usually work both at the same time. Neither employer seems to mind, for the Christian worker going about God's business is usually an excellent worker for an earthly boss as well (though God sometimes gets shortchanged in the deal).

Next time someone good-naturedly tells you not to work too hard, tell her thanks, but it's not an option. When you work two jobs, you're bound to keep busy.

Another Flood

Genesis 9:8–16

Gᴏᴅ's ᴄᴀᴛᴀѕᴛʀᴏᴘʜɪᴄ ꜰʟᴏᴏᴅ dwarfed even the worst floods we may experience, though that's little comfort for those who suffered massive losses along normally benign Midwestern rivers in 1997.

By grace, God didn't completely destroy all life during that ancient flood. Noah, his family, and a wild menagerie survived the deluge on a huge ship named *The Ark*. While Noah, his crew, and his cargo survived, you might imagine some discouraging moments, especially if you've ever been seasick. Multiply that by an elephant's stomach and a giraffe's neck and you perceive new meaning in Kermit the Frog's hit song "It's Not Easy Being Green"!

As floods commonly do, God's flood changed the face of the earth. In all likelihood, even the climate changed! Left behind were fossils of marine life in places that have baffled evolutionists, causing them to propose preposterous theories rather than stand in awe of God's power.

At the end of the flood, God gave the survivors some good news, "I establish My covenant with you: Never again will all life be cut off by the waters of a flood; never again will there be a flood to destroy the earth" (Genesis 9:11).

God has kept His promise, and we're confident that He always remains true to His word. But immediately after He cleansed the evil world through His flood, the people of this earth were back to their normal, sinful activities. Wickedness again flourished. So God sent another flood to drown evil and send sin swirling into the cesspool where it belongs. His new flood was quite creative and novel. God didn't use water. He used love.

God flooded the world with love when He sent Jesus to wash away our sins. The earth was awash with His love on that first Christmas, and the tide continued to rise right through that day when the murky surge of sin drained through an open tomb.

Jesus continues to flood us with love. It begins with a trickle of water in Baptism and grows into a lake of blessings. We ride His waves of love until that day when we settle on the heights of heaven. Just think of the stories we'll have to share with Captain Noah!

Nag Nag Nag

Luke 18:1–8

T HERE IS ONLY ONE WAY to avoid nagging, and that's for the nag-ee to do what the nag-er wants. While social scientists have other nagging problems, most common people understand that nag-ers derive a greater sense of victory when the nag-ee completes the nagged-about task with a sullen disposition and with much grumbling.

Today's Bible reading is a parable about how to wear down an arrogantly apathetic judge. This information may actually come in handy, considering the foibles of the modern judicial system. Okay, so that's not the real purpose of the parable. Jesus wanted to contrast His willingness to hear prayers with a shoddy judge's willingness to administer real justice. Of course, there's no comparison.

Jesus said, "And will not God bring about justice for His chosen ones, who cry out to Him day and night? Will He keep putting them off?" (Luke 18:7). No, this wasn't a ploy by Jesus to escape the rasping and grating of nag-ers. He assured His listeners that God hears and answers prayers. The key to understanding Jesus' answer is to acknowledge that God does indeed care and that He provides answers with precise timing.

While this parable focuses on justice, we can extend it to all situations that involve prayer. A little self-examination probably reveals that we tend to nag God in proportion to how much a specific problem or condition nags us. (My most strenuous nagging comes somewhere between 0 and 200 miles per hour on the runway!) Illness, storms, and violence yield other opportunities for nagging.

We don't need to nag God. One simple prayer gets His divine attention, and He won't miss any details. Nagging God with a hail of redundant pleas may actually signal weak faith or foster an attitude that we can persuade God to take action on our terms. Of course, God probably is immune to nagging. He knows what needs doing and He does it, sometimes even before we ask. And even weak faith is better than no faith because it recognizes—or at least concedes—God's control and care of our lives.

God invites us to pray, and His Son taught us a good one—one that covers every imaginable situation. Pray it (again) now. There is a difference between gently bringing our needs before God and nagging His eternal ears off.

Out of Court Settlement

Luke 12:54–59

I F EVERYONE HAD GOOD JUDGMENT, we wouldn't need judges. As it is, court cases abound. Even lawyers prefer to avoid court by settling out of it. (That way the only charges levied appear on the bill for services rendered.) Will social scientists of the future wonder about a society that established a comprehensive system of justice and then found ways to circumvent it? Will they pronounce our era one in which an alternative to admitting guilt was to buy off the indignation of victims? Will they see us as prone to filing frivolous lawsuits against huge corporations or famous people because it was an even better gamble than the state lottery?

Apparently, the problem isn't new. Jesus once told a crowd that "as you are going with your adversary to the magistrate, try hard to be reconciled to him on the way, or he may drag you off to the judge, and the judge turn you over to the officer, and the officer throw you into prison. I tell you, you will not get out until you have paid the last penny" (Luke 12:58–59).

We may chuckle at or decry the details of out-of-court settlements. However, we also must realize that we are part of the most sweeping and most important out-of-court settlement ever.

The court date was set by the highest ranking Judge in the universe. The problem is that He won't tell us when it is, though it matters little since we're unable to mount an effective defense.

Imagine for one terror-filled moment that we appear before God on Judgment Day. He hears our plea and decides that the evidence suggests a mandatory life sentence with no hope of appeal or parole. It's hard to imagine that and remain poker-faced!

Good thing Jesus won an out-of-court settlement for us. Long before we're scheduled to appear before the almighty Magistrate, Jesus settled the matter once for all. He erased our sins through His life, work, and death. He didn't hide our guilt in hopes that God wouldn't notice; instead, He took it away completely. He bought our freedom, and now we need not fear judgment. Even better, His resurrection arranged for us to move in with the Judge.

See you in court.

Getting Stepped On

Isaiah 51:12–23

I F YOU LIVE IN THE CITY, you take them for granted. Sidewalks, that is. Have you ever contemplated what it's like to be a sidewalk? (Being reasonably sane, you probably haven't nor have you associated with people who do.) In the privacy of your own closet or another equally out-of-sight place, imagine such an existence.

You were born wet and heavy and soon dried into a reliably hard surface, but not before some juvenile delinquents carved their initials into you. You're old now, and you've seen it all—roller skates, bicycle tires, drivers with bad aim, expensive shoes, cheap shoes, bare feet, ants, dripping ice-cream cones, chalk, etc. Perhaps the thing you most regret is that you've spent your lifetime getting stepped on. Of course, that was your reason for being.

Reality sometimes isn't too distant from imagination. It's likely that you've been stepped on, stomped into submission, rolled over, and dripped on often. It doesn't feel very good, does it? Even if you've been blessed with shelter from this sort of treatment, sin has walked all over you. Isaiah prophesied about such treatment. He said: "I will put it into the hands of your tormentors, who said to you, 'Fall prostrate that we may walk over you.' And you made your back like the ground, like a street to be walked over" (Isaiah 51:23).

Like it or not, we're in the hands of our tormentors. Sometimes we recognize them; other times they're invisible or deceptively friendly. That's how sin and sinners are. They walk all over us.

Jesus knows what it's like. He was like a sidewalk on a busy boulevard. He suffered a constant parade of sin that ground its heels into His precious body and soul. He carried that lumbering weight to the cross, hanging there to suffer all that Satan had intended for us—stricken, smitten, and stepped on.

Things are different now. Jesus lives in a city with streets and sidewalks paved with gold (or something even better). While sin still steps on us, we endure because Christ's forgiveness has swept us clean and the Spirit repairs our cracks.

Next time you go for a walk, think about that sidewalk beneath your feet and what it means to be stepped on. You might tread lightly and watch that ice-cream cone.

Something in Your I

Proverbs 21:1–5

How much does an "I" weigh? Often, it's bloated and obese, though in those who value themselves little, it's as skinny as the letter. When it comes to "I," many people imitate the current trend in gas stations—self-service. Others simply serve up themselves, perhaps preferring self-sacrifice to getting sacrificed by others. One thing is certain: There's usually something interesting surrounding the shortest word in our language. We'll examine this idea in the next few devotions.

There's something in our I. A wise sage, inspired by God, once said, "All a man's ways seem right to him, but the Lord weighs the heart" (Proverbs 21:2). The Lord weighs the heart rather than the "I" that either deprecates, exonerates, or accentuates itself. Sinners like us love that little word. It says so much about an important topic, doesn't it? It also leads to trouble.

When "I" comes first, it places everyone and everything below it. In religious people, "I" can be an insidious virus that weakens faith. The change is gradual, but you know you're in trouble when spiritual conversations emphasize what you are doing rather than what God has done. Spiritually inspired people want to do much for God, and the devil uses that motivation to scatter spores of self-righteousness. You'll find the problem in Christian literature too. Authors who encourage us to apply our faith sometimes forget to remind us why. All good things we do can only be done in response to God's great love for us—His forgiveness that enables us to apply and exercise our faith to the glory of God and for the good of others.

Another bleak side of "I" is just as bad: "I am guilty." You know you're in trouble if persistent guilt prevents you from enjoying the warmth of Jesus' love. His love is so expansive and expensive that He sacrificed His life to prevent guilt from searing your soul with the heat of hell.

There truly is something in your I. As one brought to faith by the Holy Spirit, Christ lives in you. He has removed the self-importance of "I" and replaced it with righteousness won by Christ. Next time something gets in your "I," ask Jesus to take it out. Once He does, your "I" really becomes worth something.

Irate

Romans 6:1–7

A N ANCIENT PROVERB of uncertain origin (probably the first human to taste airline food) offers this insight: "He who flies into a rage usually has a crash landing." It probably hasn't been too many days since you last took such a flight. Maybe it was at the grocery store when someone tried to cut into line. Maybe a family member committed the same extremely stupid blunder *again*. Or perhaps it was the neighbor's dog perusing your favorite tree or those kids cruising with windows open and bass boosters booming that set you off. Were you piloting the flight, or did you just watch the takeoff and landing?

Sometimes we're rightfully angered by what happens around us. We witness or hear about so much injustice and senseless tragedy. Anger, provided it doesn't send our blood pressure surging, can be a positive outlet when expressed about people and events that seem to splinter and twist God's will. Those are the kinds of things that make God irate too.

If we're really honest, we will confess that we do much to incur God's wrath. For that, God has some cross words for us. Here they are: "We were therefore buried with Him through baptism into death in order that, just as Christ was raised from the dead through the glory of the Father, we too may live a new life" (Romans 6:4). We can summarize that passage by saying that God's cross word was indeed the cross on which Jesus suffered the rage and punishment rightly belonging to us. This is nothing short of astonishing. Indeed, it would be unbelievable— if we didn't have the gift of faith. That faith is more than rote knowledge of Bible stories and creeds such as the Apostles', Nicene, or Athanasian (ask your pastor about this one if you're not familiar with it).

Faith is that personal conviction that Jesus was thinking about you and me when He hung on the cross on that bleak Friday. Better yet, faith assures us that He was thinking about us when He emerged from the tomb on that fresh Sunday morning. Even now, Jesus is thinking about us, caring for us, bringing our future in line with His will.

God isn't irate anymore. His Son brought us into His family. Forgiveness and the desire to live according to His values persist in our hearts through the work of the Holy Spirit. Because of what He has done for us, we're free to boldly claim this truth: I rate.

Icon

Isaiah 30:6–11

*I*CON IS AN OLD WORD made fashionable by the rapid growth of personal computers. Today, an *icon* is a graphic device that enables computer users to get themselves into trouble faster than they could before computers used such symbols. For example, my computer has a trash can icon on the screen. You can guess what that stands for, even if you aren't familiar with computers. (It's where much of my work is filed!)

The context of today's Bible reading really doesn't suggest icons unless you've been staring at screen savers for too long. I have, so I'll suggest that verse 8 might be applied to a more pristine context—one that involves icons as well.

"Go now, write it on a tablet for them, inscribe it on a scroll, that for the days to come it may be an everlasting witness" (Isaiah 30:8). God spoke through Isaiah because He didn't want anyone to consider His Word to be a trifling matter. Prophecies meant God cared enough to leave potent signs intended to guide believers according to His will. Perhaps we might use icons in the same way.

There's a little space on the outside margin of this page for you to doodle a personal icon that symbolizes God's love for you. Draw it now, but avoid the easy road—no crosses allowed!

Aha! Had to think for a moment, right? Plenty of situations listed in the Bible lend themselves to icons. Maybe your icon is a flaming bush like the one Moses saw or a ladder like Jacob's. Is it the head of Daniel's hushed lion or three fireproofed men engulfed in flames? Maybe you're more New Testament oriented and your icon is a shepherd's staff or, okay, even a cross.

Computer icons provide shortcuts to launch programs. The icon isn't the program, rather by the way it looks, this sign identifies a program. We need only point to it with the mouse (if you get it to quit wiggling), and it takes you where you want to go.

Use the icon you drew to remind you how much God has done for you and all sinners. Doodle it on that notepaper by the phone or, better yet, where others can see it. Maybe they'll keep their distance. Or maybe it will provide a shortcut for others to hear what you know about God's program. Would I con you?

The Evil Eye

Luke 11:33–36

TODAY WE'LL CONSIDER an eye for an I. They're closely related. We could consider at length how evil "I" can be, but let's think about the physical eye instead. Look at someone's eyes right now. (Use a photograph if necessary.) What do you see? A cornea? Red streaks? Crust? A pupil? (Ask her to get back to school!) Or can you look beyond the obvious and see lies? Flirtation? Anxiety? Affection? Anger? Evil?

It was probably a poet who said that eyes are a mirror of the soul. Maybe they are. For a moment, let's think of eyes in a way that connects pathology with the spiritual. Before we begin, read this passage: "Your eye is the lamp of your body. When your eyes are good, your whole body also is full of light. But when they are bad, your body also is full of darkness" (Luke 11:34).

Have you noticed how well eyes adjust to different conditions? For example, when you extinguish the lights in a motel room, you're immediately plunged into darkness so overwhelming that you wouldn't dare attempt a trip to the washroom for fear of stubbing your toe, running into a wall, or accidentally letting yourself into the hallway partially clad. It doesn't take long, however, for your eyes to adjust. Soon you're able to find your way around obstacles and to your destination. In other words, the darkness becomes more routine.

Isn't the evil of sin like the initial darkness when you turn off the lights? Sins, especially those "new" to us, may seem terrible at first. We don't want to skip our evening prayers or our weekly trip to worship. Or we fear God's wrath when we utter our first curse or brush against that person who seems so much more attractive than our spouse. But sin, all sin, becomes easier to commit as we become accustomed to it. It's like the shroud of darkness in that motel room. How much easier it is to navigate through our sinfulness once we spend some time adjusting!

Jesus knows how sin works. He wants to be our night-light in a sin-darkened world. Through His Holy Spirit, He enables us to see sin clearly and to shun it so we don't stub our soul. Jesus keeps an eye out for us.

Getting a Few Laughs

Mark 5:38–43

LAUGHTER EITHER REFRESHES the heart or breaks it. The first result of laughter has been clinically proven. The body benefits in several ways from laughter as long is it's the one doing the laughing. But laughter cruelly aimed at someone damages the psyche, if not more. Perhaps you've been the victim of laughter. Was it the time you slipped on the ice and provided some unscheduled entertainment? Or maybe it was the time you wore two different shoes. Then again, maybe it was the time you took the dog for a walk—and forgot the dog.

Yes, laughter can be happy, harmless, or hurtful. Consider the time Jesus got a few laughs. "He went in and said to them, 'Why all this commotion and wailing? The child is not dead but asleep.' But they laughed at Him. After He put them all out, He took the child's father and mother and the disciples who were with Him, and went in where the child was" (Mark 5:39–40).

Our own reaction to hurtful laughter probably borders on revenge. If we're trying to sew for the first time and drive our observer to stitches, we might feel like giving up. If someone laughs when we fall, our initial reaction may be to show that person what a really good laugh is. But did you note Jesus' reaction to the mocking laughter? He went about His business, and His business brought new life to a child.

When laughter is a weapon of persecution, we Christians need the Holy Spirit to give us that extra measure of patience and love. Others may persecute us with laughter when we tell them the reason we retreat when they tell a sexual joke or why we don't use their brand of blue language at work. Derisive snickers may accompany our mealtime prayer, whether it's over a sack lunch or a gourmet meal in a restaurant. It's to be expected according to 2 Timothy 3:12, which says, "In fact, everyone who wants to live a godly life in Christ Jesus will be persecuted." Laughs of ridicule can be an especially sharp sword. So hang on. You'll get over it! Someday.

While you're hanging on, do what Jesus did. Don't change a thing. You may discover that your antagonists may laugh with you rather than at you.

The Last Straw

Jeremiah 23:25–29

THE SUM TOTAL of my agricultural expertise was explained earlier in this book, so it shouldn't surprise you that for years my only understanding of the word *straw* focused on the round, hollow device used for ingesting liquids. Remember launching the paper wrapper from your straw? Or spitballs? Then there's that scientific demonstration of physics that allows you to siphon soda from one glass into your father's unwelcome attention!

When I became more educated (a freshman in college), I learned that *straw* was a farm-related product. Showing off my new knowledge, I said something like, "Oh, look at that cow chewing straw." (My friends got their healthy laugh for the day.) My farmer friends didn't know it at the time, but they prepared me for understanding this passage from Jeremiah: " 'Let the prophet who has a dream tell his dream, but let the one who has My word speak it faithfully. For what has straw to do with grain?' declares the LORD" (Jeremiah 23:28).

Grain makes nourishing food. Straw makes good bedding material and provokes allergies on the side. While unharvested grains and straw may look similar to the untrained eye, they are obviously quite dissimilar. The same is true for those who preach and teach.

Religious television and radio programs flood the airwaves today. We thank God for all the effort and interest in His Word. However, we should be careful because some preachers and teachers are merely dreamers. They provide a lot to chew on, but in the end their message is better under our feet than in our hearts. With all those spiritual messages flying into our radio and TV receivers, how can we tell empty dreams from real spiritual food?

Make no mistake. It's not always easy to discern godly from ungodly messages. The Bible enjoys a great reputation among us, and anyone holding one has entree into the hearts of believers. But we can tell if we're getting grain if we're reminded of Jesus' accomplishments on our behalf—how He opened heaven's doors through His death and resurrection. Preachers and teachers apply the Gospel message in a host of creative ways, but if the message of Christ is missing, we're getting buried under a pile of straw. Pray for an allergic reaction to such teaching. Pray to make it the last straw.

Know It All

Acts 16:29–34

NOW THAT YOU'RE HALFWAY through this book, it's time for a midterm exam. Circle the T … you know the routine.

1. T F The Pentateuch is the first seven books of the Bible.
2. T F The story of the flood is found in the book of Noah.
3. T F Herman Neutics was a famous theology professor.
4. T F Intinction is like intonation, only softer.
5. T F We must be Greek scowlers to understand the Bible.

Just what should we know so we can pass the ultimate spiritual test? Luke recorded this in Acts: "Believe in the Lord Jesus, and you will be saved—you and your household" (Acts 16:31). Paul and Silas spoke those words to their desperate jailer as he contemplated suicide to avoid the punishment mandated by the Roman government in jailbreak situations. That sentence answers the question of what we need to know—especially for the final exam.

If all we need to know for salvation is that Jesus is our Savior, then why bother with further study? Why take time to read the Bible or attend classes at church or listen to Christian broadcasting? The fact that you're reading this book indicates you already know—perhaps intuitively—the answer. We want to learn more and more about God's love for us. We want to understand how we fit into the history of salvation, which is explained so well in the Bible. God's Word to us is Good News, and we can never get enough of that.

Have you gone through times when you wondered if you knew enough to be saved? Satan sends those doubts. He hopes that you'll strive and strain to learn enough about salvation to earn it on your own. That's the dark side of knowing more about God. The devil tempts us to scrutinize God's Word, to study it so well that we think we know it all. In the process, we forget what is most important—Jesus Christ.

Continue to study God's Word. You'll know you're too smart if you can't answer this question in two words or less: Who took away your sins and saved you?

By the way, all the answers on today's midterm were false. But they weren't important. When you know Jesus, you really do know the right answer.

Graffiti

Daniel 5:1–5

I F YOU'RE LIKE MANY PEOPLE, you read in the bathroom. If you use public washrooms, chances are good you won't need to provide your own reading material. Just read the stalls. (The term "quit stalling" originated with someone impatiently awaiting available space while experiencing kidney anxiety.) Graffiti poses serious aesthetic problems for building owners, public transportation companies, bridges, garage doors, and anything else that remains immobile for too long.

Graffiti was actually invented as far back as the Old Testament. Daniel 5:5 says: "Suddenly the fingers of a human hand appeared and wrote on the plaster of the wall, near the lamp stand in the royal palace. The king watched the hand as it wrote."

King Belshazzar of Babylon suffered graffiti on the walls of his banquet room. He even caught the Tagger (to use graffiti language) in the act. Or maybe it was the other way around. God (the Tagger) caught Belshazzar in an act of defiance and disrespect. The slogan on the wall, interpreted by Daniel, foretold the king's death. The graffiti was fulfilled that very night.

Have you seen the handwriting on the wall? If God were to write on our walls, what would He say? He might enumerate the ways we disrespect Him. Would He scrawl something about how we use His name? Might He draw a picture of our wallet or purse to depict how we hoard all His material blessings instead of contributing to His work? Would He record all those evil thoughts we would never reveal to others? Would He redirect our accusations of others to expose our own faults? Would He prophesy our well-deserved death?

No!

God would take His holy finger and probably draw something like a cross. King Belshazzar's graffiti meant death because he refused to acknowledge God. This graffiti on our walls means life because it tells of Jesus who suffered death on our behalf. This graffiti on our walls reminds us that Jesus is our personal Savior who knows and loves us despite our sinfulness.

Next time you see something riddled with graffiti, let it remind you of your sinful life. But look closely—is there a cross somewhere in that tangle of lines?

Breaking the Habit

Isaiah 29:13–21

Do you have any bad habits? If not, ask your neighbor. He probably has a few to spare. (Or else he'll tell you about the habits you've been missing!) You might face future hardships if you don't have any bad habits. After all, what will the doctor tell you to give up when you're feeling poorly? Of course, there comes a point in life when you have abandoned all your bad habits and it still fails to improve your health.

Few people would claim that making a habit of regular worship is bad. But consider these words from Scripture: "The LORD says: 'These people come near to Me with their mouth and honor Me with their lips, but their hearts are far from Me. Their worship of Me is made up only of rules taught by men' " (Isaiah 29:13).

Has it occurred to you that sometimes we children of God act like we don't have a Father? Oh, it's easy to do what's expected, especially as we worship in church—when we're aware that Father is watching. We diligently follow the order of service, participating in prayers and taking care not to talk when it's the preacher's turn. If the music is a tune we especially like, we sing enthusiastically; if it's not one of our favorites, we sing anyway. But when the service ends, it's easy to completely forget Father.

Worship is more than habitual church attendance. We worship when we practice what we hear preached—when we add relationships to ritual. That's what Jesus did. He preached His sermons and led large Bible classes, and He expected people to listen and learn. He also cared about His "congregation" and expected these people to care for one another (as well as for Him). Jesus proved this point repeatedly as He demonstrated His tenderness and compassion as well as His knowledge of Scripture. Remember the time He single-handedly catered the potluck when everyone else left their pots at home?

Jesus and His Father (who is our Father too) have observed many people who've confused ritual with relationship—who leave worship nestled in pews rather than strolling the sidewalks. That's why God gave us the message we read in Isaiah. When we catch ourselves turning a good habit into a bad one, He'll help us break it. And the Holy Spirit will help us keep our good habits truly good. He has a habit of doing that. Thank God.

The Case of Getting Stoned

Deuteronomy 21:18–21

IN THE GOOD OLD DAYS, a juvenile delinquent was a kid who drank soda for breakfast and sat on the fender of a neighbor's car as he munched on three extra cookies he took without asking permission. (He probably refused to wear a hat on cold days too. Of course, those were the days when hair tonic had a higher proof than beer.)

In the good Old Testament days, when a juvenile delinquent got stoned, it meant something much different than today's terminology. Look at this Bible passage: "If a man has a stubborn and rebellious son who does not obey his father and mother and will not listen to them when they discipline him. … Then all the men of his town shall stone him to death" (Deuteronomy 21:18, 21a).

That practice probably led to the saying, "Spare the quarry and spoil the son." Those were the days when the community possessed greater importance than those who rattled its foundations with thoughtless crimes. But could God really expect parents to relinquish rebellious offspring to such punishment? Apparently He did, but it's likely that He also left some loopholes to shield the delinquent before the first stone flew. Many Old Testament laws of this type could be appealed to a reduced sentence that adequately punished the perpetrator without carrying out the death sentence.

With that little history lesson accomplished, we can place this text in a modern perspective—after all, God's Word is applicable in every age. While we're tempted to apply these verses only to young people, we should see what they mean on a more personal level.

In the previous devotional, you probably agreed that we sometimes act like we have no Father. We may even go further than that—rebelling against God as we commit our pet sins and creating other ways to act like a delinquent even if we're no longer juvenile. Does God the Father have a right to stone us for such sinfulness?

He does, but He doesn't do it. He has every right to kill us and let us spend eternity in hell. But He doesn't do that. He sent His Son to suffer our punishment, dying not by stoning but by being sinned to death. Because God did this for us, He offered opportunity and power to forgive. All this because one very big stone was rolled away to reveal an empty tomb.

Getting High on Love

Psalm 103:11–18

THE ASTRONOMER'S JOB is always looking up. (At least she won't find any puns in outer space!) If you've never gazed through a telescope at the night sky, take the time to do it sometime. Besides all those stars and planets up there, it's amazing how fast the earth spins. Look away from the telescope just for a moment after focusing on a star, and when you look back, it's out of focus.

The most powerful telescopes, even those located high on mountaintops, can't scan all of space. Even the Hubble telescope discovered that the sky's the limit. It's seemingly endless—the closest object lesson we have to explain eternity. We also can use it to describe God's love. Psalm 103:11 says: "For as high as the heavens are above the earth, so great is His love for those who fear Him."

We know God loves us a lot. We know that His love stretches farther than the entire universe. Because it is so expansive, it spurns human description. Everything we know, except the sky, has limits. For example, there's marital love. It begins sometime before the vows are spoken and the honeymoon begins but, out of necessity, much later than birth. Some people love their cars, but that love usually ends when rust spots appear and tires go bald. (Sometimes that happens with people too.) No matter what we humans love, it has either a beginning or an end or both. Not so with God's love.

He loved you before your birth. He knew you while He was still creating oaks, dolphins, ladybugs, ferns, and the Mississippi River. He loved you then, and He continues to love you though you're often unfaithful—sometimes only remembering Him when you need help or on His birthday.

Think, for a moment, of one way in which you sinned today. (Don't think too long—even if you're a big sinner.) That sin was an act of unfaithfulness, brief as it might have been. But God doesn't focus on sins. In fact, He doesn't even remember them because Jesus took them away. God loves you like He loved His Son. God's love is unconditional and limitless because Jesus fulfilled all the conditions and took away any limits when He died for you. So grab a telescope and look for that pie in the sky!

Make Like a Moth

John 8:12–18

MOTHS REALLY LIKE TO WING IT. (Ugh!) Their favorite domiciles are deep in the cool grass where birds can't catch them, in closets where they can snack 'round the clock, in my wallet where they rarely get a change of scenery, and around bright light bulbs at night.

We can learn from moths. (Wait! Don't eat your socks.) Consider how this Bible passage implies what moths can teach us: "When Jesus spoke again to the people, He said, 'I am the light of the world. Whoever follows Me will never walk in darkness, but will have the light of life' " (John 8:12).

For some reason, moths have a persistent urge to flutter near bright lights. Maybe they possess a genetic yearning for show biz. Once attracted to a light, they demonstrate tireless effort to stay within the brilliant, warm rays flowing from the bulb. (Of course, some venture too close and disappear in a sizzle.)

Christians exhibit an earnest craving to be close to their Light. Unlike the moth's scenario, however, it's not dangerous to rub against our Light. Our Light made personal contact safe, but there was a time when brushing against God meant immediate death. Moses wanted to see God, but God wisely denied his request. Instead, He allowed Moses to glimpse Him, which was enough to put a luminous glow on Moses' face for quite some time.

The problem with sinners seeing God face to face is that He is so holy that their spiritual immune system would utterly fail because of its imperfection. But people wanted to see God anyway, so God became man and came to earth in the person of Jesus Christ. Now people could see the Light. They could touch Him. They could feel His warm and gentle hands soothe and heal the hurts of their bodies. Wouldn't it be wonderful to feel His holy touch today?

We can. He touches us daily in ways we might not actually sense, but His healing and affection tenderly stroke us. He skillfully splints fractured relationships, shrinks the satanic tumors that corrode our soul, and cleanses our eyes with faith so we can see His Light and stay close to it. And when physical illness or injury closes our eyes in death, He brings us back to life where we'll live in the eternal Light. And we'll never flutter in darkness again.

Don't Horse Around

Isaiah 31:1–7

HORSES ARE NOT man's best friend. At least not this one's. Oh, I'll admit that Paul Revere probably rode a noble steed, and many a bowlegged sheriff of the old west patrolled the dusty trails, spilling coffee and donut crumbs all over the mane of his trustworthy horse. But the last horse I rode nearly killed me, though I must admit, I wouldn't appreciate getting backed into a barbed-wire fence either. But forward and reverse should be marked more clearly on those reins!

God became angry when His people trusted horses. All this must be placed in context of ultimate trust, of course. Isaiah talked about it. "Woe to those who go down to Egypt for help, who rely on horses, who trust in the multitude of their chariots and in the great strength of their horsemen, but do not look to the Holy One of Israel, or seek help from the LORD" (Isaiah 31:1).

The soldiers of Israel rarely enjoyed the latest technology in warfare. Horses greatly impressed them, as you might imagine if you've ever stood next to a stallion. They mistakenly thought that horses could win wars (and therefore peace) much as we might rely on the newest tanks or radar-evading aircraft. But God had promised to be their strength, and He told them what He thought of their weapons inventory. Horses were only flesh and bones and hair with a tail added to chase away flies. Staunch steeds were no match for God.

God intended this message for us too. We sometimes trust horses more than Him. Our horses might live under a hood and sport a horn as well as a very large price tag. Then again, a whole stable of horses is okay if we don't treat them like gods. Our horses might spend most of their time grazing in a passbook or CD certificate. This is acceptable, too, as long as we avoid turning them into objects that supplant God. Sometimes our horses take the form of self-made transportation to heaven. That happens when we figure we're good enough (or not bad enough) in God's sight just the way we are. After all, worship and prayer and stewardship are for all those sinners out there. God says "Whoa" (or was it "Woe") to that! Don't horse around. Live by that famous motto printed on what has become a horse for many: "In God we trust."

Crash Dummies

1 John 1:8–10

YOU CAN FOOL some people all the time and all people some of the time. Government officials often try both. Such may be the case of the Roswell Incident of 1947 when the alleged bodies of alleged aliens crashed into the alleged—er, the real—desert of New Mexico. For 50 years, the Air Force denied that anything had happened. Suspicious citizens doubted the credibility of the U.S. government, and years of fearful speculation followed the mysterious happenings in New Mexico.

In 1997 the Air Force told the story they should have told back in 1947. They said the bodies recovered were those of crash dummies used to test high-altitude parachute drops. (Crash dummies were at high altitudes before they could even drive cars!) Since crash dummies in bygone days didn't talk, the account is allegedly irrefutable. Some people continue to doubt the Air Force story. Who cares if the facts are supported by a document running more than 200 pages? Had the government come clean back in 1947, the Roswell Incident wouldn't have been an incident.

We can learn something about sin from this story. The Bible says, "If we claim to be without sin, we deceive ourselves and the truth is not in us" (1 John 1:8). Don't mistake this passage as one that addresses the Air Force treatment of Roswell. We're the ones who need to shun deception and concede the truth.

We can fool some people into thinking we're marginal sinners. However, the more we succeed in convincing others of our holiness, the more they'll watch to see if they can catch us in something big. Besides, other people aren't the ones who need convincing of our innocence. And it's useless to lobby our case before God. He knows what we're thinking, even if we're not actually doing it. The only ones we deceive in a cover-up are ourselves.

We need not waste time covering up. Jesus covered our sins with the cross. No deception here. The Romans didn't crucify a crash dummy that day. God knows what His Son did for us, and He is well pleased. Now the truth is out. God loves us so much that He sent His Son to take away our sins—at the cost of His comfort and life. Here's another irrefutable fact: Aliens are living on earth. You're one of them, but someday you'll go home.

138

Soaking It Up

Leviticus 18:1–20

A TEACHER ONCE PROCLAIMED that I had a mind like a sponge. I thought she meant I could absorb information many times the weight of my brain. That night while washing dishes, I perceived reality. She meant my brain was full of holes!

All of us are blessed with minds like sponges. We soak up information incredibly fast, and we usually wring it out even faster! Consider our ability to adapt to our environment. If one moves from International Falls, Minn., to the Gulf Coast of Mississippi, one absorbs information that tells him or her to either walk slower or turn into a puddle and evaporate in the southern sun. A person moving from the Gulf Coast to the Canadian border, however, quickly loses the sense of "mosey along." In such cases, our ability to absorb and process new information is truly a blessing. But consider the following warning from God:

> *You must not do as they do in Egypt, where you used to live,*
> *and you must not do as they do in the land of Canaan, where*
> *I am bringing you. Do not follow their practices. Leviticus 18:3*

God commands us to absorb only so much. Christians walk a thin line between separating themselves from the world while not removing themselves from it. Think for a moment how religious beliefs and moral standards have changed since you were a teenager. Perhaps much water has passed over the sponge since you were a teen, and the change is shocking. We tolerate more immoral behavior than ever before. In matters of faith, we are urged to believe that as long as someone believes in anyone or anything that transcends humanity, it's not only okay, it's actually good. It's about these matters that God alerts us.

Human nature is bound (as in chained) to absorb its culture as a matter of either survival or sensual pleasure, unless someone can break the fetters. We know that Someone well. Jesus broke the bonds that so solidly connected us to Satan. He whacked away at them and pried them loose with the cross. He freed us to absorb His love and wisdom. We refuse to soak up evil because we're free and empowered to obey the real God rather than cultural customs and idiosyncrasies. As we absorb His abundant love, we're free to wring it out on others so they can soak it up too.

Counting Your Blessings

Luke 11:27–32

THE LYRICS OF AN OLD SONG claim that if worry deprives you of sleep, you should count blessings rather than sheep. It's probably good advice. All that bleating will rob you of rest. And when you think about it, you are richly blessed, aren't you?

1. *The Holy Spirit gave you faith. As a believer you recognize your bless-ings, and you also can see them where others see only travail or trouble. You personally know the Giver of those blessings.*

2. *Your senses are working. You see the pages of this book, and if noise distracts you, thank God you can hear. You feel the differing textures of your surroundings, and you smell. No, not you. I mean …
well, you know what I mean. Put the book down and have a snack. Unless it's one of those taste-free varieties, you probably enjoy the flavor. (If one or more of your senses don't function, you're blessed with increased intensity in other senses to compensate.)*

3. *God gave you this day your daily bread. (You asked for it, didn't you?) Not only bread, but everything else you need for survival, maybe even prosperity. If you're a little hurt that God hasn't given you as much as the proverbial Joneses, remember that the more one has, the more one is tempted to feel self-sufficient and, thereby, the more one is tempted to discard faith.*

4. *Somebody loves you. That person might live with or near you or perhaps he or she sends thinking-of-you cards. Maybe you see this person every day and the love is so routine that you take it for granted. Maybe he or she lives elsewhere or only in memories. Even if you're terribly lonely, God loves you so much that He sent Jesus who loves you so much that He died for your sins. Now the Holy Spirit loves you so much that He keeps you faithful, even when you're tempted to roam.*

5. *And then there's this: "As Jesus was saying these things, a woman in the crowd called out, 'Blessed is the mother who gave You birth and nursed You.' He replied, 'Blessed rather are those who hear the word of God and obey it' " (Luke 11:27–28).*

Jesus enabled you to hear God's Word, which mercifully assures you that even when you don't obey Him, Jesus obeyed for you. You're saved! You have God's Word on it.

Silence Is What?

Acts 18:1–11; Zephaniah 1:7a; 1 Peter 2:15

Have you heard about the mime who was arrested? The officers wondered if they should tell him he had the right to speak up.

There are times when silence is golden. Note three advantages of silence:

1. You're an unlikely candidate for leading a neighborhood or congregational committee.

2. More people will agree with you.

3. Silence is a wicked weapon during an argument.

The Bible treats silence several ways. The first appears in Zephaniah 1:7, which says, "Be silent before the Sovereign Lord, for the day of the Lord, is near." As much as God invites us to address Him in prayer, sometimes it's best to be silent. In our silence, we listen to God. We're likely to hear His voice speaking passages from the Bible or whispering comfort in the nonverbal language of faith that our souls hear.

At other times, silence isn't so golden. Acts 18:9 says: "One night the Lord spoke to Paul in a vision: 'Do not be afraid; keep on speaking, do not be silent. For I am with you, and no one is going to attack and harm you, because I have many people in this city.' "

Jesus is with us too. God willing, as you read this book, you're not facing the potential persecution that Paul encountered. Persecutors in civilized society are generally more wily and sly than life-threatening, which is scary. Can you sit next to someone on the plane and tell him what you know about Jesus? Does Jesus' love creep into normal conversation—or just creep away? How hard it is for some Christians to witness! It might help to remember you're not in it alone.

A third concept of silence appears in 1 Peter 2:15: "For it is God's will that by doing good you should silence the ignorant talk of foolish men." Peter suggests that behavior expresses more than words. Good Christians are also good neighbors, good citizens, good church members. They live good lives. Oh, foolish people will point out the many ways good Christians aren't always good at being good. You know where you fall short, so it's clear that you can't rely on your own goodness. But you don't have to. God is a good forgiver, and that suggests one more way to silence foolish people.

Sweetheart Laws

Psalm 119:97–104

A STRANGE TITLE to be sure, but if the legal system can claim grandfather clauses, then it's also possible to have sweetheart laws. Not that many people would fall in love with the whole harem of laws that keep the judicial system—as well as criminals—running.

Laws are funny things. We have a love/hate relationship with them. On one hand, we hate those laws that make us pay more taxes or drive slowly or jump through hoops to obtain services purchased with our tax money. On the other hand, we love those laws that allow us to call the police on that loud party next door or that prohibit neighbors from keeping a herd of buffalo in their backyard or that require the courts to consider our lawsuit regardless of how frivolous it is.

How do you feel about God's Law? It certainly keeps us in line, and the glut of civil laws seems like a modern Leviticus built on the foundation of the Ten Commandments. But, of course, we must obey the laws—both in spirit and in action. That's the hard part. That also reminds us of the complete definition of God's Law—including the part that condemns us if we don't obey even one part of it.

David had feelings about God's Law. He spoke them in Psalm 119:97, which says: "Oh, how I love Your law! I meditate on it all day long." This is the same David who broke the Law in serious ways, including adultery and murder. Yet David assures us that he loved God's Law and that the Law was worth remembering.

Like David, we don't want a God who surprises us like a stop sign that lurks behind overgrown brush. We want to know what He expects so our lifestyle can be consistent with His will, which brings us to another reason to love God's Law. It shows us our shortcomings—sins, in less genteel language. We just love to know about our sins, don't we?

Love God's Law even if it subpoenas your conscience. Knowing your sins enables you to confess them point blank, candidly bold in your faith and trust that Jesus earned forgiveness for every sinful act—a real Sweetheart Law. Then God's laws lead us to reform, with the guidance of His Holy Spirit. And God is full of more forgiveness when we wallow in our imperfection. Instead of holding God's Law in regretful "Aw!" we can hold His law in loving "Awe."

Seeing Red

Exodus 15:1–18

IF YOU'RE OLD ENOUGH to remember television in the black-and-white era, you probably have a special appreciation for color. Do you remember your first exposure to what we now accept as routine? Perhaps, like me, you gazed transfixed, wondering how it was possible for the electronic picture box to devise such a miracle. All the while, we looked out our windows and didn't wonder a bit at the glittering spectrum. The only way to account for such a paradox must be the shock value of seeing something new.

It's silly to ask if you've ever seen red when speaking of the physical color (unless you're color blind). Most of the time, "seeing red" refers to temper and anger and sometimes even blood. But if you'll forgive (another) pun, we also can claim that the newly escaped Israelite slaves certainly could Sea Red with their backs pressed against a hostile shoreline.

How frightened they must have been. Fear easily leads to anger, and they probably were ready to surrender to the Egyptians as soon as they surrendered Moses to the sea. All this was new to people whose heritage was 400 years of submission and slavery to a powerful and cunning nation. They only knew the red of splitting blisters on their hands or weeping welts from the master's whip.

Could anything good come from the Red Sea? When hope seemed lost, they experienced something new. They sang about it for years afterward: "Pharaoh's chariots and his army He has hurled into the sea. The best of Pharaoh's officers are drowned in the Red Sea" (Exodus 15:4).

What do you see when you see red? Look beyond the fiery emotions the phrase suggests and see salvation instead. Think of the Red Sea. Think about blood too—blood oozing from the wounds in Jesus' hands, feet, and side. Not a pretty picture, but that's what makes red a color to celebrate. Jesus suffered and died for our sins. He liberated us from certain slavery to sin, releasing us to live in the hope of certain salvation and joyful service to God.

Why not wear something red today or tomorrow? It's a color usually noticed in clothing. If someone comments about your color choice, tell them about how you were rescued and by whom. But if nobody notices, that's okay too. Look in the mirror and Sea Red.

White Out

Isaiah 1:1–26

FEW PEOPLE APPRECIATE my generosity. To this day I can't understand why my secretary was offended when I gave her a 55-gallon drum of Wite-Out for Secretary's Day. My brother-in-law wasn't too pleased either when I consented to let him drive my new car. I thought the January whiteout would keep him from being distracted. Come to think of it, my fifth-grade teacher didn't like anything I did for him either. He threw away my art, craftily entitled "White House in a Blizzard." So much for appreciation.

It's not too hard to imagine that Isaiah liked white. Here's why: " 'Come now, let us reason together,' says the LORD. 'Though your sins are like scarlet, they shall be as white as snow; though they are red as crimson, they shall be like wool' " (Isaiah 1:18).

White has long been a color that symbolizes purity. (Okay, so white isn't officially a color. Tell that to the Seven Dwarfs!) Clothes-washing detergents polish their image with claims of the brightest whites, and toothpaste thrives on sparkling smiles. Of course, what advertisers don't mention is that white is quick to show dirt and deterioration.

Purity is one attribute of God. He created the first humans to be pure—without sin. Who knows how long they enjoyed that status, but when they smudged themselves with sin, the blemish couldn't be hidden. Not only did God notice the grime, but that single sin soiled human life forever. Of course, we've added a lot more filth of our own, so we can't blame our first ancestors for the continuing grit of life.

No stain exists that God can't remove. We're among millions of Christians in God's daily load of wash. Not a day passes that God doesn't take away our sins and make us pure again. Admittedly, sometimes we're like a child who wants to avoid cleanliness to the same degree that a grandmother craves it. We easily can become content living in our sins. After a while we accept it like an active child accepts dirt behind his or her ears. At those times, we need someone to remind us that "cleanliness is next to godliness." The old cliché is true when we speak of sin, isn't it?

Take advantage of God's cleansing action today and every day. Forgiveness is His brand of correction fluid, and unlike the earthly Wite-Out, it doesn't just cover our mistakes, it completes erases them.

The Grass Is Always Greener

Psalm 23:1–6

GREEN IS GOOD (unless it's the color of envy or skin). It's the color of nature, coming in many different shades as it works to nourish the plants on which it's spread. Green often symbolizes nurture, tranquility, and wealth. (No wonder money is green!) The favorite psalm of millions uses the word in this context: "He makes me lie down in green pastures, He leads me beside quiet waters" (Psalm 23:2). The picture is one of rest, peace, and contentment. What a colorful way to illustrate God's love!

Green was likely the first color God painted as He commanded plants to grow for both food and beauty. It was a sprig of green that cheered Noah when the dove brought him evidence of dry land after bobbing on floodwaters for a year. The palm branches spread on the road to Jerusalem were green, a refreshing carpet of honor for the Savior of the world. Green was probably the first color Jesus saw when He emerged from the tomb on Easter, walking into the garden where a friend mistook Him for the gardener. Green has indeed been associated with many blessings.

Green is no less appreciated today. Metropolitan areas have recognized the value of greenways where hurried inhabitants can relax in country-like serenity. Farmers look for that first shoot of green to pop through the soil, a sign of life and livelihood. Campers luxuriate in the cool beauty just outside their tent flap. Green also adorns the altars of liturgical churches for most of the year, reminding us that God is always with us.

Wear something green today or tomorrow. Chances are others won't notice it as they did when you wore red. But let it remind you that God's love is as lush as a rain forest. He wants you to rest in His love and completely trust in it as the psalmist suggests. God fills you with life and wants you to be a portable oasis, rambling through the deserts that spiritually dehydrate those who don't know Him. As you move toward the better things of life, it's also good to remember that the grass truly is greener on the other side of the fence—the fence that separates life on earth from life in heaven. You're headed there, even though you're in the valley right now.

Yellow Jack

Leviticus 13:29–37

Today's challenge is to use the title phrase in a sentence. For example, "Never poke fun at a burly mechanic, even if he's using a yellow jack." Better? How about, "The yellow jack was afraid to lift the car." Best? "The ship hoisted a yellow jack and remained in quarantine for weeks." Yes, the real yellow jack is a flag that announces forced isolation of a ship in port. Usually it's for good reason because the cargo may infect and even kill unprotected civilians.

Yellow may be the favorite color of bananas, but for today, we'll consider the more disgusting aspects of the color. We'll begin with Leviticus 13:30, Because you've probably paid little attention to this obscure verse, get a magnifying glass. "The priest is to examine the sore, and if it appears to be more than skin deep and the hair in it is yellow and thin, the priest shall pronounce that person unclean; it is an itch, an infectious disease of the head or chin." It seems the priest was also a master of maladies, especially those that made people unclean in God's presence.

What disagreeable things can you associate with yellow? It's not a healthy color for eyes or skin or paper. Its hue often is associated with cowardice and infection. Even traffic signals take a cautious approach to yellow. Then there's yellow journalism (which may include puns) and the stinging shock of angry yellow jackets. And as we learned today, there is the yellow jack of separation and exclusion.

The devil enjoys raising the yellow jack on us. He's sure to inform God about our pitiful sinfulness and how it endangers heaven's holiness. A close inspection reveals the devil's truth. We are, as we confess, sinful and unclean. But that flag will never shame us because Jesus decontaminated us. He scrubbed away our sins with His own blood and immunized us with His righteousness. For His Son's sake, God will not place us under quarantine.

If one of those Old Testament priests were to examine us, he wouldn't see any yellow hairs on our souls. We are made clean by Christ. We have permission to enter the port of God's kingdom. Take down the yellow jack and hoist high the cross.

Feeling Blue

Exodus 27:1–19

B LUE OFTEN DESCRIBES emotions as well as pigment. Generally, it's not an emotion we enjoy—sulking, down-in-the-dumps, depressed. Sometimes, however, there's perverse rapture in such a state of mind and heart. An entire music genre grew from experiences that made people forlorn and downcast. It could well be the music of sinners too.

Since my Father left me,
I don't know what to do.
I feel so lonely, brokenhearted, out of touch, and blue.
What can I do? What can I do?

How horrible if sinners were left to moan that dirge. No perverse pleasure in this misery. It's a song of doom. It has legitimate basis in reality. Sin separates us from God. Without Him, we're nothing but an organism playing out its last days in hopeless despair.

The cure for the blues is repentance—returning to God who always welcomes us. We look forward to the warm embrace of His forgiveness and reconciliation. Though we sing the blues many times, God's patience and mercy endure forever.

Blue can be as buoyantly blissful as it is depressingly despondent. Blue is the color of royalty and majesty. Blue was a color used to honor God in Bible days, as this passage that describes the tabernacle suggests: "For the entrance to the courtyard, provide a curtain twenty cubits long, of blue, purple and scarlet yarn and finely twisted linen—the work of an embroiderer—with four posts and four bases" (Exodus 27:16).

We're approaching that day when God finally will get His glory due—from believers and nonbelievers alike. Look at the sky on the next clear day and imagine it as the courtyard outside heaven. It's the first place that we'll see our Savior's welcoming smile when the world ends. Beyond that blue portal lies the King's mansion, probably colored in hues we never imagined. And He will share it with us. That's one color scheme that will never become boring! Singing the old blues will be a thing of the past. Our new blues will sound like a royal anthem befitting our move into a regal new home.

Wear blue today or tomorrow. Let it stand for the princely presence of God in your life. Because of Christ, you're a bit blue-blooded yourself.

Show Biz

Luke 18:9–14

L OTS OF PEOPLE pursue the glamour of show business. We probably would have more actors than you could shake a stage at if the public liked the wannabes as much as they liked themselves. As for actresses, they would last longer if their hourglass figures didn't suffer from the shifting sands of time. Show business is intense and tough, largely populated by people who really don't want to be themselves—or at least people who want to act like somebody else.

Jesus told a parable about a man who thought he was on stage every time he prayed. Luke 18:10–11 says: "Two men went up to the temple to pray, one a Pharisee and the other a tax collector. The Pharisee stood up and prayed about himself: 'God, I thank You that I am not like other men—robbers, evildoers, adulterers—or even like this tax collector.' "

The Pharisee knew he had an audience, and he went to prodigious oratorical lengths to impress those watchers. He attempted to play the hero in a scene where the other character—a despised tax collector—was at best a scandalous cheat and at worst a diabolical villain. The stage was the temple and the action was prayer. The most memorable line is repeated above. The lead character expected applause as a hero.

The hero's true identity was thinly disguised in God's sight. He was a fake, the kind of actor who would hire a team of publicists to tell the world about his humility. His prayer was one of praise and thanksgiving—for himself!

Do you know people like that Pharisee? It's bad enough when these self-adorers appear on film, but it's even worse when they wear the costume of Christianity. Maybe you have a little acting experience yourself. Have you ever said something like, "And you call that being a Christian?" Or have you shined the spotlight on the obvious miscues and forgotten lines of Christians you might consider understudies?

The true stars of Christianity know they don't have to act. They can be themselves—even pathetically sinful selves—and God will still love them. His forgiveness is like a legendary epic (as if He needed the stuff of legends). We stars realize with gratitude that the only one who deserves applause is our Savior, Jesus Christ. Next time you're in church, why not bring down the house?

Frequent Failures

Matthew 1:1–17; Haggai 1:5–6

IF THE DEVIL awarded bonuses to those who fail the way airlines award bonuses to frequent flyers, we would win a trip around the world but never get to the airport. In fact, failure is so rampant that one author wrote a book about it. It was so successful that it sold three copies.

What does failure have to do with the Bible readings listed above? Did you fail to make a connection? (Sorry about that.) The list of Jesus' ancestors seems well-rooted as far as family trees go. If we were to conduct a background check of those people, however, we would discover that even the rich and famous on this list were haunted by serious failures. Abraham passed off his wife as his sister to save his life. Isaac was careless with his will. Jacob walked funny. Ram had a penchant for fleecing people. Nashon had trouble spelling. David surrendered to lust. Solomon grew cynical in old age. So the list goes. (I probably failed to uncover the whole truth about some of the characters above.)

If Jesus' ancestors had trouble with failure, you know what His brothers and sisters of this age face. Not to depress you or anything, but nearly everything we do is a failure in some sense. Listen to the words of the prophet Haggai: "Now this is what the LORD Almighty says: 'Give careful thought to your ways. You have planted much, but have harvested little. You eat, but never have enough. You drink, but never have your fill. You put on clothes, but are not warm. You earn wages, only to put them in a purse with holes in it' " (Haggai 1:5–6).

True, isn't it? No matter what we have or what we do, we never experience ultimate and final satisfaction. If we did, we would have heaven on earth, and we know that's not its true location.

There is something that defies failure, however. It's the power of God through Jesus Christ. The salvation Jesus earned on the cross of Calvary makes Satan a failure. Try as he might, Satan may cause us to stumble, but supported by God, we'll never fall. Empowered by the empty cross of Jesus Christ, we need not fear failure. He will not let us fail to join Him in heaven.

Super Sermons

Acts 17:1–12

PITY THE POOR individuals who don't have to leave the house to hear a sermon! Many of us go to church for that experience, and many preachers long to preach an immortal sermon. (Too bad some confuse *immortal* with *eternal*.) In fact, some poor preachers feel they're getting through to the congregation when they see a lot of heads nodding. But before we become too critical of preachers, we can recall that good listening usually makes good preaching.

Luke describes good listening in Acts 17:11. He noted, "Now the Bereans were of more noble character than the Thessalonians, for they received the message with great eagerness and examined the Scriptures every day to see if what Paul said was true."

You might think that the Bereans listened so well because they had a talented, fluent, dynamic preacher like Paul. But Paul claimed that he wasn't much of an orator. In fact, he probably didn't even make his college debate team. But those Bereans knew how to listen. Then they checked out the facts of the sermon!

We would do well to emulate the Bereans. Where do you start? Next time you listen to a sermon, make some mental notes of the chief points. (Well, maybe you better write them on paper.) Record the sermon text, and reread it in a Bible that has cross-references. Read those texts too. Or buy a study Bible that explains passages. (Your local Christian bookstore or your pastor is a source of advice on what translation to read.) As you study more about what you hear, you'll probably turn into a preacher yourself.

Too late for the seminary? Maybe. But most great sermons are preached from faces, hands, and feet rather than tongues and lips. Compassionate eyes reflect Christian concern, and smiles illustrate the joy of salvation. Helping hands are reminiscent of the service Jesus performed. Then there are those sermons that come from the sole. (Yes, it's spelled right.) Our feet carry us many places in a day, which provides opportunities to preach sermons with the rest of our body—lips, tongues, and larynx included.

Maybe now you're convinced that you're a preacher. But have pity on the nodders in your "congregation." They may be in danger of getting whiplash.

Exercise Equipment

1 Timothy 4:6–14

AREN'T MODERN INVENTIONS WONDERFUL? Exercise equipment is a good example. People can build their bodies in the privacy of their own homes with machines that manipulate every conceivable muscle (and a few that aren't so conceivable). You can purchase walking machines, skiing machines, weight-lifting devices, and other contraptions that might have been outlawed even in the Dark Ages as instruments of torture. My own experience with exercise devices is limited, unless you count teeter-totters, swings, and jungle gyms.

The craze surrounding physical fitness undoubtedly has many origins. Some people like to keep that which God called His temple trim, fit, and efficient. Others feel it's the avenue to attractiveness; some hope remaining physically fit will help them live longer. All are good reasons when kept in perspective, and they suggest some parallels in the realm of faith as well.

Consider Paul's words to young Timothy: "Have nothing to do with godless myths and old wives' tales; rather, train yourself to be godly. For physical training is of some value, but godliness has value for all things, holding promise for both the present life and the life to come" (1 Timothy 4:7–8).

Paul wasn't suggesting that exercise is worthless, but he knew what happens to taut tummies, bulging arms, and broad chests. Gravity is vicious as the years pass, and fitness training is no guarantee of extended life. Paul also might advise, "Exercise your faith as well as your body because when your body goes, God will keep your faith strong."

No one wants a flabby faith any more than they want a frumpy physique. Therefore, someone should commend you for exercising right now. The Holy Spirit uses exercise "machines" such as devotional books, group Bible studies, chat sessions with Jesus, worship services, and the sacraments to flex and pull and twist and pump weak faith into fit faith. When faith is strong enough, God even allows adversity to push it to its limits, thereby making it firmer and even more brawny.

Maybe you've heard phrases such as "buns of steel" or "abs of steel." What can you claim? With the coaching of the Holy Spirit as you diligently exercise in God's Word, you have a soul of steel. (And it won't collapse, warp, or rust with age.)

Ring around the Platter

Matthew 23:23–28

AREN'T MODERN INVENTIONS WONDERFUL? Of course, they aren't always consistent with their reputation. Take dishwashers, for example. Maybe it's because I owned an early model (two hands, a washcloth, and a towel) that I wasn't satisfied with the electrical kind. I was especially dissatisfied with its effectiveness on paper plates. It didn't do well with bones or gravy that had been dried-on for more than 11 days either. If you left coffee in a mug more than three weeks, well, the dishwasher didn't make a dent in that either!

My dishwasher must have been the Pharisee model. Listen: "Woe to you, teachers of the law and Pharisees, you hypocrites! You clean the outside of the cup and dish, but inside they are full of greed and self-indulgence. Blind Pharisee! First clean the inside of the cup and dish, and then the outside also will be clean" (Matthew 23:25–26). Wow! Those were some of the harshest words our Savior ever spoke.

Squeaky clean on the outside, but ring around the soul on the inside. That describes the condition of anyone who tries to masquerade as wholly holy on his or her own. Those who flaunt their facade of goodness anger us, just as they did Jesus, but sometimes the situation is more pathetic.

Think of a well-known person who, by all appearances, is someone everyone would consider good. Got a name in mind? What evidence does this person demonstrate to support this reputation? Perhaps it's large donations to worthy causes or hours of personal labor to help those living in ramshackle squalor. Maybe it's someone who participates in every fund-raiser at the local school or who chauffeurs the neighborhood kids to soccer practice. As a Christian, however, you know what the ultimate measure of goodness is, don't you?

Does this person believe that Jesus is his or her Savior from sin, death, and the devil? If not, all the philanthropy and volunteer hours in the world won't make this person good in God's judgment. How easy it is for outward goodness to deceive both the do-gooder as well as those who observe the goodness! As good as this person might be, he or she needs your witness, empowered by the Holy Spirit, to be truly good. Maybe you can start by offering to help with the dishes.

A Sandwich to Remember

Acts 2:40–47

AREN'T MODERN INVENTIONS WONDERFUL? Another fascinating one is the bread maker. Older bread bakers remember the loving punches inflicted on dough, though no loaves were pummeled in anger. It was just something bakers kneaded to do. Next came the dough hook, which butted dough with nary a drop of sweat required of the baker. Now we have this machine that does everything but eat the bread.

Bread has long assumed religious significance. There was the unleavened bread baked by the children of Israel as they packed for their escape from Egypt. There was manna in the desert when they were far from bakeries. Finally, there was my mother's bread, which once reminded the family of the bricks baked by the Israelites while still captive in Egypt.

Jesus compared Himself to life-giving and life-sustaining bread. When He instituted the Lord's Supper, He didn't break a fish or a leg of lamb. He broke bread and told His followers to remember Him when they ate it. Together with the wine, we celebrate today His presence and receive the forgiveness He won for us on the cross.

Beyond Holy Communion, we can continue another tradition that helps us remember Jesus' sacrifice. Acts 2:42 suggests something we can copy: "They devoted themselves to the apostles' teaching and to the fellowship, to the breaking of bread and to prayer."

We "break bread" every time we eat, and we eat several times each day (except for those who partake in one continuous meal). This presents the perfect opportunity to pray. Although we're hungry and don't want the food to cool, we can have a few brief words with God about more than just our meals. (After all, it's not like He's a waiter who doesn't want to hear how your day went.) There's also the fellowship aspect. If you eat alone, it's probably the time when you're most lonely. But you can find a cure for that loneliness if you pull out a chair and invite God to sit with you. Then you can pray and eat simultaneously. If you're so blessed to have companions at the table, enjoy their fellowship and be a source of joy for them as well.

Whatever your meal, remember the time Jesus ate and prayed and led fond conversations with His friends. Even that routine summer sausage sandwich can be something to remember.

Keep Your Antenna Up

Luke 12:35–40

Aren't modern inventions wonderful? (By now you would probably appreciate one that would turn off reruns of the first sentence.) I cite cellular telephones as yet another example. In days of yore, you couldn't go to a baseball game and be bothered—I mean, remain in touch—with important business clients (or the cleaners or the fish market or the travel agent). You would have to enjoy the game completely independent of infringements on your time. Now you're never more than 11 beeps away—even when you don't want to be.

In fairness to Motorola, Ameritech, Cellular One, and all others who might take offense at the first paragraph, let me say that cellular telephones are one of God's technological blessings. They give us added measures of safety and peace of mind. They also offer good subject matter for thinking about our relationship with Jesus.

The Bible says, "Be dressed ready for service and keep your lamps burning" (Luke 12:35). Were Jesus talking today, He might say, "Remain available and keep your antenna up." Unlike a demanding supervisor who insists that you're always available by phone, pager, fax, or smoke signal (even though you're expected to exercise discretion when contacting him), Jesus sets a perfect example for us.

We're aware of Jesus' hours—simultaneously available to everyone 24 hours a day. He responds to our needs, small or large, and He's faster than a microwave signal in relieving our guilt with forgiveness. His willingness to serve us demonstrates how we can respond to Him and to those who need us.

If you're out in the public at all, you interact with or at least observe many needy people (and I'm not talking about the homeless). Among their numbers may be a family member, your boss, the kid across the street, the widower in the next apartment, the driver stopped on the shoulder of the highway, the salesperson at the store, or the man standing next to you on the elevator.

With a smile on your lips, a Scripture verse in your heart, and a friendly word on your tongue, you might be God's answer to that person's prayer. Let Jesus know that you're always available. And keep your antenna up!

Seeing but Not Sawing

Acts 28:23–31

THE SCENE IS PROBABLY repeated at countless county fairs throughout the summer. Ingredients include a skilled, muscular artist, chain saws of several lengths, and a small forest of very large tree trunks cut into manageable pieces. No, these aren't the makings of a horror movie. Together, they provide a fascinating demonstration of wood sculpture—fashioning an anonymous chunk of trunk into an aesthetic masterpiece.

A respectable audience filed onto the bleachers awaiting the three o'clock show. The trunk was about a yard high and two feet thick. As the man began hacking—I mean, sculpting—more spectators gathered, wondering aloud what this unique sculptor was making. Then a strange thing happened. As the crowd began to recognize the sculpture as some type of animal, they began to leave. When the remaining audience identified the outline of a moose, several more rows left. Relatively few people remained to applaud the artist's completed masterpiece moose.

The county fair scene may make us wonder if Jesus and His apostles didn't face the same disappointment as they proclaimed God's Word. We read in Acts, "For this people's heart has become calloused; they hardly hear with their ears, and they have closed their eyes. Otherwise they might see with their eyes, hear with their ears, understand with their hearts and turn, and I would heal them" (Acts 28:27). Sound like the crowd at the fair?

Anytime we're quick to criticize, we risk receiving what we give. Most of us sometime suffer drooping eyes and clogged ears when it comes to God's Word. How often doesn't our Bible reading fade from enthusiastic anticipation to an agonizing "How many more verses in today's reading?" Our good intentions at the beginning of the sermon lapse into daydreaming or shift to that wasp that is buzzing near Mr. Felton's ear. If we need more to confess, how about the prayers that go unsaid because we're in a hurry or too tired?

Like any good actor, speaker, or chain saw artist, the audience won't affect the presentation. Jesus continues to preach His Word through the Bible and those chosen to preach and teach it. We're free to take our embarrassing guilt to the very Person we offend. He forgives and encourages us to listen attentively and to hear more of the good things He wants to tell. When it comes to His Word, it's worth sticking around to the end.

News Flash

Malachi 3:13–18

A N ARMED MAN in Issaquah, Wash., surrendered to police after blasting four shots into the hard drive and one shot into the monitor of his computer. Police evacuated his apartment complex, but apparently the cybershooter wasn't dangerous to anyone unless that person was named Compaq, Acer, or Dell. If you have any familiarity with computers, this is known as a fatal error.

As the shooter discovered, computers aren't always friendly. In fact, they're either coldly efficient or distantly indifferent. Computers perform complex tasks in seconds, yet they cannot think, and regardless of how cute the screen saver, they have no feelings toward you whatsoever. Even if you shoot them.

According to the prophet Malachi, God's people once felt that God was cold, indifferent, and unsympathetic toward them. Malachi 3:14–15 says: "You have said, 'It is futile to serve God. What did we gain by carrying out His requirements and going about like mourners before the LORD Almighty? But now we call the arrogant blessed. Certainly the evildoers prosper, and even those who challenge God escape.' " Spoken like the true modern-day people they were! And they would feel just as modern today, wouldn't they?

It irks most of us that evil plunders the earth's population seemingly without rein, often escaping the punishment it deserves. Murderers go free on technicalities, unreformed rapists use parole to prowl again, and coworkers openly blaspheme God and end up promoted anyway. Worse, Christians in some parts of the world are hunted like animals and cruelly persecuted. It's enough to make Christians feel their faith is futile.

That's sin talking. God never promised Christians any special treatment. In fact, He warned us that life could be hard—or even short—because of faith. So when we feel that faith is pointless or feel sorry for ourselves, we know the devil has infiltrated our mind and soul. We can repent and ask the Holy Spirit to help us recognize God's strength in the midst of our weakness. We can expect the same assurance that was given to Malachi's crowd: " 'They will be Mine,' says the LORD Almighty, 'in the day when I make up My treasured possession … And you will again see the distinction between the righteous and the wicked, between those who serve God and those who do not' " (3:17–18).

Revelation from Research

Revelation 2:8–11

CHURCH ATTENDANCE prolongs life. A respected journal of public health studied longevity in two groups of people—those who regularly attended worship and those who didn't. The annual death rate was 36 percent higher in the group that didn't attend church regularly.

This study spanned 28 years and included more than 5,000 subjects. Actually, they could have discovered the same thing in a few minutes had they listened in Sunday school. (One side note: The government reacted favorably to this research because it can collect several more years of taxes from at least one segment of society.)

God revealed this: "Be faithful, even to the point of death, and I will give you the crown of life" (Revelation 2:10b). Remaining faithful to death usually includes a lifestyle of regular worship. Simply going to church, of course, doesn't guarantee salvation. Faithfulness includes trusting God, living according to His will, talking to Him regularly, loving and serving others and, because we aren't consistently good at any of the above, asking and accepting forgiveness.

The research study didn't differentiate between Christians and non-Christians. The results were solely attributed to healthier lifestyles and supportive social and emotional interaction. It only makes sense that happy and healthy people would live longer. But to be genuinely happy and healthy, we depend on faith. Oh, not our own. It's often weak and sickly. But God's faithfulness is what makes us live longer.

How old are you? Perhaps God has been faithful to you for many years. In fact, He was faithful even before you were! He sent the Holy Spirit to deliver faith to your soul. That faith soon circulated to your intellect and emotions, but it requires constant maintenance. God faithfully does that—by the day, even by the minute if necessary. He loves you even when you neglect or avoid Him. He also takes advantage of those times when you're weak or sick or depressed or disgusted to bring you closer to Himself.

God is faithful until death. Not His death, of course, but ours. Because of His faithfulness, we'll be another statistic that indicates longevity runs in God's faithful family. Those researchers were right. Faithful people do live a long time.

Last Things First

John 5:24–30

CHRISTIANS TALK A LOT about eternal life. Sometimes it's hard to distinguish between assumptions and biblical revelation. We'll spend the next few devotions on heavenly things, examining the few scriptural passages on this subject. I admit from the outset that we'll never comprehend the true nature of heaven until we're there. We also can thank God that He used more space in the Bible to proclaim heaven as a gift than He did to describe it.

Those desiring a room in the heavenly mansion must have advance reservations. Yours are made, thanks to the gracious service of the Holy Spirit. The Good News is that eternal life begins right here on earth. Jesus said, "I tell you the truth, whoever hears My Word and believes Him who sent Me has eternal life and will not be condemned; he has crossed over from death to life" (John 5:24).

Faith is the joyful beginning of eternity with Jesus, which certainly has implications for how we live. Think how you would like to live in heaven. Wait a minute. If you see heaven as a place of rest, that doesn't mean you should practice for the future now! No, heaven is where we'll know completely why the Holy Spirit led us to love and serve both God and other humans.

However we envision heaven, we know it will be happy, and because eternal life begins here on earth, we can be happy already. Maybe "satisfied" is a better word. Skirmishes with sin punctuate our current phase of eternal existence, and we often come away with scars. That's all part of crossing over "from death to life."

Content in what the future promises, we trust God to make the earthly stage of eternity one in which we share our faith with others and worship our Savior with regularity. Faith reminds us to confess our sins and seek the Spirit's power to live according to God's will.

Do you remember the moment you "crossed over from death to life"? For some, it happened before they knew what was happening—Baptism as an infant. For others, it came when they were more aware of this gift. In all cases, the Holy Spirit brought the gift freely, with no merit or even comprehension on our part. Isn't that a great way to kick off the future?

Watch That Second Step

1 Corinthians 15:35–49

THE FIRST STEP toward eternal life is easy. We do nothing except receive the gift of faith from the Holy Spirit. But watch that second step. It's a doozy.

You've probably heard several jokes about death and taxes. At least death doesn't get worse with each legislative session! Dying isn't something which we look forward to experiencing, except in our "later" years when we anticipate a reunion with those who have gone before us to our Father's heavenly mansion. As we grow older, we realize just how much life on earth is encrusted in sin and misery. But we enjoy it anyway—the people and places and things that are gifts from God. In fact, God wants us to delight in His gift of life on earth. The danger is cherishing this life more than our hope of relocating closer to Him in the future.

The apostle Paul addressed the paradox of dreading death versus hoping for heaven. He said, "But someone may ask, 'How are the dead raised? With what kind of body will they come?' How foolish! What you sow does not come to life unless it dies" (1 Corinthians 15:35–36).

We'll investigate the "body issue" in tomorrow's devotion, so let's more closely consider the issue of physical death now. The Bible teaches that the dead will be raised. Not just those who died in Christ, but all people. We will join the crowd that rises from the dead. (The only way we won't rise is if Jesus returns before we die.)

This will be the first time we'll truly fathom the depths of God's limitless power—power unbridled by human intellect or suppressed by human emotion. Everything will seem new and exciting—just the way a fresh start should be! But before we get giddy, we should remember we're talking about death.

If we didn't die to sinful existence, we could not live in heaven. That death came when the Holy Spirit brought us to faith. Physical death is another matter—a reminder of how sin destroyed God's plan. But the most hopeful way to view death is to use Paul's familiar example from agriculture. Seeds fall from plants at the end of their season. They seem to die and dry out until they descend underground. Then they grow into fresh plants that don't resemble their former condition as seeds.

We're dead and planted rather than dead and buried. When Christ returns, we'll forget all about our seedy existence in the past.

New and Improved

1 Corinthians 15:50–53

L ET'S EXAMINE your advertising awareness. Think of your television viewing. What type of product seems most prone to the "new and improved" angle of advertising? It's probably detergent—dish, clothes, tub, toilet bowl, tile, and carpets alike. How much better can detergent get? Soon those dirt stains will flee from the mere shadow of a new and improved, biodegradable, super-economy, lifetime-size plastic bottle! (That's when I'll volunteer for the cleaning chores!)

The greatest new and improved cleaner ever developed is really quite simple. God was its inventor. Its liquid form—mixed with a powerful formula—cleans the worst stains of sin. Rather than washing a pair of blue jeans, this cleaner works on human beings. God applied this cleaner—water and His Word—to us in our Baptism. It changed spiritual life forever, though we still live in a body that will someday return to the earth from which the first model originated. That's when we can expect the next version of "new and improved."

Paul explains, "Listen, I tell you a mystery: We will not all sleep, but we will all be changed—in a flash, in the twinkling of an eye, at the last trumpet. For the trumpet will sound, the dead will be raised imperishable, and we will be changed" (1 Corinthians 15:51–52).

Some Christians worry and wonder what happens to loved ones blown apart in tragic accidents or what God thinks of cremation. When you think about it, though, would you find the remains of Peter, Paul, or John? God doesn't need remains any more than we need our present bodies after death. He'll find us and shape us into something new and improved. You'll still be you and I'll still be me, but we wouldn't want our old bodies in our new home. (It's bad enough that people laughed at us on earth without giving the angels cause to do the same thing.) Sin will no longer wrinkle our faces, drop our hair, bulge our tummies, or crack our joints. We'll be remade, this time using heaven's specs. But John tells about the best change of all:

> *Dear friends, now we are children of God, and what we will be has not yet been made known. But we know that when He appears, we shall be like Him, for we shall see Him as He is. 1 John 3:2*

"We shall be like Him." That's the last time we'll ever hear "new and improved."

Never Seen Before

Revelation 21:1–4

ONE OF THE MORE difficult adjustments to make when thinking about heaven is to forget about life on earth. As you approach the proverbial pearly gates, will you check your passbook to see if you can handle the down payment on your new home? Will you need to fill out a pile of forms (in triplicate)? Will you be stuck with higher taxes because they have to fill potholes in those streets of gold? Of course, the major problem with questions such as these is that they entirely dodge the point of eternal life in heaven.

In Revelation 21:1–4, John describes heaven in radiantly generic terms. (As far as we know, John was the only one to see what was never seen before or since.) John first emphasizes that God lives with humans. God personally—oops, divinely—makes tears, pain, and death extinct. He moves us from a corrupt, defunct earth to what John calls a new heaven and a new earth. Who can even begin to contemplate the glories and ecstasy of living directly in God's presence?

We won't need the moon because night will disappear; we won't need the sun because God's glory will brighten our lives. We'll be free forever from bad relationships, automobile crashes, pseudoscientific theories, human arrogance, long freight trains, dirty diapers, traffic jams, fattening foods, pornography, flat tires, gangs, fierce storms, ferocious animals, and … Wait a minute. All these are what will be gone. Except to say that we'll live in God's holy presence, we haven't concluded what that experience will be like.

Paul summarized eternal life in heaven by quoting this from Isaiah: "However, as it is written: 'No eye has seen, no ear has heard, no mind has conceived what God has prepared for those who love Him' " (1 Corinthians 2:9).

No, we can't accurately imagine life in heaven. That's not to say that we can't dream about escaping the pitfalls, pain, plundering, and plagues of earthly life. It's not to say that we can't fantasize about mansions, sparkling streets, beautiful gardens, and thunderously whooshing sighs of contentment. Our best approach to envisioning heaven is to realize that we can't even begin to know what's good for us.

Fed Up

John 4:31–34

A MERICA GROWS enough food to provide each citizen three square meals a day. Rounded off, if you'll excuse the expression, the average American is served more than half a ton of food annually, much of which goes to waist. Which brings us to this question: What are you having for dinner?

The Bible is the Book of Life in more than one way. It deals not only with the extraordinary power and love of God, it also highlights the common events such as births, burials, marriages, and meals. In Jesus' time, meals probably were simple but tasty. Like His disciples and us, Jesus needed to eat. After all, that's an element in the nature of humankind.

Pressed by curious, ailing, sin-stricken, and sometimes hungry crowds, Jesus didn't always get to eat "on time." This apparently concerned His disciples because they urged Him to eat. But He said He already had all the food He needed, prompting the disciples to wonder where He stashed His lunch box. Jesus' response? " 'My food,' said Jesus, 'is to do the will of Him who sent Me and to finish His work' " (John 4:34).

Clearly Jesus was fed up, though not in the usual way. Our Savior meant that spiritual nourishment comes not only on the receiving end—through Bible study and participation in worship and the sacraments—but also on the giving end as we do God's will. That's like saying that the farmer gets nourished not only by eating his produce, but also by distributing it to others. That makes sense when you think about it. When the farmer gives, he also gets something in return. We call it making a living.

It's time for us to be fed up also. First, in the usual sense, we're fed up with sin's ruinous effects on life—ours and others. As we ask forgiveness and receive a barn-load of mercy, we become more fed up, this time on the bounty of God's Spirit. Then it's time to be like Jesus—fed full on living as God pleases and serving others mounds of our Father's forgiveness and love.

Now that you're feeling fat and sassy, burn up some of those spiritual calories. If you get hungry before the next scheduled meal, you won't have to distract yourself to deter your craving for a snack. Here's one case where you can snack at will. His!

The Case of the Divine Dice

Jonah 1:1–12

I F YOU EVER WANT to see a living (albeit faulty) definition of strong faith, watch a gambler at his favorite slot machine. Another instrument intended to give you nothing for your money is a pair of dice. If you ever have opportunity to throw them, do a good job—three or four hundred feet should do the trick.

If you've read the entire Bible, you've come across lots of instances when it seems as though God condoned and even blessed gambling. In particular, we find several cases of individuals making decisions by throwing an ancient version of dice called "lots." The disciples cast lots to determine who would replace Judas. Going back to the Old Testament, priests used lots to assign temple duties and to choose which goat would be sacrificed and which would be set free on the Day of Atonement. Then there was this case: "Then the sailors said to each other, 'Come, let us cast lots to find out who is responsible for this calamity.' They cast lots and the lot fell on Jonah" (Jonah 1:7). As in all gambling, there are winners and losers. The question here is "Which one was Jonah?" (Think about that later.)

If it's true that gambling is part of God's won't (the opposite of will), why did God allow and even ply His holy will using what seemed to be devices of random chance? The answer is as slippery as greased dice, but experts think casting lots was common in the cultures of Bible times. God has been known to use the stuff of ordinary life to convey His will, thus it appears that God once revealed His desires through this method. Therefore, casting lots involved neither luck nor statistical probability. Instead, it was God's graphic way to impart His decisions. He manipulated the dice, so to speak. (Check this out in Proverbs 16:33.)

The good news about casting lots is that they've been cast off in this era, except where they're abused in the current gambling craze. Better yet, when it comes to the most important decision of our lives, there won't be any lot casting. Judgment Day will come, and God Himself will discern true faith from unbelief. He will not play games with our eternal lives. In fact, the decision is already made. Jesus decided our future, and He took no chances. He died for our sins and returned to life so we might win. It's a sure thing.

Complaint Department

Psalm 55:1–23

WHEN ALL ELSE FAILS, COMPLAIN. But be careful. If something doesn't work, it might very well be you! Consider my first snow thrower. One winter morning as I was confronted with several inches of fresh snow. I announced this would be the last time I would shorten my life by shoveling the driveway. My wife calmly suggested, "Why don't you buy a snow thrower?"

I trekked to the store and made my purchase. I got the box home and began to complain about the assembly instructions. "Must be a translation from a dead language," I said. My wife, an expert in translating written instructions, threw them out, then mustered the parts into a machine.

I took my lifesaving machine outside, pulled the starter rope and … pulled the starter rope and … drove the machine to the shop. There I complained bitterly, loudly, and (I thought) convincingly about its stubbornness. The clerk smiled. She flipped the starter switch (marked clearly in English, French, Spanish, and German), gave a gentle yank, and it roared to life. I've been a more cautious complainer ever since.

Should I have prayed over the machine before I complained? After all, Psalm 55:22 says, "Cast your cares on the LORD and He will sustain you; He will never let the righteous fall." Prayer might have been wise in this situation—I could have stopped and asked for patience, perseverance, the ability to ask for help sooner, etc. Perhaps these verses are more helpful, though, when we find ourselves grousing about other people.

Human relationships, durable as they may be over time, are often fragile in the short term. When ties become strained, the easiest thing to do is to complain. Maybe it's only a mumble grumble—mercifully out of earshot of the intended target. But carping is carping.

Complaining may provide some measure of immediate relief in a tense situation, but it rarely has lasting, positive effects. That's where Psalm 55:22 comes in. It's not the kind of psalm we use against someone. Instead, our Lord wants us to cast all our complaints on Him because He cares for us. He'll plant His suggestions in our hearts, though it would be good to search His manual—translated clearly from ancient experts that include Moses, David, Matthew, and John. Best of all, this Complaint Department actually comes to you.

They're Here

Acts 2:36–41

NEXT TIME you see a crowd, try this little exercise. Growl loudly to determine how much attention you can attract. No, don't! Someone (or something) may growl back—more loudly and with bared teeth. Try this instead, especially in a sports arena or in the line waiting to use the washroom on a plane. Narrow the crowd down to an estimated 3,000 people. Imagine that each person is headed to hell. Now that's a dreadful thought. Then contemplate what it's like to convert each of those 3,000 people to belief in the Savior, Jesus Christ. Sounds like an impossible mission.

You may think you're just an ordinary Christian—faithful and willing to serve Jesus but limited in your calling and abilities. You're certainly not missionary material. After all, you get homesick going to the mall! But you do have a mission and a mission field.

Listen to what happened when Peter preached to a curious crowd that was hoping to hear some good news—er, Good News. "With many other words he warned them; and he pleaded with them, 'Save yourselves from this corrupt generation.' Those who accepted his message were baptized, and about three thousand were added to their number that day" (Acts 2:40–41).

You and I may not be persuasive Peter, but a multitude of people need to know what we believe. They're just like that throng that Peter confronted—members of a "corrupt generation" who need to know, as Peter worded it, how to save themselves.

No, Peter didn't mean that literally. Sinners can't save themselves. The people in our crowd can't either. We need to preach a powerful sermon, but don't be frightened. We don't actually need eloquence or creativity to deliver an effective message. We need the Spirit's power—the same Spirit that worked the conversion of 3,000 people after Peter's discourse. That Holy Spirit enables us to live as Christians, and He makes us capable of sharing our Good News through what we say and do.

What we say and do is important to our crowd. They suffer from corruption every day. When they see you coping with similar situations, they might be interested in knowing where you get your strength. There's your opening. And if you can't respond with spiritual conversation, talk to God about the lost mass out there. They're here, waiting.

No Small Feet

Isaiah 52:8–10

HIS BARE SOLES made a dull *thud*, then skidded on the smooth stones. Small pebbles squashed into the nerves of His feet, which were already aching under the load of timber slung over His shoulder. Those feet seemed so small as they walked their last steps.

But those stones weren't the worst part of the process. Now there was the spike, driven through flesh and muscle and wood. All this for sins our feet were too inadequate, too wayward, to bear. Could these be the feet of Isaiah 52:7? "How beautiful on the mountains are the feet of those who bring good news, who proclaim peace, who bring good tidings, who proclaim salvation, who say to Zion, 'Your God reigns!' "

Next time you pull off your shoes at the end of a long day, think of Jesus' feet. You'll probably feel worse. That's okay because your conscience is reminding you why you need Jesus. Those sad, tired, painful feet that plodded to the cross were also the feet of the divine Messenger. He not only delivered good news, He was the Good News.

We don't know Jesus' foot size, though some "scholarly" research will undoubtedly announce such a discovery at a future time. (Given the way gym shoes are promoted by the feet of sports heroes, what would the companies do with Jesus' feet?) No matter the size, Jesus' feet were the right size to do the job. And they were indeed beautiful compared to the sinners' feet deformed by spiritual corns, fallen arches, and fungus.

If you're done stretching your feet and feeling guilty, pull off your stocking and massage your soles. By now you may have guessed what's coming next: Think of Jesus massaging your soul, relieving it of guilt and pain, healing both emotional and physical sores that rob you of contentment and comfort. Look closely at your feet. Imagine them as perfect—ready to take you on your walk with Jesus.

You are walking with Jesus. He's talking to you too. His life and wisdom and love are an open book, 66 units long. Joining you is the Holy Spirit to guide your footsteps on this earthly portion of the path to eternal life, with its piercing pebbles and slippery rocks. But you'll stay on your feet with the powerful Spirit supporting you. By His power and blessing, you'll be tap dancing to angelic music someday. And that's no small feat.

Gimme Gimme

Exodus 16:1–36; Numbers 11:6

So what has the Lord done for you lately? Has it been anything substantial since the drama of your birth or the miracle of your faith? Or has it been more or less routine or even ho-hum?

How easily we forget the miracles and blessings of everyday life! How easily we want more and more and MORE! But if you want a really bad example of G & G—greed and grumbling—read this: "The Israelites said to them, 'If only we had died by the Lord's hand in Egypt! There we sat around pots of meat and ate all the food we wanted, but you have brought us out into this desert to starve this entire assembly to death' " (Exodus 16:3).

These were the same Israelites whom God had rescued from slavery in Egypt. Did they remember the whippings and long hours in the hot sun? No. Now they preferred food to freedom. So God delivered food fresh to their tent flap every day for 40 years! Yet hear this: "But now we have lost our appetite; we never see anything but this manna!" (Numbers 11:6).

You would never be like that, would you? So what has God done for you lately? Sometimes daily breath and bread, family and friends, unfettered church doors and uncensored sermons, blood pressure and allergy medication, and a modestly functioning brain become so mundane that we don't count them among our blessings. Once in a while we hunger for a spiritual extravaganza of sorts. We can be pitifully like the Israelites.

God was the God of Israel. He cared for them like no one else. God is the God of all people. He cares for them like no one else. When we're hard pressed to remember what God has done for us lately, we can check the pulse of faith. Do you believe you're a sinner, doomed to eternal failure and punishment? Do you still believe that Jesus saved you? Do you believe that God forgives you for the sake of Jesus Christ?

In a world characterized by a gimme-gimme attitude, it's nice to know you can hunger for something without offending our God of many blessings. Ask Him for more and more and MORE faith. Be a glutton for forgiveness. Feel your soul stretch to capacity with the Holy Spirit's power. Go ahead. Put down this book and ask for it now.

Would You Buy This?

Hebrews 11:1–7

MARKETING IS THE ART and science of making a product attractive and available to consumers. Consider the market research and strategy that went into the Edsel. (For you post-Edselonians, the Edsel was a highly touted car introduced by Ford in the late 1950s. It disappeared soon after.) Every year, hopeful manufacturers introduce their own variety of Edsel to the public in the hopes of demand that far exceeds supply. Not coincidentally this will mean profits. It's probably feasible for effective marketing to create demand for boats in Death Valley!

This leads us to the subject of marketing faith in Jesus. The best marketing consultants would consider this to be the supreme challenge. Well, perhaps not. They're often in the business of selling unbelievable claims. But would you want something that had a reliable history, though some critics question the validity of its claims? Would you desire something that had incredible, indescribable potential that couldn't be accurately measured? Would you really trust its value and integrity if you could have it for free? Would your neighbors think any less if you parked a pink Edsel in front of your house?

Marketing faith in Jesus probably doesn't seem too complex to believers. Our faith is rooted in God's Word. We believe what He says, not because of clever marketing strategies but because the Holy Spirit provided faith to believe these inconceivable assertions. Furthermore, we take comfort in knowing we're not the only ones involved in this faith thing. "By faith Noah, when warned about things not yet seen, in holy fear built an ark to save his family. By his faith he condemned the world and became heir of the righteousness that comes by faith" (Hebrews 11:7).

Does this suggest that we should look for a good used Edsel or shop for a ski boat in the Sahara? Faith in Jesus is more than buying something worthless on earth. It's rejoicing in the gift of forgiveness and salvation, trusting that God makes good on His astonishing promises. It's trusting that the best things in life are indeed free.

Going Out for Business

Matthew 27:45–50

R EMEMBER THE "Going Out of Business Sale" signs that popped up regularly in store windows? They became so prevalent that consumers didn't trust them. Then by the time they verified the shopkeeper's honesty, it was too late.

I wonder if merchants ever advertised a "Staying in Business Sale"? In a way, that was the message of a cleverly worded ad that appeared weekly in the newspaper. Being an astute and ethical business student in college, I yearned to uncover deceptive advertising. I had one particular appliance store in my sight when I discovered that my sight had failed me. "Going Out for Business" looks a lot like "Going Out of Business" to eyes accustomed to the more familiar message. What a deft twist on a stock slogan!

That catchphrase might remind us of Matthew 27:50: "And when Jesus had cried out again in a loud voice, He gave up His spirit." The handwritten sign tacked to the cross might well have said, "Son of God. Going out for business." Prior to this time, everyone crucified went out of business for good. Could the public expect anything different?

Maybe some in modern society have the same disillusioned perception of Christians. Religion doesn't seem as popular today as it once was. True religion, that is. Christians are often denounced for outdated morality and chided because they frequently fail to practice what they preach. It's true that sometimes you can't tell believers from unbelievers by the way they act.

Jesus is going out for business among us, and our weakness only confirms His strength. Christ is in the business of forgiveness, and He'll always have a steady clientele. You and I alone could keep Him working overtime. Remarkably, He's never too busy. He never has so much business that He becomes out of touch with us, though He has His Spirit on the road to rustle up more business.

How comforting to know that Jesus makes our business His business. Because He releases us from sin's devastating grasp, we can ask Him to make us more like Him in the way we think and live. We trust that He will continue to call on us despite our regular disloyalty to Him. Pray that He never simply minds His own business. We know that in the end, we won't do business with anyone else.

Build One Today

Joshua 4:1–24

WHERE ELSE BUT IN CHICAGO could you find a statue of Lincoln in Grant Park and Grant in Lincoln Park? Sounds like someone mixed up their monuments. But this incidental bit of urban trivia brings us to the subject of memorials.

What is your favorite national shrine? Is it the Washington Monument in D.C. or Lincoln's Tomb in Springfield, Ill.? Is it the wall that lists the names of those who died in Vietnam? Is it the Wahabahoochit Monument, which is dedicated to the city council that shortened the name of Wahabahoochit, Maine, to Ooch? Mine is one dedicated to the memory of memory. It's a hollow skull inscribed with the words ... Actually, I can't remember the inscription.

People erect monuments in memory of significant events. Take Joshua 4:20–22 for example: "Joshua set up at Gilgal the twelve stones they had taken out of the Jordan. He said to the Israelites, 'In the future when your descendants ask their fathers "What do these stones mean?" tell them, "Israel crossed the Jordan on dry ground." ' "

It's likely you have a memorial monument adorning a wall in your home or wrapped snugly around your finger or perhaps hanging from your ear or neck. Christians favor the cross as a fitting memorial to the slain and risen Christ. No event in history parallels this incident in immensity and consequence. Of course, the cross isn't a welcome tribute in all places. So what can you do?

Build your own monument. Build it anyplace—on your desk, in your backyard, cradled in the cup holder in your car, on the kitchen counter, at the corner of your workbench ... You get the idea. Use anything—a pile of paper clips, pebbles, parking receipts, mugs, or bolts will do just fine. Every time you see them, let them do for you what Joshua's stones did at Gilgal. If anyone questions your little pile of memory makers, tell them it's a memorial to memory—the memory of what Jesus did for you on the cross. If someone reduces your little monument to memory, remember the monumental pile of sins that only one Person could (and did!) destroy.

One other thing. If someday you forget all the memorials you've ever seen, be sure to remember the answer to "Who's buried in Jesus' tomb?"

You Don't Know What You're Doing

Matthew 6:1–5

SOMETIMES IT'S MERCIFUL that you don't know what you're doing. Suppose you're in a restaurant and this gorgeous food server of the opposite sex asks, "Wanna neck?" Quickly agreeing, you get handed a piece of chicken.

Other times, not knowing what you're doing provides entertainment for others. For example (and I'm speaking from experience), you might attempt to dock a pontoon boat in gusty winds and rolling waves as the conservation agent, who is waiting to check your catch of the day, watches from the pier.

At still other times, not knowing what you're doing is efficient. For example, if you had to know why you shouldn't step on the gas pedal before starting the car, it would increase your travel time or result in expensive research.

As you can see, it's not all bad when you don't know what you're doing. Jesus thought so too. He said, "But when you give to the needy, do not let your left hand know what your right hand is doing" (Matthew 6:3).

Jesus implied that the true motive for service and charity comes from deep within the Christian heart. So deep, in fact, that the stimulus for charitable work stems from the power of the Holy Spirit by the grace of God and for the sake of Jesus Christ.

Jesus knew the pitfalls of generous stewardship and service. That's why He warned us. Good deeds get noticed. Sometimes they earn public recognition with a plaque or a seat on a governing board. That's not wrong; we should thank and honor those who respond to the Spirit's inspiration. The problem is that praise too easily seeps from the heart to the head. When that happens, we're tempted to forget how good God has been and focus instead on how good we are. It happens in the smallest of ways, perhaps even as the offering plate is passed in church.

Our Savior didn't die and rise simply to get the praise He so rightly deserves. He saved us because He loves us. Oh, it made headlines all right, but it never went to His head. Although He did so much for us, we often respond with disobedience, even rebellion. Yet because He loves us, He doesn't let His left hand know what His right hand is doing. His love is truly blind. Because it is, we too can serve others in blissful ignorance.

Heavy Wait

2 Peter 3:1–9

THE LADY ON THE PHONE cheerily promised that the repairperson would arrive at 8:30 A.M. to fix the air conditioner. Now it's 9:30 A.M., and no repairperson. You can think of three reasons why the individual is late:

1. *He can't locate your home.*
2. *His truck overheated and he's stranded in an air-conditioned service shop.*
3. *The dispatcher never told him about you.*

You call the company, and you're again cheerily informed that there was an emergency. "My air-conditioning is broken, the comfort index is 113, and he has an emergency?"

"Yes," the voice says. "His wife forgot to include his iced tea, and he had to have his tea. Will 2 P.M. be okay?"

Waiting is a common problem recorded throughout history. Sarah couldn't wait to have a child. David couldn't postpone his lust. God's chosen people were impatient for the Messiah. We're waiting for Jesus to come again. And it's been a long wait.

Here's what the Bible says about waiting. "But do not forget this one thing, dear friends: With the Lord a day is like a thousand years, and a thousand years are like a day. The Lord is not slow in keeping His promise as some understand slowness. He is patient with you, not wanting anyone to perish, but everyone to come to repentance" (2 Peter 3:8–9).

If ever there was a good excuse for delays, this is it. Other believers waited, perhaps impatiently, for Jesus to return. But our Savior's delay resulted in your salvation. More than half of the world's population still does not believe in Jesus, and He patiently allows time for them to come to faith too. That's not to say He'll wait forever. Forever is reserved for after judgment. All this suggests that we need to keep busy while we wait.

Pray that unbelievers will respond to the Holy Spirit's call to faith—before it's too late. Share your faith through whatever ability or resources you have so others may know Christ through you. And don't tire of waiting or lose confidence in His promises. The Dispatcher does indeed have your name written in His book. He will be here soon.

Flashback

Ephesians 2:1–5

Flashback is a literary technique frequently used by people just released from the hospital. In the comfort of their own living room, they can share the exact moment when that strange pain ambushed them. They vividly recall the ride to the hospital when every pothole—yes, every crack—jolted them with pain. Then there was the emergency room and that doctor that looked as if he had just graduated from high school. And that snippy nurse! Finally, the blood samples, x-rays, MRIs, and poking. Why, it took an extra week just to recover from all the tests!

It's often more enjoyable to look back on certain events than it is to experience them. As we look back, we recount abnormal life situations without the real-time pain, fear, and uncertainty. We might even embellish the event a bit—for dramatic effect.

One flashback that doesn't need elaboration is our condition prior to salvation. Ephesians 2:1 says, "As for you, you were dead in your transgressions and sins."

Let's use flashback right now. From the safety of wherever you are, relive that time of horror, anxiety, or helplessness when you faced the most life-threatening experience humans ever face. You were actually soul dead—another victim of epidemic sin. You might have provided just the culture where sin grows most rampant. Or maybe you were a tiny baby unable to recall your inherited sin. In either case, the cure was the same—lifesaving faith in Jesus Christ.

Like many serious diseases, sin is curable, but it recurs to chronically inflict life with pain and anxiety. That's why we remain on medication once the initial healing is accomplished. That medication is daily repentance and forgiveness. It comes in capsule form—small but potent doses of God's Word in Bible readings, meditation on God's Word, prayers, and hymns. Group therapy helps too. It's good to join other Christians who are recovering from sin as they meet weekly to flashback on their former condition, learn how to live in a sin-infected world, and praise their divine Physician. We also participate in another form of therapy as we meet frequently for a Holy Meal with soul-healing results.

Next time someone wants your attention as they flashback on their heart surgery, be patient. Maybe they'll give you opportunity to share your brush with death.

Fill in the Blank

John 10:17–21

DESCRIBE CHRISTIANS by filling in the blank: Christians are D_____. Being a Christian, you probably answered something complimentary such as "saved" or "forgiven." But think for a moment how someone not fond of Christians might fill in the blank. Some might say, "Christians are bizarre." Of course we might excuse them because so many churches advertise themselves that way during the Christmas season.

Antagonistic unbelievers of Jesus' time filled in the blank this way: "Many of them said, 'He is demon-possessed and raving mad. Why listen to Him?' " (John 10:20). Along those same lines, I prefer to fill the blank with this: Christians are loony. Now before you write a nasty note to the publisher or to me, let me explain. Loons provide an excellent comparison with Christians. (I hope.)

If you've never seen a loon up close, go to Mercer, Wisc. You still might not see one in the flesh, but the residents erected a huge statue of a loon at the south entrance to the town. Real loons aren't nearly as large as the statue, but they're generally bigger than ducks. They're beautifully colored in black and white. They have long bills and curiously webbed feet that don't allow them to walk on dry land. Up to this point you're probably wondering if there is any—point, that is.

Christians are like loons for two reasons—their song and their unrecognized strength. Loons warble plaintive cries that make them sound hauntingly sad and vulnerable. Yet loons are strong underwater swimmers, able to remain submerged as they torpedo beneath the surface in pursuit of prey. Because I have never seen a skinny loon, they are, apparently, quite successful.

Christians might sound like whiners, or at least doleful and powerless, to some observers. However, this is not so. Our song, if I may include you among the loony ones, calls Christ into our lives. Yes, it's a cry that sounds feeble to those who don't know us well, but it's our normal song sung in confidence that the Savior always responds. Beneath our outer beauty (Christians are beautiful!) lies fortitude and stamina provided by the Holy Spirit.

Don't let it bother you if someone thinks you're loony. Just sing your tune.

The Case of Long Lives

Genesis 5:1–32

A LTOGETHER, METHUSELAH LIVED 969 years, and then he died" (Genesis 5:27). Methuselah lived so long ago, rumor has it that he had only three digits on his social security card. Not only did he live long ago, but he lived for a long period. (It's ironic that he almost lived long enough to die in the flood. So much for the blessings of old age!) Many others lived to astonishing ages, as Genesis 5 attests. And mandatory retirement was unheard of, as Noah would be happy to tell you.

Now for the question first phrased by an ancient, unknown 3-year-old. "Why?" Why did people live so long in those early Bible days? What accounts for such exceptional longevity?

Wherever questions arise, so do answers—even if they're only theoretical. Some who have studied this phenomenon believe that the world's environment was more hospitable—in effect, these individuals lived during the truly good old days. Scholars surmise that the climate included mild temperatures with complementary levels of humidity. Because the climate was so agreeable, serious illness was rare, food was plentiful and nourishing, and air was pure. Besides, these were the pre-life insurance days, so adults had to live longer to adequately care for their families.

Yes, the last statement was absurd. And we also must admit that speculation about why people lived so long is a bit silly. In fact, it's downright distracting. While the list of ages in Genesis 5 provides information God thought useful, we should be careful to prevent our curiosity from consuming our faith or directing our attention away from the main theme of the Bible.

God's Word is the history of salvation. We also may think of it as the future of salvation. God proclaims His love for sinners and reveals what He did to establish a wonderful relationship with us. He reports in detail why He sent Jesus, what Jesus did, and how we benefit from Jesus' life, death, and resurrection. God promises that while our years on earth are unlikely to be as many as Methuselah's, we will live forever, which should be long enough to satisfy anyone. When it comes to forever, what difference does it make how many years we spend on earth?

The Other Side of the Gate

John 10:7–9

GATES ARE USUALLY ERECTED FOR A REASON—either to keep something in or to keep something out or both. Normally they serve as a portal for limited access to an otherwise secure area. In the case of our family dog, the secure area just happens to be the rest of the world. When the dog exits its pen, look out! First, she'll sit on you, effectively trapping you under her considerable weight; then she'll either lick or bark you into submission, depending on her mood.

Think of all the gates you see. Better yet, think of your own gate—if you have one. How do you feel when your gate is closed? Do you feel the same when gates belonging to others are shut? How do you feel when you discover your gate is open? Again, would you feel the same seeing an open gate elsewhere? Depending on your point of view, gates can mean either threat or welcome, entrapment or escape, anxiety or security.

Jesus compared Himself to a gate. He said, "I am the gate; whoever enters through Me will be saved. He will come in and go out, and find pasture" (John 10:9). Jesus is the gate that separates eternal life from endless doom. No one has ever entered or refused to enter any gate nearly as important.

For believers like us, every gate can make us feel good, secure, and able to escape the devil's power. Our world is filled with sin and hostility. It's a dangerous place. But the gate to safety and salvation is open, inviting us to escape to Jesus' protection and care. It's a whole different world on the other side of the gate.

John saw a gate in his glimpse of heaven, which is recorded in Revelation. This gate sparkled with jewels, a prelude to the heavenly city in which we'll someday reside. The gate is open to us and all believers. In fact, it's open to everyone right now. Someday, though, that gate will close forever. If statistics are right, only about 30 percent of civilization will be on the good side of the gate. Pray that others hear and believe the Gospel. Hold the gate open and welcome those who want to enter. And when Satan saunters by, probing your defenses, be sure to show him the gate.

Fearless Fear

1 Samuel 12:20–24

Hollywood heroes don't know the meaning of the word *fear*. They probably don't know the meaning of too many other words either. Then there are those more common people who fearfully flee something that isn't pursuing them, just like Davy Crockett. Yes, Davy used to loiter outside my bedroom window, twirling his coonskin cap in a way that would have struck Santa Anna with terror. It certainly drove me to the sanctuary of my parents' bed. Forget the Alamo. The United States would have won had Crockett done his deeds outside the windows of that fearsome force from Mexico!

The Bible includes a unique mixture of phrases that seem to emphasize a paradox of fear. Take this verse for example: "Be sure to fear the LORD and serve Him faithfully with all your heart; consider what great things He has done for you" (1 Samuel 12:24).

Fear has absorbed modern meanings that may cloud the biblical concept of fear, especially as it relates to God. Some may ask, "Why would anyone fear someone who did great things for them?" You probably know the right answer already, so the next paragraph is blank. Write in your response. (Fear not. No one except you will read it.)

Good work. Let me share another answer. Fear of God is like fear of a cement truck. These trucks are large and heavy. Even a minor altercation with one probably would have major consequences, including hefty hospital bills and prolonged traction. Because we are aware of what a cement truck can do if we fail to respect it, we focus on its positive aspects. For example, it can lay a foundation for a house.

We need not fear God as long as we fear Him. We're in trouble only if we refuse to acknowledge Him as the supreme power in all the universe. When we recognize God's power to slay or to save, we appreciate what He has done for us through Jesus Christ even more. And God did it all for sinners like us, who, from time to time, don't fear Him or grow complacent about Him. But God loves us, and He did the greatest thing anyone could ever do. He saved us from our sins and continues to forgive us every day.

Maybe we're the ones who don't know the meaning of the word *fear*.

Sromur

Jeremiah 51:33–48

THEY USUALLY GET THINGS BACKWARD. That's why I reversed the spelling of today's subject. It seems that if you want someone to believe you, tell them it's a rumor—it's more convincing than telling the truth. Too bad baseless rumors round so many bases. They apparently caused God's Old Testament people some problems too. Jeremiah says, "Do not lose heart or be afraid when rumors are heard in the land; one rumor comes this year, another the next, rumors of violence in the land and of ruler against ruler" (Jeremiah 51:46).

Have you noticed that rumors rarely spread good news? "Rumor has it that the company will downsize next month." "I heard that Nora and Ted are separating." "The produce department is displaying salad posters. It must be their way of saying salads will cost more lettuce." "John said that Frank heard from Jared who was talking to Al that the price of Bumble & Tumble stock will plummet."

In those hours after the first Easter dawned, rumor had it that someone had stolen the body of a freshly executed criminal. It's a rumor that some preferred to believe and perhaps still do. Even Jesus' disciples thought it was a rumor when the women returned from the cemetery and reported a mysterious encounter with an empty tomb and a glorified Friend. But there's nothing like a few facts to ransack a hot rumor!

Jesus rose from the dead just as He had promised. He crippled the devil's stranglehold on our souls as predicted by the prophets. He provided tangible proof to all doubters by a show of His hands and feet.

Perhaps we would prefer rumors to truth's pain, but the fact is that we're devout sinners. Yet our faith convinces and assures us that Jesus took away our sins and continues to forgive us despite our obstinate attitude. All these truths appear in the one book we can trust without exception—the Bible. No need for rumors of a Messiah or hearsay of salvation or gossip about some vague Gospel. We have the truth. We have it in clear language. We have God's Word on it.

Rumors are ordinary annoyances of life, stimulating speculation or anxiety as we wait for their failure or their confirmation. Good thing God left nothing to idle speculation regarding our salvation. We *know* for *sure* that everything *God* told us about *Jesus* as the *Holy Spirit* spoke through *Holy men of God* is *true*. That should end any rumors to the contrary.

Owner's Manual

Ecclesiastes 7:19–22

IT OFTEN SITS ABANDONED in what we used to call the glove compartment. They probably don't call it that anymore and for good reason. How many drivers actually keep gloves in there? But back to the subject—the owner's manual for a car. If cars have an owner's manuals, perhaps faith can have one too. So we begin an "owner's manual" series that compares various working (or otherwise) parts of a car to the workings of faith in the life of a Christian.

The first topic is the air bag. Cars always have had air bags, but they usually sat in the backseat and shouted commands to the driver to avoid accidents, wrong turns, and an otherwise relaxed travel experience. Incidentally, old-fashioned air bags, for all their effort, did not reduce the number of accidents. At least modern air bags save people from the deadly consequences of their mistakes.

Backseat drivers would love this passage: "There is not a righteous man on earth who does what is right and never sins" (Ecclesiastes 7:20). The Law orders us around, and because it's always right, it also condemns us when we don't comply. Perhaps that's the worst part. The "I told you so" factor grates at us, yet anyone who has ignored the righteous contentions of a backseat driver has experienced that irresistible human urge to be contrary.

Good thing the Gospel is like the modern air bag. It saves us when we crash. And crashing is inevitable. We run head-on into sin and its folly. We race through stop signals erected by the Bible, though sometimes the impact comes from ignorance or at the initiation of a traveling companion. Our clash with sin would claim our lives except that the Gospel cushions the blow and allows us to walk away scared and scarred but still breathing.

There really is no planned way to use an air bag. It activates only when it's needed—only in dire circumstances. The Gospel, however, helps us not only in dangerous situations, but also during routine living. It's comforting to know that Jesus loves us, and the Gospel encourages us to respond to Jesus' love through obedience. When we fail, it explodes into action, bringing forgiveness and restoration.

Next time you sit behind an air bag—or in front of one—say a silent prayer of thanks to God for your spiritual air bag.

Air-Conditioning

Ruth 2:1–16

THE FIRST AUTOMOBILES were completely air-conditioned. Originally, air-conditioning involved rotating levers on the door until sufficient comfort levels were reached. In the 1950s, the only cars with air-conditioning were luxury models. Today, it's hard to buy a car without it. In fact, larger cars and vans have individually controlled air conditioners so every passenger can maintain a personal comfort level. Some cars even have a thermostat that delivers constant temperatures summer and winter. But these innovations will never please those who feel an uncomfortable draft no matter where they sit.

One by-product of faith is a lot like air-conditioning. It provides comfort no matter what the environment inflicts on us. Ruth of the Old Testament knew that comfort. " 'May I continue to find favor in your eyes, my lord,' she said. 'You have given me comfort and have spoken kindly to your servant—though I do not have the standing of one of your servant girls' " (Ruth 2:13).

Ruth was an uncomfortable young lady in a land that was inhospitable to women. As the reading implies, she knew it only too well. She felt less worthy than the least of the servants. That's exactly how it is with us sinners. Good thing we can cool ourselves despite the scorching heat of sin and warm ourselves against the frigid enmity of the devil. That's what the Gospel does. It bestows comfort in the face of sin's antagonizing discomfort.

Look forward to the next time temperature makes you uncomfortable. Let it remind you of sin's attempt to wreck your comfort. Then imagine the comfort of a cucumber cool or toasty warm car and bask in the luxury of controlled comfort. Let your comfort remind you that Jesus took the heat for your sins and warmed the deathly cold of the grave. His love for you is always there, as routine as air conditioners and heaters in cars but still a luxury you could never afford on your own.

Salvation's comfort is the standard equipment of faith. And don't worry about a draft. God knows just the comfort level you need.

Keeping It Clean

Ezekiel 36:24–27

EVERY CAR OWNER'S MANUAL includes instructions on how to keep the vehicle clean and looking new. This process, too, has evolved. It used to be that owner's manual refused to waste pages on the obvious, but new car finishes are finicky and easily defaced by improper cleaning methods. In the "good old days," it was a family event to take your car to the car wash. The experience was punctuated by "oohs" and "aahs" as chains dragged the car through whirling sponges and chamois, often extracting radio antennas and license plates in the process. Today, "no touch" commercial enterprises clean your car for only a little less than the monthly payment! (But they're still not responsible for the antenna.)

Ezekiel had the right idea about keeping clean, though he was more concerned with the spirit than with the bumpers. We find these words in Ezekiel 36:25: "I will sprinkle clean water on you, and you will be clean; I will cleanse you from all your impurities and from all your idols." Put another way, Ezekiel assured believers that God's cleaning method is guaranteed to remove the bugs, tar, and grime of sin.

If you've ever attempted to remove a summer-evening-drive-in-the-country's accumulation of deceased bugs from your windshield, you can understand how relentlessly sin clings to us. Scrape as you might, you're always left with some reminder of an insect's anatomy. It takes a powerful application of water and soap to wash away the smears and blotches.

God's water is simple water, but it carries the force of God's Word. It makes us squeaky clean and looking like new. Once that water is applied in Baptism, all future washes at the well of forgiveness are certified to keep us looking as pristine as the day God first washed us.

Martin Luther taught that we must daily wash away our sins by the power of the Spirit because, like a freshly washed car, we soon become soiled. We keep clean by recognizing our dirty sinfulness, asking forgiveness, joyfully accepting it, and allowing the Spirit to polish us with power to resist further blemishes. Most of us have quite a coat of wax! But thanks to our patient heavenly Father, who faithfully cleans us every day and keeps us fit to remain His pride and joy. If only cars had such doting owners!

Cruise Control

Joshua 24:1–15

A N ELDERLY FRIEND never capitulated to the temptation of cruise control in his new cars. He feared an uncontrollable spin off Route 66 right into space, ending in a crumpled heap somewhere on an isolated corner of Pluto. Too bad he missed the perverse pleasure of explaining to a state trooper that something must be wrong with the cruise control!

As any owner's manual will explain, cruise control doesn't work unless the engine is running. Faith suggests the same thing. We can't cruise along with Jesus unless faith is alive. Joshua might have understood the workings of cruise control because this faithful man, powered by the Spirit, set his life on automatic. In his words: "But if serving the LORD seems undesirable to you, then choose for yourselves this day whom you will serve, whether the gods your forefathers served beyond the River, or the gods of the Amorites, in whose land you are living. But as for me and my household, we will serve the LORD" (Joshua 24:15).

Joshua cruised along, serving God, and he had no intention of breaking the Law. We can learn from his inspiring example. Our God-given faith enables us to choose our course and purr along toward our destination of eternal life and happiness. We need not race off after sinful diversions or creep along wondering if we'll really meet Jesus in person. Faith allows us to cruise with Jesus at a constant pace, trusting Him to keep us moving toward our destination at just the right speed.

Like cruise control, faith sometimes requires us to slow down when obstacles get in our way. Satan would love to keep us stuck behind him, like a sports car trapped behind a slow-moving truck on a two-lane highway. He tempts us to race into the other lane and into a head-on crash with oblivion. But Jesus knows that the tempo of faith needs constant attention and adjustment. Sometimes we need to slow down and sometimes we need to speed up to remain on the road to heaven.

When Joshua reached his journey's end, he probably looked back fondly at the trip. He forgot the hardships that faith's walk sometimes involved and remembered with gratitude how God made his service enjoyable—how the Spirit kept him moving with no effort on his part. That's how faith and trust work. They keep us going by God's power when we would otherwise tire easily and perhaps stop altogether. So stay on the road, set the cruise control, and enjoy the trip. You'll arrive safely and right on time.

182

Clear View

1 Peter 1:2–6

Y OUR FAITH, whether new or old, comes equipped with front and rear defrosters. Your car has the same features, and you know how driving is more efficient when you can see where you're going. And those rear defrosters enable you to shudder when some maniac tailgates you. As for the side windows, especially those bordering the backseat, defrosting remains a challenge, but that's okay. We wouldn't want to deprive any generation of children from etching artwork on the frost or fog!

Faith permits 360-degree vision. We see where we're going (though we're limited in how far ahead we see), we know where we are now, and we also look back to where we've been. All this is for good reason, as we read in 1 Peter 1:5: "Who through faith are shielded by God's power until the coming of the salvation that is ready to be revealed in the last time."

Where are we going? That's a fundamental Christian question, and we're well-versed in the answer. Of course, it always helps to maintain clear vision, so let's review what we've seen.

When we look behind us, the view is breathtaking. We see where faith has taken us and how well it has preserved us, not only on smooth highways and in good weather but also down rocky roads and through treacherous storms. Our progress through a faith-filled life gives us confidence to proceed.

Then there's the side view. Faith keeps us aware of what's happening around us. Sometimes the view is good; sometimes it's frightening. Sometimes we relax and enjoy the pleasures of faith; other times we strain our vigilance to avoid sin that seeks to sideswipe us, cut us off, or run us off the road. Faith alerts as well as comforts us.

Finally, there's the view forward. We're confident of our final destination, but we're far from seeing all that lies ahead. Faith doesn't assure us of perpetually good times, but it does suggest that our faith gets stronger when we pass through ordeals and distress. The secret is looking beyond temporary hardship to the God who will provide eternal pleasure in the company of our Savior.

Oh, yes—one more tip for clear forward vision: Wear your Songlasses.

News Flash

John 18:28–32

THE WHOLE NEIGHBORHOOD knew when I tracked mud across the kitchen floor. We heard the same kind of news flashes when any of my friends brought home a stray dog, forgot to flush the toilet, left the refrigerator door open, or brought home a bad report card. But here's a news flash that tattles on footprints so old they're fossilized: Anthropologists (in my neighborhood we called them *mothers*) spotted the remains of a barefoot stroll through wet sand after a rainstorm. They claim the prints belonged to a woman who could have been an early human.

As much as muddy feet have been castigated throughout history, Jesus urged believers to associate with others regardless of their cleanliness. This was quite revolutionary. The Jews regarded people as unclean for a variety of reasons—more than even most mothers would boast. Sinners—those who weren't genetic or devout Jews—were especially filthy. We catch a glimpse of this thought in today's Bible reading: "Then the Jews led Jesus from Caiaphas to the palace of the Roman governor. By now it was early morning, and to avoid ceremonial uncleanness the Jews did not enter the palace; they wanted to be able to eat the Passover" (John 18:28). The governor's palace was no place for a devout Jew, especially on the eve of a holy day.

Jesus wanted His message broadcast to sinners. That's why He visited them in their kitchens and wandered among the most seriously defiled. That's one reason the church leaders of His time refused to believe that He was the long-awaited Messiah. The long list of rules that served as criteria for acceptance didn't include such irrational behavior.

It's a good thing Jesus broke the rules. He accomplished His purpose on the cross—the dirtiest of all places! He came to us, sinners though we were, and gave us faith. He still comes to us—sinners though we are—and reminds us that we're forgiven but in need of renewal.

Jesus wants the faithful to get their feet muddy and leave their tracks among the sinners who need the Gospel so desperately. We are not to shun the world of unbelievers. Rather we are to walk through it. We don't have to worry about soiling ourselves or that which we treasure. Jesus still washes His disciples today!

The Surgeon General Has Determined ...

Acts 20:7–12

SOME PEOPLE PROTECT themselves by listening only to sermons on the radio or TV. They figure it's safer than waking suddenly to the rap of an offering basket against their chest. It's also more comfortable because they don't need to worry about someone recognizing them as the subject of the sermon. Others are deluded into thinking it is healthy to wake revitalized and invigorated after a good sermon. But be advised that the surgeon general has determined that sleeping during sermons may harm your health. Research from Acts 20:9 confirms this theory:

> *Seated in a window was a young man named Eutychus, who was sinking into a deep sleep as Paul talked on and on. When he was sound asleep, he fell to the ground from the third story and was picked up dead.*

It's easier to diagnose the Eutychus Syndrome in others than it is to detect it in yourself. (A sore neck after church is one symptom. An icy handshake from the preacher is another.) There was a time, however, when all of us were much like Eutychus—only worse. We once were dead in our sins.

Before the Holy Spirit granted us faith, we gradually were falling into a deep and fatal sleep. Oh, an examination would report that our eyes were open, our hearts pumping, and our lungs rhythmically inflating, but we were slipping away as insidiously as when we close our eyes in boredom. Sin is a real killer. (Too bad the surgeon general doesn't warn people about that!) Like falling 30 feet to the ground, sin dealt us death.

Eutychus' story had a happy ending as Paul, by God's power, revived him. Our story ends mercifully as well. Jesus, by His power as God, resuscitated us to continue living and serving Him and others. He breathed life-giving and sustaining faith into our cold, stiff souls. He applied heavy doses of forgiveness so sin's cancer would disappear and we could live to share our faith with others.

If you find yourself snoozing next time you hear a sermon, you'll probably be unable to resist. But when the sermon-ending "Amen" sounds, stretch your arms, give a mighty yawn, and hope the pastor didn't throw an "Amen" into the middle of the sermon. Better yet, thank God that He woke you in time. Not in time to go home, but in time to wake you from sin's lethal slumber. Next time, take a nap before church.

The More the Merrier?

Romans 5:15–21

ONE OF THE MORE successful commercial ventures is the so-called outlet store mall. It's so called because it usually is a super-effective outlet for bulging wallets and it tends to maul credit card limits. The best outlet malls are located at interstate highway interchanges and advertised by billboards and traffic backups for several miles in any direction.

Today's Bible reading sounds much like an advertisement for a sin mall. (Again, *maul* is the preferred word!) Listen: "The law was added so that the trespass might increase. But where sin increased, grace increased all the more" (Romans 5:20). Before you spend all your faith on a sin spree, consider the risk of potential deception here.

The self-indulgent side of us wants to view this passage as an invitation to "shop till you drop" at Satan's Outlet Extravaganza. After all, we may reason, the more we sin, the more grace we get. Sort of a win-win situation. Of course, that's a misapplication of the passage. The bright side of this passage warms the soul of sinners who realize that God doesn't observe a credit limit for sinners. He neither condones sin nor does He hold it against those who claim Jesus as Savior.

Sin ruins our lives. It makes us unhappy, sick, despondent, and sometimes even dangerous. Certainly, God never wanted us to be this way; therefore, He hates sin and refuses to tolerate it. On the other hand, God loves sinners. Despite our past, God accepts us as His children for the sake of His Son, who died to eliminate our debt. The more sinful the sinners, the more thankful they are because they owe their lives to the Lord many times over.

The devil's main competitor has an outlet store too. Grace comes in many sizes, but there isn't much variety. The only kind we can trust is God's. It's durable and comes with a lifetime guarantee. Best of all, it's free.

Think about the kind of sinner you are. If this takes a long time, don't worry. On the other hand, if you don't think you have many sins, perhaps you should examine yourself more closely. Our tendency to compare sins committed and forgiveness accepted may dull us to the magnitude of gratitude we owe our Savior. If we thanked God for forgiving each sin committed, we'd be too busy to concern ourselves with much else. Including outlet stores.

Wipe Out

Acts 19:1–12

L IKE EVERYTHING ELSE, it doesn't cure the common cold. It does offer a relatively cheap and effective treatment. It comes in two varieties: disposable or reusable. It fits nicely in a pocket or purse. Experts of illusion may borrow it from unsuspecting volunteers to demonstrate sleight of hand. I once loaned my handkerchief to such a person. His trick didn't work, which he blamed on contaminants. I think he succeeded in something, though. The next time I sneezed, I snuffed rabbit fur up my nose!

It didn't involve prestidigitation, but handkerchiefs played a role in the New Testament. Luke reports, "God did extraordinary miracles through Paul, so that even handkerchiefs and aprons that had touched him were taken to the sick, and their illnesses were cured and the evil spirits left them" (Acts 19:11–12).

God used ordinary handkerchiefs to wipe out sickness, both physical and spiritual. Of course, the handkerchiefs were only object lessons employed to demonstrate God's power and love. He could have used anything. He could have used nothing. Instead, He gave us something wonderful to talk about and appreciate.

God's reasons for performing miracles through Paul were twofold. First, God demonstrated His love for people by treating that which bothered them most at the time. You know what it's like—being so sick that you think of little else except how miserable you feel. God showed He loved the whole person and didn't isolate the soul or deliver a litany of "everything will be all right someday." He knew how to get people's attention. That being accomplished, people's minds and hearts were open to the second and more important purpose. God wanted sinners who are sick with sin to come to faith, repent, and be saved. He wants us to remember what He's done so we stay as close to Him as He is to us.

Let your box of tissues or your handkerchief serve as an object lesson of God's presence in your life too. Know that He continues to heal today even those who don't recognize the "medicine" of the Great Physician. God continues to build bodies with inexplicably complicated and effective immune systems. And remember how God sent Jesus to mend your broken soul and wipe out sin's death grip. You might want to use that handkerchief to blot the sweat of relief from your brow or dab the tears of joy from your cheeks.

187

Look at the Numbers

Isaiah 53:1–12

THE WORLD RELIES ON NUMBERS. Companies are downsized or expanded based on numbers. Research often results in statistics that are completely contradictory to other statistics that prove the opposite. Statistics can support just about any position. In reality, we probably can agree on one thing—statistics support statisticians!

The Bible uses numbers to make a point too. Most of the time, the numbers are symbolic or figurative. We'll examine that type of number in the next few meditations, but for now, we'll stick to more concrete numbers. Today's theme is that salvation—for us—is as easy as 1–2–3.

1. *Jesus lived. God promised a Savior, one whom His people could see and hear. He undoubtedly knew ahead of time that a true God/true Man wouldn't be understood or accepted any better than a burning bush or a cloud in the wilderness, but some would believe. Many would be people who had never heard God's promise. Jesus had a mission among people even before He officially began His short public ministry. He needed to live in perfect obedience to God. Easy as 1–2–3 for Jesus, right? Probably not. The Bible recounts how the devil made Jesus His pet project. Jesus resisted all temptation, and He dedicated His perfect obedience to us.*

2. *Jesus died. No doubts here, and it was no accident. Isaiah predicted, "Surely He took up our infirmities and carried our sorrows, yet we considered Him stricken by God, smitten by Him, and afflicted. But He was pierced for our transgressions, He was crushed for our iniquities; the punishment that brought us peace was upon Him, and by His stripes we are healed" (Isaiah 53:4–5). Isn't it frightening to think about God being dead? Even for a minute? For God and His people, 1–2–3 takes on more meaning. You know what happened on the third day.*

3. *Jesus rose. One and two would mean little if it weren't for three. Because Jesus rose from the dead, we will too. His defeat of the devil also defeated the power of sin. Sin is a terminal condition, but thanks be to Jesus, it's not permanent.*

We're on our way to see Jesus right now. If you believe that, you have saving faith. And talk about something easy as 1–2–3, it's faith—the free gift of the Holy Spirit planted in you by His mysterious power. The old kindergarten rhyme is true: "1–2–3, Jesus loves me!"

The Worst Number

Revelation 13:11–18

FOR YEARS NOW, sensitive citizens have whimpered about their loss of identity. Yes, it used to be that your name was replaced by a number, but that's no longer true. Chances are that your name has been replaced by many numbers—social security and credit card numbers; telephone, fax, and mobile numbers; PINs; etc. Just about the time you begin to remember the more frequently used numbers, you lose your card and get a new number!

Many Christians would recoil in horror if 666 became one of their numbers. Why? Revelation 13:18 explains: "This calls for wisdom. If anyone has insight, let him calculate the number of the beast, for it is man's number. His number is 666." This is no cartoon beast either. The beast of Revelation is Satan at his worst—the devil both pathetic and powerful as he still seeks to overthrow the Savior. Sometimes the most dangerous enemy is one who is already defeated and embarks on a blaze of terror and revenge. That pretty well describes the devil's case.

Some Christians fear that Satan will one day initiate a rampage especially aimed at ruining life as we know it. However, it's probably safe to assume that we're already embattled. Satan's weapons need not include a nuclear arsenal or a deranged dictator. He is a master of camouflage, and he's disguised his 666 into the number 1. The devil has already convinced a large segment of society to believe they are number 1. Is there a better way to coerce people to ignore or despise the true Number 1? Just think how the devil dances when he watches all the number 1s trying to prove they really are number 1. That's when they turn the attack on themselves into a war on others.

On our own, we'll destroy ourselves—if not in this world, then for eternity. Christians sometimes participate in the 666 campaign, and it's not always against their will. But when we adopt a different identity— the identity of a forgiven child of God, our will is no longer ours. It's God's. And God's will is to save us so we may live with Him forever.

Believers by the Gross

Revelation 7:1–4

How populated is the place you live? Would you describe the populace as dense or sparse? Or would you claim that even sparsely populated areas can have a dense population? What is the perfect-size community in which to reside? Of course, you probably would enjoy any size population if all your neighbors were as good as you, right?

Have you ever wondered how many people heaven will hold? John in his divine revelation from God reports, "Then I heard the number of those who were sealed: 144,000 from all the tribes of Israel" (Revelation 7:4). Talk about a planned community! The anticipated population sounds a bit disappointing, though, perhaps even distressing. Only a thousand gross? And all from Israel?

Like much of Revelation, the blessed 144,000 is symbolic. Theological scholars suggest that 144,000 interpreted figuratively should be understood to mean this: a lot. (*Throng* or *multitude* begin to sound pretty acceptable here!) With the number's meaning now in perspective, perhaps another concern alarms you. What's this about Israel?

Relax. Jesus includes you among the Jews even if you're not Jewish. Again, theological scholars explain the comforting news that "Israel" is just another term for God's chosen people. God's people come from all races and ethnic backgrounds. When you think about it, it's so much more efficient, word wise, to call us "Israel" than to announce a federally approved and mandated nondiscrimination policy.

Symbolic numbers interest many people. (I hope you are one of them because we have a few more "number" devotions to go!) But we must be careful not to let numbers steal the stage from the real focus of the Bible. Those figurative numbers are only stage props to help us understand the whole story of God's love for sinners. It's comforting to know that a weird number like 666 stands for the devil's limited (albeit considerable) power. It suggests that he can't permanently harm the 144,000—the millions of Christians past, present, and future who live in God's forgiveness and celebrate Jesus as their Savior.

You and I were counted when heaven's population was announced. Invite others to join the throng or multitude or whatever you want to call it. If anyone questions the size of Christ's kingdom, just tell them to stretch the number—a lot!

1,260 = 3.5

Revelation 11:1–12

As you can tell by the equation above, some of us learned new math. The difference between new math and old math is that you're never wrong in new math. This especially appeals to people like me who maintained a solid D average through elementary and high school. College math was harder, and I didn't do so good. (I did weller in English.)

Despite what you may think, 1,260 does equal 3.5, or as it's sometimes stated, "time, times, and half a time" (Daniel 12:7). You'll find these numbers and this term used throughout the book of Revelation. How shall we understand this equation?

"Time, times, and half a time" translates in time (days or years) to 1 + 2 + 0.5 or 3.5. In the same way, 1,260 in days adds up to 3.5 years. Certainly, this is something you've wanted to know for years—at least 3.5 anyway. So how is all this related to the Bible? Revelation 11:9, 11 says: "For three and a half days men from every people, tribe, language and nation will gaze on their bodies and refuse them burial. ... But after the three and a half days a breath of life from God entered them, and they stood on their feet, and terror struck those who saw them."

That's just one instance of a passage that uses one form or another of the 3.5 equation. It's important because it symbolizes a limited time. Reading the situation described in those passages, we might sense relief that such harsh events are limited in duration. Considering our own times on earth, we can figuratively say that we'll go to heaven when we're three and half years old.

You evaluate the quality of life based on your general health and your age. As age progresses and health deteriorates, life often becomes less enjoyable. That's the cumulative effect of our sin-sick world. We long for better times when not only can't we read the eye doctor's chart on the wall, we can't even see the wall! We may feel less threatened by death when it has already robbed us of loved ones, which leaves us lonely and living with memories. As we age, we become increasingly alarmed by the seeming epidemic of violence, immorality, and injustice in our world.

Take heart. Sin's rampant reign lasts only 3.5 years in God's math. It will end, but don't bother counting the days. God knows when the time is up.

A Perfect Seven

Job 5:17–27

N O SELF-RESPECTING Olympic gymnast would be pleased with a consistent round of sevens for a final score. And someone referring to his or her beloved as a "perfect seven" could expect a lengthy silent treatment—or maybe its opposite. In biblical terms, however, seven is indeed the perfect number. It symbolizes completion and wholeness.

The number seven appears in this context in several books of the Bible. People understood the number's meaning in those days and used it as a literary device to deliver spiritual messages. Though we don't use this number in the same way today, perhaps we should. For example, if you have some paper handy, pencil in a large seven on several sheets. Leave your sign in various places. If you get tired of the way the number seven looks, make seven colorful dots or lay seven pennies out where you (and maybe others) will notice.

Some may misinterpret your sevens as symbols of luck. Somehow the perfect number became perverted. Christians need not subscribe to luck, though perhaps we should say that no one needs to believe in it. *Luck,* along with its cousin's *fate, fortune,* and *destiny* are inventions of idol minds that refuse to trust God.

God's love is a perfect seven. We hear of it in Job: "From six calamities He will rescue you; in seven no harm will befall you" (Job 5:19). God's care and concern know no limits. He continues to love and protect us well beyond what we could ever expect. He never runs short of power to defend and nurture His children. Christ's forgiveness of our sins gets the highest score too. Thank God it's always one higher than what we accumulate.

Yes, it's safe to say that we're not perfect sinners. We're sixes at worst. (Applied conservatively, we're all at our worst—maybe even 6.9s!) How comforting to know that Jesus earned perfect sevens on the cross and beat us by a close score. Even better, He shares His victory with all the losers, which makes them—us—winners.

Now back to the sevens you inscribed and littered. Maybe someone will ask if you're superstitious. Of course, they could think you have some compulsive behavior and flee your presence immediately. But if they ask, share your faith. Tell them about the Perfect Seven in your life. Maybe Seven will be a winning part of their lives too.

Idolatry

Habakkuk 2:18–20

DATELINE: Kilauea Volcano (Hawaii), Aug. 12, 1997, Associated Press. (Okay, so the flash is a bit dim.) Fiery lava oozed down the mountainside engulfing a 700-year-old temple, the site of many ancient human sacrifices. Active temple worship occurred as late as 1819. In 1989, lava flow destroyed the visitor center, but it didn't succeed in exterminating the idol site until now. Some would like to see the place eventually restored to perpetuate the culture.

Dateline: Judah, 626 B.C. (give or take 30 years), *Babylonian Globe Democrat* quoting Habakkuk who spoke for God in the Bible: "What profiteth the graven image that the maker thereof hath graven it; the molten image, and a teacher of lies, that the maker of his work trusteth therein, to make dumb idols?" (Habakkuk 2:18 KJV). Now he knew what he was talking about!

The Kilauea incident brought an unintentional new meaning to the old biblical phrase "molten image." Lava incinerated and buried the old arena of idolatry, though it did not affect those who still worshiped the heritage if not the false god who had accepted human sacrifices there. Habakkuk's words, printed here in King James Old English, however, endure. Nor will they ever be consumed because they are the words of our true God—Father, Son, and Holy Spirit.

Over the years, Satan has dressed himself in the clothing of various idols. He's taken the form of golden calves, Asherah poles, trees, and other dense objects. He's been quite effective, too, because people often prefer to believe in what their sinful selves stand for. It's not hard to understand this because idol worship often involved bloody appeasement via helpless children or young women, sexual orgies, intoxication, and various human efforts to earn a base god's approval. That's consistent with much of what society still worships—or at least tolerates.

We don't need idols, past or present. We have a God who, incredibly, sacrificed Himself to save us. The blood was His Son's, and He went on to fill us not with wine, but with the Holy Spirit. And the Spirit fills us with ecstasy through liberty from sin and death. The day is coming when the last vestiges of idolatry will disappear into the lake of fire that John saw in his revelation. The last traces of sin will disappear with Satan, never to attack us again. The Good News is that the devil already feels the heat.

Mission Statement

John 20:24–31

BIG BUSINESS has discovered the mission statement. Mission statements usually sound noble and grand. Most translate to two simple words that everybody understands: Make money. Or it might be more precisely translated as: Make lots of money. Would you like an example? Acme Universal Widget and Wowsit aspires to legally extricate as much money as possible from 98 percent of the population of New Brunswick by supplying fur-lined, electronically heated swimwear for men and women.

Those involved in writing mission statements—whether corporate, educational, or congregational—know how difficult the task is. You want to say things "just right," so when the project is a group endeavor, it's a daunting task to get everyone to agree on wording. The most well-worded mission statements—especially the commercial species—are sufficiently confusing so nobody really knows what the mission is. (After all, there are only so many ways to say, "Make money.")

Christians have a clear mission statement. It was a snap for our loving God to pour it into John's pen. "Jesus did many other miraculous signs in the presence of His disciples, which are not recorded in this book. But these are written that you may believe that Jesus is the Christ, the Son of God, and that by believing you may have life in His name" (John 20:30–31).

God's mission statement allows no deception or confusion. All our Lord's miracles and every inspired word recorded in the Bible have one purpose, one goal: that people of every nation and every generation may have eternal life. It doesn't even cost money. In fact, it took a severe loss to abide by God's mission statement.

Christians merge under God's mission statement not only to enjoy salvation, but also to act so others will join them now and forever. Our mission is the same as God's, though we're often inept at executing it. But the Holy Spirit is with us so we, as forgiven sinners, can tell other sinners how they, too, can join the cause. The Spirit equips us to live as missionaries through what we say and do in our homes, workplaces, recreation areas, and neighborhoods. Sometimes the mission is hard. But with the Spirit's help, it's never impossible.

Oversleeping

Judges 16:18–22

H AVE YOU EXPERIENCED the panic that often accompanies oversleeping? Then again, "panic" is probably too extreme to describe the reaction. Perhaps the most notorious oversleeper was Rip Van Winkle, who slumbered for 20 years. That just illustrates the dangers of forgetting to set the alarm clock. Besides, it couldn't happen again—not in an age of subwoofers, motorcycle engines, and inconsiderate neighbors.

Samson of Bible times discovered the consequences of sleeping too long. Of course, in his case, a 10-minute nap would have been too long! Read on: "Then she called, 'Samson, the Philistines are upon you!' He awoke from his sleep and thought, 'I'll go out as before and shake myself free.' But he did not know that the LORD had left him" (Judges 16:20).

Samson's sleep involved more than closed eyes and relaxed breathing. He overslept spiritually. He was too occupied wallowing in sensual and self-deceiving pleasures to notice—or even care—that he was being had. Samson provided the classic model of taking God for granted and becoming careless. He left the Lord.

Not an upbeat day for devotional material, huh? On a brighter side, isn't it good to receive reminders of dangers? We're thankful for these messages when they appear on the roadside or when we hear them on the radio, but sometimes we rebel when they come from the Bible. It's no more welcome than hearing about severe storms in the vicinity, but it is just as useful.

On an even brighter note, it's good to know that the Lord will not leave us—unless, of course, we break the relationship. Jesus loves sinners. That's why He went through such extremes to take away our sins. Like Samson waking after Delilah's strength-sapping haircut, we're powerless to fight the devil. While Satan whirls his chains around us, Jesus steps in and announces that we belong to Him—that we have His power to snap the chains and fling them into the devil's face.

Stay awake in the Spirit. Talk to Jesus when you get spiritually drowsy. Grab those chains and chuck them at Satan. All Christians have this strength and power. No wonder cartoonists picture the devil as red-faced!

Seeing Things

2 Kings 6:15–23

THE INVOLUNTARY JERK STARTLED ME. No, it wasn't the guy sitting next to me in the theater. It was either a slow-moving gnat or one of those enigmas known as "floaters" that sail smoothly across aging eyes. Just try to explain your sudden reaction to "things" that others find invisible.

Today if you talk about seeing things—even floaters—you risk acquiring an instant reputation that puts a lot of space between you and others. If you're a Christian who sees things, you'll likely be labeled a fanatic. But people of God—people with an "in" because of Jesus Christ—have a long record of "in"-sights.

A verse from today's Bible reading underscores this point. "And Elisha prayed, 'O LORD, open his eyes so he may see.' Then the LORD opened the servant's eyes, and he looked and saw the hills full of horses and chariots of fire all around Elisha" (2 Kings 6:17). Despite the impending onslaught by fierce foes, God's almighty army formed a protective barrier around His people. Although anyone who dared to look saw the invading army, only those who looked beyond themselves saw salvation.

The same is true for us. Perils surround us. It is ironic, but the most menacing threat is the sin of complacency. We become so accustomed to "life as usual"—generally good life as usual—that we fail to perceive its dangers. You know how it is. When things go well, we sense no need to trust God. If life goes really well, we trust ourselves more and more—until the invading army of sin appears, showing its ugly side. Then, because of self-reliance, we wonder how we'll cope with the brewing trouble.

At times like this, we need to see things—things like Elisha's friend saw. Things like an army of angels to defend us from death and the devil. But most of all we need to see Jesus. The only way we can see Him is through eyes of faith opened by the Holy Spirit.

Do you see Him? You do if He's real enough to talk to in your prayers. You do if you understand the cross as something more than jewelry. You do if you see Him offering His body and blood for you in a meal of bread and wine. You do if you can close your eyes and see Him inviting you to heaven. Seeing things now? You can be sure it's not your imagination.

Continuing Education

Ezra 7:6–10

DISCOVERIES AND THEORIES increase by the day. Those who don't keep up are left behind. It's true for medical professionals, educators, engineers, computer programmers, construction workers, and even waste managers. Those who wait to learn from their mistakes usually receive an extensive education too—too late to be helpful. What was studied and practiced in the past must be restudied and practiced anew.

Today's reading deals with a student of God's Word, Ezra. We read, "For the gracious hand of his God was on him. For Ezra had devoted himself to the study and observance of the Law of the LORD, and to teaching its decrees and laws in Israel" (Ezra 7:9b–10).

Ezra kept up with God's Word. Although nothing had changed about God, He repeated His promises (as well as His threats) through people like Ezra. However, we must take care not to give Ezra more credit than he deserves because that would rob God of the credit.

The "gracious hand of His God" was on Ezra before he ever studied God's Word or observed His laws. God has never looked for people worthy enough to receive His blessings and love. Instead, God mercifully lavished undeserved love—grace—on Ezra and also on us. He also filled us with faith so we know what He's done. Once recognizing and claiming God as our own, we're free to fruitfully study His Word.

God's grace empowers us not only to study, but also to learn—and there's a difference. If you study every medical text available and pass the certifying exams with the highest grades, it means nothing unless you actually practice what you've learned. It would be silly to endure such stringent study and then refuse to use what you've learned for the benefit of others. It's the same with God's Word. As we continue our education in His Word through private and group study, we become better prepared to practice what Jesus preached. It would be a shame to keep all that Good News to ourselves, so practice we must.

Practice is a comforting word. Here on earth, even our Christian practice never makes perfect. But Jesus died for our imperfections. He equips us to practice our faith without fear of failure because forgiveness is always a confession away.

God bless you as you continue your education in His Word. Don't forget to practice every day.

Nothing to Cry About

Lamentations 3:18–26

WATCH THE FACES of people coming out of Sunday services, or worse, going in to worship. Looks like some of them consider Lamentations their favorite book of the Bible, right? However, some of the most comforting and stirring words of Gospel appear in (of all places) the Old Testament book of sorrows, Lamentations. That shouldn't surprise us.

Here is a beautiful example of grace from Lamentations 3:22–23: "Because of the LORD's great love we are not consumed, for His compassions never fail. They are new every morning; great is Your faithfulness."

The prophet Jeremiah, writer of Lamentations, had much about which to mourn. But isn't it just like God to turn around the worst situations with His love? In the middle of bad times, God's faithful people can trust His care and compassion. His supply of mercy and love never dwindles. In fact, its abundance seems to increase proportionately in times of adversity. God is a faithful Father and provider.

Faith is a funny word. We often use it to describe those who believe in God. In those terms, we know faith comes in a variety of shapes, sizes, and quantities. And consistent with the Lord's compassion as proclaimed in Lamentations, we know that even the smallest atom of faith is sufficient for salvation and immortality. The tiniest grain of faith brings the believer into the very presence of the Savior.

Then there's the faith ascribed to God. God's faithfulness is anything but tiny. It's monumental, magnetic, and mmmmm, mmmmm, mmmmm! While our allegiance strays, He remains loyal even when there's absolutely no justification for such loyalty. When we forget the One who loves us beyond description, He loves us enough to remain, waiting. Even when we abuse and misuse His name, God remains open rather than defensive, patiently waiting to hear our repentance and mercifully restoring our broken relationship.

With all this faithfulness surrounding us, we're strengthened and encouraged to face even dismal or painful futures. Every wound, disease, disappointment, discouragement, injustice, setback, or loss is like that little scratch we had on our knee when we were four and our mothers said, "It's nothing to cry about."

Nothing to Laugh About?

Genesis 17:15–18:12

CONSIDER THESE ANSWERS to some common questions about laughing:

Q: Are there different kinds of laughter?
A: *Yes. Ho ho. Ha ha. And hee hee—or to be more gender correct: (s)hee (s)hee. If that answer isn't what you expected, here's a different one. Yes. Laughter may be described as gleeful, scornful, polite (as when strangers laugh at your jokes), or merciful (as when friends laugh at your jokes).*

Q: Because this is a religious book, does the Bible ever mention laughter?
A: *Yes, several times in both Old and New Testaments. We also might imagine Jesus laughing in delight at the wedding reception and when He was surrounded by little children.*

Q: Did any famous Old Testament characters ever laugh?
A: *Yes, and they were married (to each other). Case in point: Abraham and Sarah (a.k.a. Sarai before she laughed).*

Q: How would you characterize their laughter?
A: *Abraham was rolling on the floor (desert), doubled over in delight. Sarah's laugh was cynical. By way of evidence, read the following: "Abraham fell facedown; he laughed and said to himself, 'Will a son be born to a man a hundred years old? Will Sarah bear a child at the age of ninety?' " (Genesis 17:17), and "So Sarah laughed to herself as she thought, 'After I am worn out and my master is old, will I now have this pleasure?' " (Genesis 18:12).*

Q: What is the point?
A: *We sometimes dupe ourselves into thinking that worship, Bible study, and prayer—foundations on which the Spirit builds faith—include nothing to laugh about. Yet laughter is most certainly appropriate when we consider what God has done for us. We're entitled to laugh with scorn at the devil, whom Jesus defeated by dying a sinner's death and returning to life in a victory only God could accomplish. We can flash a cynical smirk when the devil or any of his supporters accuse us before God because God already has declared us innocent for Jesus' sake. Then we're able to laugh in joy here on earth because what lies ahead dilutes any present sorrows or afflictions. Someday we'll roll around the heavens, laughing forever as Jesus tickles our souls with His everlasting love. Just be careful you don't fall off a cloud!*

Nothing to Sneeze At

2 Kings 4:18–37

HERE IS A LITTLE KNOWN FACT with which to impress your friends or to keep adversaries at what they consider a safe distance. Among the thousands of words printed in the Bible, *sneezed* is one of them. You'll see it in person later; but first, this digression.

Maybe Bible translators should take a closer look at the creation account in Genesis—focusing particularly on the creation of man. Given the present state of human quality, rather than breathing the breath of life, maybe God sneezed when He held that dust up to His nostrils. That would explain a lot, but of course it wouldn't be consistent with the fact that Adam and Eve were created perfectly and in God's image. So don't give the theory a second thought.

God's compassion and power are nothing to sneeze at, though in one case, a young boy actually did as we hear in 2 Kings 4:35. "Elisha turned away and walked back and forth in the room and then got on the bed and stretched out upon him once more. The boy sneezed seven times and opened his eyes."

This was no allergy! The boy was dead only moments before. It started as a headache, and a short time later, he died in his mother's lap. Understandably, the mom didn't accept her son's death. If you read the entire story, you're impressed with the mother's faith in God's kindness and power as exercised through the prophet Elisha. You can imagine the outburst of joy in the other room as the family heard the small sneezes behind the closed door.

There could be enough sneezing on Judgment Day to send an allergist's convention into ecstasy. Some of those sneezes will be a symptom of sickness as unbelievers and disbelievers wake to the eternal company of Satan in hell. These are the unrepentant sinners who sneezed at God's invitation when presented with the Gospel. Then, by God's grace, there will be us—perhaps sneezing in delirious joy as we come alive for the second and last time. The company of heaven will shout praises as we rise to the occasion. Their welcome will certainly exceed that which the little boy experienced. Even Elisha will greet us. I can only guess at what he would say. I think "God bless you" would be fitting.

Old Friends

John 15:9–17

SOMEONE DEFINED *friends* as two or more people who are angry at the same person. Someone else compared friends to appliances—the less they are used the longer they will last. Friends can also be relatives, but more often they're people with whom you can choose to relate.

Look back in your personal history, and think of one of your best friends. Close your eyes (don't try this while reading), and remember one of the good times you had together—perhaps a time when you laughed together or simply luxuriated quietly in each other's company. When you open your eyes, quickly find a mirror. Are you smiling?

Where are your old friends now? When did you see them last? Probably at a reunion or a wake. How did the conversation go? Many old friends find conversation faltering after a few minutes. How can things change so much after 10 or 20 or 30 years? How did we slip away, both becoming someone different?

Time tends to thin even the thickest friendships. To help time along, there's always distance, especially in a mobile society such as ours. All this makes one yearn for friendships like the ones you used to have. Speaking of former friendships, what can happen to a 2,000-year-old friendship?

Among Jesus' many heartwarming words are these: "I no longer call you servants, because a servant does not know his master's business. Instead, I have called you friends, for everything that I learned from My Father I have made known to you" (John 15:15).

Sharing intimate secrets and desires are common characteristics of friendship. Jesus shared His dreams and His knowledge with us. His most fervent dream was that everyone would live with Him someday. He even died to make that dream reality.

We can't allow ties with our oldest Friend to slip away. We can remind ourselves of great times together like Baptism and Holy Communion. We can think about the times our Friend came to help, and how we owe Him our very life. Yes, we can do something we probably haven't done with other old friends—talk to Him regularly. You'll probably find that, in this case, you won't run out of things to say. Why not give Him a call right now?

Good Judgment

Romans 2:1–4

ONE WONDERS if good judgment exists. It isn't always evident in our judicial system where criminals sometimes go free on "technicalities" and innocent people serve harsh sentences for crimes they didn't commit. If it isn't bad enough that we question the judgment of those we employ in our judicial system, we also question the judgment of those we love most—our spouses. (Hint for the day: Never, under any circumstances, question your spouse's judgment. He/she married you!)

Romans 2:1 offers the definitive judgment on judgment. "You, therefore, have no excuse, you who pass judgment on someone else, for at whatever point you judge the other, you are condemning yourself, because you who pass judgment do the same things." In other words, it appears that good judgment is no judgment.

Should we believe that whatever anyone wants to do is acceptable because the Bible tells us not to judge? Should we consider ourselves blessed equally with those who believe in other gods or who choose to believe only in themselves? Should we smile approvingly at our acquaintances for their promiscuous pleasures and lewd language because "Who are we to judge?"

Like a multiple choice quiz, the answer is "none of the above." Paul's point to the Romans addressed self-righteousness—a concept that remains an issue with us. You know from experience that judging others isn't nearly as complex as judging in courtrooms. Lawyers don't get in the way of private judgments. There aren't two sides, only one—and it's yours. It's so easy to see the faults of others that we wonder why they can't see them. But they question the same thing about us!

The other point Paul implies is that God knows everything necessary to make the right judgment. The wicked will get what's coming to them. As for us …

If we all got what the Judge says we deserve, heaven would contain Father, Son, Holy Spirit, and legions of angels, but no humans. We're too guilty to live freely in such company. Yet God will judge us, but His judgment will reflect what Jesus did on our behalf. You know the story. It never changes. Jesus lived, died, and rose to take away our sins. God sent His Son to earth with that mission in mind. When you meet God in heaven someday, be sure to compliment Him on His good judgment!

Lousy Logic

Romans 5:18–6:2

L OGIC IS AN EXERCISE of human intellect (which already begins to explain its limitations). For example, simple but authentic logic suggests that the horsepower in automobiles should not exceed the driver's I.Q. Conversely, the driver's I.Q. must exceed the posted speed limit. Logic suggests that this would greatly reduce traffic so you and I could get home faster.

Often it seems that logic is a college course rather than an extension of common sense. To prove this point, let's examine the logical implications of Romans 6:1–2, which reasons, "What shall we say, then? Shall we go on sinning so that grace may increase? By no means! We died to sin; how can we live in it any longer?"

Paul confronted Roman logic. He might have said, "Look here. If you hit your thumb with a hammer, it hurts. When the throbbing subsides, you feel better. However, do you hit each finger in turn with a hammer so you continue to feel better?" Paul might have said it that way, but it was probably more logical to say it the way he did. Anyway, it was especially logical because God told Paul to say it that way.

Only those looking for loopholes in God's will would suggest that we should sin more so we can receive more forgiveness. That's never been the intent of forgiveness, though mercifully it operates that way, which is not logical at all. Why would God continue to forgive sinners as they stupidly or sullenly or stubbornly plod through the same sins while adding new ones to their repertoire? The illogical answer is that God loves us. It really doesn't make sense, does it? That's precisely what makes His love so wonderful. We don't deserve it and can't earn it. He gives it freely, and He gives it often.

Getting back to Paul's point, God's grace and mercy is no reason to keep on sinning. Along with forgiveness, God has given us the power to hate sin and fight it. Motivated by God's perpetual forgiveness and His Holy Spirit, we seek to use forgiveness less and less as we struggle to live as He wants. "Why sin when you don't have to?" is the logic to which we ascribe. But when logic—good logic—fails us, we're always welcome to do the illogical: We can count on God's forgiveness once again. That's common Christian sense that hits the nail on the head, not the thumb.

But ...

Galatians 5:1–6

THE ENGLISH LANGUAGE includes several one-word expressions that are frequently spoken when at a loss for words and stalling for time until adequate verbiage slides down neurons (or nasal passages) from brain to tongue. One such word is *but*.

For a word that has little meaning by itself, *but* peppers vocabulary with regularity. For example, "I know I'm late, *but* ..." or "Yes, that's a good point, *but* ..." Then there's the stuttering triple *but* when you can't get an excuse in edgewise with an aggressive accuser.

But has a role in spiritual matters too. Consider the following passage: "It is for freedom that Christ has set us free. Stand firm, then, and do not let yourselves be burdened again by a yoke of slavery" (Galatians 5:1). No, you didn't miss anything. *But* doesn't appear in letters, but it certainly looms in attitude. In this case, it's a really big *but*.

The "yoke of slavery" is dogged discipline of the Law, especially as the Jews considered it in the apostle Paul's time. They believed they needed to obey God's Law perfectly to please Him, which they did. That wasn't the bad part. Some believed they could do so and boldly claimed that they did. The temptation to assimilate that attitude remains infectious among believers today.

The conversation goes something like this: "I know Jesus died to take away my sins, *but* I must do something to help my salvation along." Or: "I know lots of Christians are kind of weak when it comes to obeying God's will, *but* I'm pretty good at it. At least I try." Sometimes it even takes this twist: "Those people will never get to heaven, *but* I'm working hard to get my reward."

Paul says we're free, and in many other Scripture passages, he also says our freedom is free. Throughout the history of salvation, as noted in the Bible, people have searched in vain for ways to earn a way to heaven. Despite God's constant reminders that we are incapable of such effort, and that attempts to earn salvation are unnecessary, people have persisted in their quest. Perhaps they don't realize that doing so is abject self-centeredness and idolatry. Yet we all fall to this temptation. When that happens, the Holy Spirit reminds us of the most fundamental truth of Christianity: We are saved by God's kindness and mercy—solely by grace. No *buts* about it.

204

What?

2 Samuel 12:1–13

B

Y ITSELF, *what* is an innocent word. Yet it's often uttered with an attitude, especially when it comes from someone "caught in the act" or at least suspected of perpetrating one. If you could spell it, it might look like this: Waaaaaa-t? Then it's followed by a righteous excuse or declaration of innocent ignorance. For example, a puddle of orange soda soaks into the white carpet. Mom enters the room. After she composes herself, she asks, "What is that orange spot on the floor?" Missy, looking as though she just woke from a long nap, responds, "Waaaaaa-t spot?" While the impending tempest boils behind mom's eyes, Missy hurriedly continues, "Waaaaaa-t? I was just sitting here wiggling my toes ..."

Sinners, when confronted with their "acts," may utter something akin to "Waaaaaa-t?" After all, it isn't pleasant to be caught in the act or reminded of past ones. Human nature pushes our guilt button, and we can't tolerate it. The natural response is to deny wrongdoing or plead ignorance.

Pleading ignorance might convince others, but not God. It doesn't fool our inner self either. But when you're guilty, you don't want to be. Perhaps you fear the consequences. Besides, there's always the other person who's more reprehensible than you!

King David (a man with lots of public face to lose) sat in judgment of one of those "other guys" when Nathan reported a malicious injustice. (See today's Bible reading.) At the time, David didn't realize that Nathan was speaking in hypothetical terms. He didn't get it that Nathan was revealing David's own grievous sin. David pronounced harsh judgment on the other guy. When Nathan revealed the culprit's identity, David did the right thing. He resisted the urge to spout a defiant "Waaaaaa-t?" Here is what happened: "Then David said to Nathan, 'I have sinned against the LORD.' Nathan replied, 'The LORD has taken away your sin. You are not going to die' " (2 Samuel 12:13).

Sin is so much easier to see in others than in ourselves. There's always a wealth of ways to justify our actions—as most courtrooms seem to prove. But there remains only one way to deal with sin. Confess it. Not only does God already know about it, He is eager to forgive it because it makes His Son's life and death worthwhile. So when you feel like saying "Waaaaaa-t?" shake the urge and confess instead.

If ...

Matthew 4:1–7

SOMETIMES THE WORD has a flavor of anticipation: "*If* I save $3 from every paycheck, I can purchase a new car for cash by the time I'm 101." At other times it's colored with regret: "*If* only I hadn't spent so much money on lottery tickets, I'd have enough to play for this $75,000,000 purse." Finally, there's the conditional *if* of challenge: "*If* you work hard and flatter your boss, you'll be promoted to an office with a view of the water cooler."

Religion is full of *if*. "*If* I try really hard, I'll be a better person, and God will save me." That may be the worst spiritual fallacy ever uttered. There's nothing conditional about our behavior. It's universally imperfect. Take a moment and think about "How I want to be" versus "How I am." Since you really know yourself, and no one else is involved, you have the opportunity for brutal honesty. Things don't look so good, huh? We need not fret about the *ifs* of earning a home in heaven. Christ bought us a beautiful place with His suffering, death, and resurrection.

Next, let's consider the *if* of religious regret. "*If* only I had a better job, a faithful family, more time, a Bible I could understand, a pastor who preached exciting sermons, I'd get closer to God—you know, go to church and Bible class." Here is the *if* that blames God for weak or evaporating faith. Yet God is patient. Even slothful sinners have opportunity to repent and enjoy God's grace.

Finally, we have the spiritually challenging *if*. The devil thought he was clever in this confrontation with Jesus: "The tempter came to Him and said, 'If You are the Son of God, tell these stones to become bread' " (Matthew 4:3). We Christians hear versions of this *if* often. "*If* God loves you Christians so much, why does He permit you to get cancer or suffer deadly accidents or fight through bitter divorces like everybody else?"

The truth is that people universally enjoy God's blessings as well as suffer the consequences of a sin-afflicted world. The real difference is how the believer views these life experiences. Even the worst experiences turn out well for Christians.

If we must have *ifs* in life, then only one *if* can count: *If* we believe Jesus took away our sins, we'll live forever with Him in heaven. *If* only more clung to that Good News!

Uh ...

Mark 9:14–27

IF TIME IS MONEY, a few well-placed *uhs* are worth millions. *Uh* is what you say when you don't know or can't remember an answer. For example, "Where are your teeth?" Answer: "*Uh,* I think I left them under my pillow. No, that was 60 years ago. *Uh,* now I remember—last I saw them they were fizzing in a little cup on top of the flush box." (Have you ever wondered why the tooth fairy doesn't leave teeth under your pillow? *Uh,* maybe not.)

Jesus' disciples seemed to utter (or was it *uh*tter?) a lot of *uhs* while accompanying Jesus. There was the *uh* when Jesus told them to find food for thousands of hungry people. Their response to Jesus' command? Maybe there's no Greek equivalent for it. However, my guess is they blankly looked in the Savior's eyes and said, "*Uh,* sure." Then they shuffled away, scratching their heads. Then they returned with, "*Uh,* the stores are closed, and *uh,* we think, *uh,* these people should go home."

Uhs probably were common companions of miracles. In another incident, the disciples were stuck with an *uh* when they were unable to lure a demon from a possessed boy. The spectators demanded to know why. " 'O unbelieving generation,' Jesus replied, 'how long shall I stay with you? How long shall I put up with you? Bring the boy to Me' " (Mark 9:19).

Uh can be an ugly word when it stands for uncertainty and doubt. How long can Jesus tolerate us when we wonder if the Bible could be wrong? "*Uh,* do we really go to heaven when we die?" "*Uh,* how can I prove that God created everything?" "*Uh,* why would God love sinners?" "*Uh,* how can babies have faith even before they coo?"

Uh, the Good News is that doubters and other varieties of "*uh*-ers" often keep their God-given faith despite doubts. (Most of us know that from experience!) Doubt and faith coexist, and sometimes this relationship is even good! Doubt drives us to prayer and Bible study because faith hints that God has answers to our questions, even if we don't always understand them. Once we accept the fact that we don't need to understand the farthest reaches of God's goodness and will, we can trust Him. That trust is so strong, we wonder how we ever could have doubted. (Did Thomas ever know that feeling!) It's almost as if we should say, "*Uh,* huh!"

Well …

Proverbs 28:1–18

WELL HAS EVOLVED from little more than a hole in the ground to a one-word expression of helpless guilt that is often accompanied by a vocal tone suggesting naive innocence. Perhaps you haven't heard it used this way unless you're around young people or are addicted to *Dick Van Dyke Show* reruns. Indeed, anthropologists will someday discover that *well* originated with Mary Tyler Moore (playing Dick Van Dyke's wife). She massaged the term to perfection every time she was unable to explain some irrational behavior. Jack Benny did well with it too.

Along the same lines, there exists another mutation of the *well* response to guilt. It sounds like this: "Ooooh, *welllll.*" We use it when we know that what we have done is irreversible, such as, "My diamond earring fell down the drain and washed into the septic tank. Ooooh, *welllll* …"

Sinners caught in the act may respond similarly, but doing so suggests that (1) we're unsure of our Savior's supply of forgiveness and/or (2) we don't take sin seriously. In both cases, sin remains sin, and God takes sin seriously even if sinners do not.

Proverbs 28:13 puts it bluntly: "He who conceals his sins does not prosper, but whoever confesses and renounces them finds mercy." In other words, nothing from human invention or ingenuity protects us from the truth or consequences of sin. (Speaking of old TV shows, wasn't there one by that name?)

Hiding our sins from God is like trying to hide a Dodge under a doily. Spiritual futility isn't funny, though. It's terminal. Thank God, it's also unnecessary.

The concept probably is foreign to the business and political world, but in God's kingdom, confession spurs prosperity. Confessing sin means we agree with God (and probably many others) that we are indeed imperfect and even evil. Confessing sin also means we're confident that God will not hold our sins against us because He sent Jesus to take them away. Now that's authentic prosperity!

Well, so much for *well.* I even avoided a well-worn temptation to call *well* a deep subject. Like the *well* of helpless guilt or casual excuse, sometimes it's better to leave well enough alone.

Get Wet

Zechariah 12:10–13:2

Ever since some Old Testament child discovered that a stout branch swished and splashed in a swift-flowing stream created both visual and tactile amusement, humans have been fascinated by the aesthetic value of water. Thus, we have fountains.

Haven't fountains flowed a long way? Two fountain displays in Chicago prove the point. Magnificent old Buckingham Fountain charms thousands of visitors each year. Its beauty lies in its architecture, as well as the spewing water illuminated by colored lights. A short distance away are the fountains of Navy Pier, which are totally devoid of visible structure. They're simply streams of water arching over walkways and tempting small children (and adults who wish they were children) to get wet. The water itself is the attraction in these winsome, whimsical displays.

If you've just made it through what had to be the world's longest paragraph devoid of the divinity in a devotion book, you're probably strong enough to stomach what's next. Perhaps you've heard or sung the spiritual, "There Is a Fountain Filled with Blood." Picture the best fountain you've ever seen and replace the water with … with … with the reason some hymnals now contain the reworded and less graphic title "There Stands a Fountain Where for Sin." How strange that in a society that watches violence any given night on TV, we have to sterilize a graphic hymn!

Every once in a while, and probably more often than we would like, it's good to picture the price of our sinfulness. What a reviling sight! That Jesus died a gory, inhumane death on the cross should be enough to make us sick, especially when we know that it should be our blood filling the fountain. But the fountain filled with blood really isn't meant to nauseate us. Instead, it solemnly reminds us of the immense thanks and praise we owe to Jesus.

You'll probably want to leave this devotion with a different picture of fountains, one more familiar and refreshing. So let's close with words from Zechariah 13:1: "On that day a fountain will be opened to the house of David and the inhabitants of Jerusalem, to cleanse them from sin and impurity." From that fountain flows the water of Baptism, cleansing us from the stains of sin and rejuvenating us for an unending life of joy. Jump right in and splash around!

Speedy Delivery

John 6:61–69

A MONG THE WORLD'S most clever inventions are the wheel, indoor plumbing, nose hair scissors, and mailboxes. Though you've probably taken mailboxes for granted ever since you could reach the slot, perhaps you'll give them the respect they deserve after today.

Mailboxes are models of forethought in design and functionality, as proven by only minor changes in appearance over the years. You can put things in, but only authorized individuals can take things out. They shelter their contents from the weather, yet they're open constantly. How else would you pay your bills in places like Moose Tail, Alaska?

Mailboxes remind me of Jesus, but that's not to suggest that He'll be late in arriving or wedged in the pages of a mail-order catalog. Mailboxes and Jesus have one thing in common: They are the only way to reach inconvenient places like Moose Tail or unapproachable places like God's kingdom. One of Jesus' disciples said it this way: "Simon Peter answered him, 'Lord, to whom shall we go? You have the words of eternal life' " (John 6:68).

Consider what we deposit in mailboxes: thoughtful greeting cards, bill payments, business correspondence, charitable donations, and sweepstakes entry forms. For the most part, we're confident they will arrive safely, on time, and far more efficiently that if we delivered them personally. Then consider our deposits in Jesus: sins, friendly greetings, pleas to extend our "credit," requests for guidance and assistance, and hopes for a flourishing future based on something more certain than a sweepstakes number. And Jesus delivers!

As Peter acknowledged, Jesus is the only way to eternal life. When Jesus took away our sins on the cross, He delivered us to God's very doorstep. Neither rain nor sleet nor ice nor snow nor dark of night nor Satan nor sin prevented Jesus from making His appointed rounds. And we even go first class!

As with mailboxes, we sometimes take Jesus for granted. We're so accustomed to His matchless love that it's easy to forget how well it works. So next time you stamp an envelope and drop it in the mail, pause for a moment to thank whomever it was who invented the mailbox. (Probably somebody's Uncle Sam.) Then pause for a while long to thank Jesus, who takes you where you want to go.

A Carpenter's Tears

1 Peter 2:22–25

THEY BOUGHT THE OLD HOUSE. What impressed them most about the structure? The woodwork. That seems to be the stock answer when anyone asks about old houses. It's ironic that people who lived in old houses before they were old houses often painted over the rich grains and luster of the woodwork because the decor was old! It's enough to make a carpenter cry.

Then there was the era when people didn't like the "modern" woodwork in their homes because it was too sterile. So they applied "antique kits" to make the wood look rich and warm. Sometimes it turned out cheap and gaudy, but at least it was antique. It's enough to make a carpenter cry.

My aunt and uncle's house had the best woodwork, but only in the kitchen. It was red. Against the contrasting yellow walls, it warmed the artistic embers of this young boy's heart. I thought it was cool. It was enough to make a carpenter cry. The truth, of course, is that woodwork is nothing unless it adorns comfortable and happy surroundings.

Jesus worked wood. He probably learned cutting and assembling and fastening at His earthly dad's workbench. How Joseph must have marveled at Jesus' potential as a master craftsman. Could it even be that Joseph was a little disappointed when Jesus took on a different career? Was it enough to make a carpenter cry?

Jesus remained in the woodworking field. In fact, He became a master craftsman. The Bible says of Jesus, "He Himself bore our sins in His body on the tree, so that we might die to sins and live for righteousness; by His wounds you have been healed" (1 Peter 2:24). When this Carpenter cried from the cross, the whole universe heard, even to the very depths of hell.

Jesus fashioned the rough, unfinished wood of the cross into a work of art. He transformed that crude, lethal lumber into a symbol of forgiveness and unconditional love. His work remains functional as well as beautiful even today. Jewelers forge crosses into ornaments often worn by people ignorant of what the symbol represents. Yet for millions of us who believe, it's a reminder of what Christ has won for us.

You might not buy (or excuse!) a house based on the beauty of its woodwork, but never cease to praise Jesus for His.

Citizenship Quiz

Romans 13:1–7

WHY DO WE HAVE GOVERNMENT? In a comprehensive survey, here's what a half dozen citizens said:

- *So we have something to grumble about.*
- *To take politicians from obscurity to infamy.*
- *For an effective way to spend taxes.*
- *To continue the tradition begun by George Washington when he threw a dollar across the Potomac River. Not only was that as far as a dollar ever went, we've gone one up on George by flinging many more dollars across whole oceans!*

The survey didn't include God, but here's what He said: "Everyone must submit himself to the governing authorities, for there is no authority except that which God has established. The authorities that exist have been established by God" (Romans 13:1).

Governments spend thousands of words legitimizing their existence. They place these words in national museums but not before placing them in documents called constitutions. Then, in a noble effort to grow good citizens, they make school children memorize every paragraph and amendment. This is not to criticize government (which is still legal at the time of this writing), but wouldn't it be better if we listened to what God has to say in Romans 13? As we all know, however, that would be illegal because we're supposed to separate church and state!

Isn't it good that God doesn't treat us like we treat Him. Here He is, encouraging—indeed commanding—loyalty, allegiance, and obedience to our government, even though government can't officially acknowledge His influence. Isn't that just like God?

Citizenship aside, we treat God unfairly, even badly. Yet He remains our faithful leader, though we could question His fairness. He doesn't give us what we deserve. Instead, He blesses us with far more than anyone could justify. He distributes earthly blessings without bias—both to those who love and honor Him and to those who deny or decry His rule.

All governments have their heroes, and God's kingdom is no different. Jesus single-handedly won the most critical war ever when He crushed sin against the cross. No wonder we worship Him! Here's more good news: None of this was paid for with taxpayer money.

Naming Names

Romans 15:1–13

ON A SCALE OF 1 TO 5, how would you rate your faith? If you find this exercise incomprehensible, think of it this way: Suppose you found yourself in church and when the collection basket is passed, you have only a $20 bill. (This places a test of faith on crudely practical terms, doesn't it?)

Okay, have you rated yourself? Now think of someone whose faith probably would rate lower. Aha—lots of people fit this category, right? Finally, think of someone whose faith you would rate higher than yours. How does it feel to rate lower?

After all that evaluating, shouldn't we just forget it? Besides, God tells us to leave the judging to Him. Should we not name names? God has this to say: "We who are strong ought to bear with the failings of the weak and not to please ourselves. Each of us should please his neighbor for his good, to build him up" (Romans 15:1–2).

When God orders us not to judge others, He really means that we, of all people, aren't qualified to condemn. God could have ended the world before we came to faith, but He patiently waited for us. His patience continues, and its primary purpose is to bring more people into His heavenly kingdom. Besides, we're unable to peer into our peers to see the condition of their souls. This doesn't mean we ignore those whose faith appears weak—especially those who clearly expose their weaknesses.

What can we do for the apparently weak? We can adopt God's patience, though this may be tough. How long can you comfort and assure those believers who seem ever so forgetful about taking their troubles to God? How can you deal with that friend who persists in a pet sin (such as homosexual behavior or drug or substance abuse) despite professing faith in Jesus as Savior? Then there's that person who looks back at you from the mirror every morning—the one who intimately knows your spiritual weaknesses and persistent sinfulness—and won't free you from guilt.

Jesus is God of the sinners and the weak. He saved us despite our weakness. Now He empowers us to pray for others who are weak. So go ahead, name names. Be sure to include your own.

Here Today

John 3:27–36

Have you noticed how we work so hard to make life easy? You've probably discovered that the best things in life are free. It's all the "second bests" that cost so much. With all the getting and losing in life, no wonder some call it a game. Some game. By the time we learn the rules, we're too old to play! How good to know that despite the occasional chaos of life, we're still in it! And things will only get better.

So much of life seems devoted to improving its quality. Scientists, engineers, educators, counselors, and physicians combine the latest technology with personal creativity to refine everything from door handles to artificial hearts, mosquito abatement to lip gloss, anxiety-filled nights to dousing heartburn. They even meet with some success.

However, for every new, life-enriching invention, there is at least one life-marring discovery—one new indication that sin continues to make life on earth less satisfying. Therefore, it's fitting to remember what the Bible says: "Whoever believes in the Son has eternal life, but whoever rejects the Son will not see life, for God's wrath remains on him" (John 3:36).

Not only is the best thing in life free, it already has been discovered and it's surprisingly simple. Believe in Jesus and you have eternal life, and eternal life begins the moment you believe. In other words, we're living for eternity right here, right now! Not that we won't be moving someday, but when we do, it's certain to signal upward mobility.

Some might view this scriptural concept of eternal life as somewhat premature. How often haven't we thought of eternal life as commencing with death? But living here, living now, knowing we'll live forever suggests a few things about how we live.

We live like we've got nothing to lose. Why hold grudges and bitter memories when we can forgive as Jesus forgives? Why mourn the passing years (or months or days or minutes) when we still have all of life ahead of us? Why focus so much attention on ourselves when we could work to serve others? (We'll have a long, long time for rest and recreation later.)

Enjoy life. Ask God to help you cope with its challenges and down times. Praise God for all the good times. Thank Him for putting you here. Always remember that your future is out of this world.

Gone Tomorrow

Philippians 1:18–26

WHAT ARE YOUR PLANS FOR TOMORROW? Next week? Next month? What are your hopes for next year? God willing, those plans will reach fruition. God willing, they may not. The only significant factor is God's will. Yet this is not meant to sound pessimistic or fatalistic.

Listen to the apostle Paul: "I am torn between the two: I desire to depart and be with Christ, which is better by far; but it is more necessary for you that I remain in the body" (Philippians 1:23–24). Paul was eagerly willing to be here today and gone tomorrow, though if God kept Him alive, he recognized its purpose. That's a great, godly philosophy for life and death.

Speaking of a life and death philosophy, have you ever thought about living life backward? In some ways, it's a reality for Christians. We begin with death and progress through life. Paul, in another letter, said that faith begins with the death of sin. When the Holy Spirit implants faith in our soul, it takes us from the catacombs of sin into fresh new life.

For many of us, our date of death was the day we were baptized. Now we're living that part of life between death and entirely new life. Like Paul, we sometimes yearn to escape our present stage of life in favor of living in greater spiritual, emotional, social, and physical ease. Yet that might not be God's will. In that case, it is God's way of saying that we still have a purpose on earth.

Just what is your God-given purpose? Are you like Paul—in the company of others who need your witness and service? Probably. Even if you're seriously ill or homebound or physically challenged, others need you. They need to see how you face life's hazards and hardships. If you're prosperous, healthy, and happy, others need to see how you handle that particular challenge too.

The neat thing about starting life at death (of sin) is that all our plans for the future are certain. Whatever happens to us today, we can trust God to do what's best. It may mean that we're here today and gone tomorrow. By the way, if you're gone tomorrow, we'll know where you went.

At Your Doorstep

Romans 10:14–21

WHO DELIVERS YOUR NEWS? My newspaper comes regularly early every morning. And I'm doubly blessed because I don't need to bend down to pick it up off the driveway. Our dog does it. By the time I get the paper into the house, the dog has even digested some of the news for me! How's that for service?

It's convenient to have the newspaper delivered each day. It's probably the only way I'd ever routinely read the comics—er, news. Newspaper delivery reminds me of the Gospel—God's Good News delivered to our very soul by the Holy Spirit. Romans 10:17 says, "Faith comes from hearing the message, and the message is heard through the word of Christ."

Now it may be stretching the point to compare the Holy Spirit to a paperboy (if you'll excuse an old-fashioned term with no sexist undercurrent intended). Paperboys of yore usually accommodated their customers. It wasn't so much altruism as straightforward economics that provided the motivation. A happy customer meant a healthy tip. So if you asked the paperboy to leave the paper inside the storm door, he did. If you asked the paperboy to balance the paper on his nose while ringing the doorbell, he probably did. Good paperboys delivered newspapers according to their patrons' needs.

The Holy Spirit delivers the Good News according to each individual's needs too. He knows how best to leave faith folded snugly in our souls, waiting to be unfolded and read and believed. But even the best paperboy never brought the paper into the house, sat down at the breakfast table, and read the news for the customer. The Holy Spirit leaves that to us too. If we want the news, we must accept it. The Holy Spirit's call to duty does go beyond that of the paperboy's, however, because the Spirit helps us as we read the news—a quiet, invisible partner who encourages us to believe and respond to God's love through Jesus Christ.

By the way, I didn't tell you everything about my delivery dog. If I don't keep her on a leash while she retrieves the paper, she likes to deliver parts of the paper to various neighbors. While that would leave me with serious gaps in the news, it's a good model for people to follow when they receive the Good News. Spread it around. Take it to the neighbors. Who knows? Maybe you'll get a generous tip.

Good News—Section I

2 Timothy 1:8–12

NEWSPAPERS ARE GOOD FOR MANY THINGS. They let us know what happened—mostly bad—since the last edition. They keep us informed of what's expected to happen—such as meetings, weather predictions, upcoming trials, and local government (with the last two often in the same article). Newspapers have certain "advantages" over radio and TV news too. For example, they can be employed as a portable wall to discourage breakfast conversation or curled rigidly to smack bugs. But enough about newspapers. On to Section I—the big news.

Newspapers boldly confront you on the front page. Headlines scream, shock, scare, or sadden. Sometimes, like when the home team wins a championship, the news lifts our spirits. If we had to narrow the Good News to a front-page headline, perhaps it would be 2 Timothy 1:10: "But it has now been revealed through the appearing of our Savior, Christ Jesus, who has destroyed death and has brought life and immortality to light through the gospel."

Granted, that headline would take up the entire front page, but at least it's worth reading. It's even a direct quote! It's the most important event of the day—in fact, the most important announcement in all history. It's a scoop to fulfill the most avid reporter's dreams! For us, it's even better because it reveals Good News.

Good News, like most Section I stories, is surrounded by bad news. Surrounded may be too tame a description. Inundated would be more accurate. Just analyze the first section of your newspaper. You probably can count the good news articles on one finger. Bad news is far more typical. That truly reflects real life. So much sin and its companions suffering, destruction, and violence! It makes us yearn for Good News.

God's Good News gives our souls a lift. It tells us that even in the glut of horror, fear, and sadness, Jesus is our Protector, Comforter, and Savior. He is a real life Hero, powerful enough to frustrate the devil's attempts to rape our souls and strangle us with sin.

Most headlines lead to longer stories. The same is true with the Good News. Write your own story now, even if you only pen it in your mind. Review your personal news event—the Who, what, when, where, why, and how of your salvation. Just be sure to give WHO the most space.

Good News—Section II

2 Corinthians 5:11–15

A T WHAT AGE did you begin to understand why people read the obituaries as if it were a nationally syndicated column? (Excuse me if you haven't reached that age yet.) I must confess that I read them now too. I'm always relieved when I don't find my name listed.

Obituaries reveal much about people, or rather, what others thought important about the deceased. The number 1 priority seems to be family—who is left behind and who went ahead. Then comes the suggested memorials that often provide clues about what killed the person or which organization the deceased favored.

Even God's Good News has an obituary page, and you can guess the most prominent name. Jesus does deserve top billing! How might His obituary read? Try this: "And He died for all, that those who live should no longer live for themselves but for Him who died for them and was raised again" (2 Corinthians 5:15).

While some people weep when they spot the name of a relative or an old friend in the obituaries, we need not feel sad about seeing Jesus name. There are several reasons for this. Surely we mourn the fact that our sins caused Jesus' death. But in God's grand plan to save us, Jesus did exactly what needed doing. He obeyed His Father, lived a sinless life, and shed His blood that we might be saved. Jesus did God's will, and He did it for us.

Perhaps the most important reason not to mourn is that Jesus didn't remain dead. The Son of God rose from the tomb, demonstrating to all believers what would happen to them. Death has claimed millions for far more than three days, but to those whose earthly lives have ended, time isn't important. Isn't it wonderful to think of all our loved ones who will wake and rise just as their Savior did 2,000 years ago?

Were an obituary written for Jesus today, it would list the usual particulars—born Christmas, died Good Friday, rose Easter. There's no body to lie in state or grave to visit, but memorials of praise to God would be appreciated in lieu of flowers. The list of Jesus' siblings probably would consume the entire Sunday edition of the *New York Times* and more. Somewhere in that long list of famous people like Esther, David, Peter, and Paul, you would find your name. So weep if you must, but make your tears droplets of joy.

Good News—Section III

1 Kings 18:41–46

IT'S OFTEN THE FIRST SECTION located by a large segment of the population. Readers eagerly scan the columns to learn how their favorite pack of millionaires fared. Were they trounced, or was victory won by a scant margin? What indiscretions did they commit, and what did they have to say about themselves? Where do they stand in the win/loss column? What are their chances for future fame? Yes, the sports section makes for exciting reading.

Are you a sports fan? If so, you've probably enjoyed about the same ratio of pleasure to aggravation that gamblers experience. Even the great athletic dynasties eventually tumble as players are traded or sold like shares of stock. But to give sports credit where due, without pastimes such as baseball, how would kids ever learn the national anthem?

Would the Good News have a sports page? You may remember Paul's talk about running the spiritual race with perseverance and striving to win for God. A lesser figure on the sports page, however, was an old man named Elijah. One of today's athletic apparel clothing companies would have offered him a generous reward for endorsing its running sandals according to this news report: "Meanwhile, the sky grew black with clouds, the wind rose, a heavy rain came on and Ahab rode off to Jezreel. The power of the LORD came upon Elijah and, tucking his cloak into his belt, he ran ahead of Ahab all the way to Jezreel" (1 Kings 18:45–46).

Old Elijah sounds like a speedy mudder in the fourth race at Jezreel. What were the odds of Elijah beating a horse? The odds were very odd. In fact, it was no contest because "the power of the LORD" fueled Elijah's sprint. Elijah, humble prophet that he was, probably didn't think of this as a race. (Maybe he just wanted to get in out of the rain!)

Next time you read the sports section, think of Elijah. Think of yourself too. Are you a winner or a loser? Count your name in the win column, not because you can throw a touchdown, whack a goal, fling a 97 m.p.h. fastball, arch a three pointer, or KO the devil. Instead, you have God's power to fight sin and to score victories of grace and mercy in His name. You are indeed a winner, coached by the Holy Spirit, and clinging to the triumphant robe-tails of Jesus. The best news is, He'll never trade you to another team.

Good News—Section IV

Zephaniah 3:14–20

THEY WON'T KEEP YOU current on events like the front page does, nor will they promise riches like the financial section. You might sacrifice delicious recipes, forego the marvels of new home furnishings, and be less conscious of new fashions as well. But never, never skip the section of the newspaper with the comics. Why is Sarge socking Beetle today? Is Snoopy starting another book from atop his doghouse? How has Hagar's wife tamed the lovable Hun this time? Then there's Dilbert, simultaneously exposing and suffering corporate folly.

Comic strips break the tension of breaking news. Although they create plots of their own, we know they're not real. Often they reveal some of life's foolishness and invite us to laugh at ourselves. For a few moments, we have the opportunity to eavesdrop on the thoughts and behavior of people we'd either love to meet or want to avoid.

God doesn't need comic strips. He only needs to look at the pages of human history—our personal history included—to observe many of the same situations we scan in the comics. Much of what He sees isn't funny. In fact, it's enough to make a Creator cry. Our mistreatment of others, the environment, and everything else under His bright sun must make God shake His holy head in rueful acknowledgment that such things really exist in the world for which He had such high hopes.

Certainly, God must have His lighter moments too. Zephaniah 3:17 says, "The LORD your God is with you, He is mighty to save. He will take great delight in you, He will quiet you with His love, He will rejoice over you with singing." Yes, maybe God smiles just a little as He watches your attempts to do His will. He's pleased that you want to obey and honor Him. He probably grins as He anticipates that time when you'll join Him in heaven, never to bumble around again. He looks into your heart and reads your thoughts, knowing your hopes and worries, your insecurities and courage, your failures and successes, your tears and laughter.

Next time you read the comics, think of God reading your life. Do something today to delight Him. Give God a good laugh. While you're at it, laugh along with Him.

Good News—Section V

2 Timothy 4:1–5

ONE SECTION OF EVERY NEWSPAPER seems to have limited criteria for its writers. It seems like any knucklehead can make it into print. People with fine ideas like your own—well, they don't seem to get many opportunities. Still, an occasional writer must really be wise. She thinks so much like you! The news may depress you, and the comics may brighten your mood, but nothing has the potential to boil your blood or invigorate your intellect like the editorials.

Perhaps you've read the weepy words of someone who considers himself broad-minded. However, in your humble opinion, he's confusing a broad mind with a fat head. Have you noticed how easy it is to assert a conviction based on a few facts? Very few?

The Bible warns against misguided, impaired opinions and those who support them: "For the time will come when men will not put up with sound doctrine. Instead, to suit their own desires, they will gather around them a great number of teachers to say what their itching ears want to hear" (2 Timothy 4:3).

Both opinions and editorials make ears itch. Sometimes they make ears red too. God sets us straight with the words recorded in Timothy, and He's not just expressing His opinion. So many viewpoints run counter to God's teachings. Equally many spite His will. Then there are notions that seem benign but cover some sinful abscess. Among these inflammatory biases are the ideas that we control our own futures and that all lifestyles and behaviors are okay. Such ideas are wicked whispers in itching ears. Perhaps the most dangerous ideas, however, involve beliefs that sin doesn't exist or that somehow we can save ourselves by being good.

Who needs opinions when we have Jesus—the same Jesus that blots out our sins and sends His Holy Spirit to help us fight our evil, human inclinations? Who needs convictions to the contrary when we have forgiveness and salvation for free, having done nothing to earn it? Why deny sin's existence when we observe the glut of tragedy-making headlines or the pangs of our personal tragedies? We have a real God who loved us so much that He sent His Son to take the form of a man, one named Jesus, to suffer and die and defeat sin. For us. That's no opinion. These are facts boldly reported in the Bible. Isn't it great to agree with a real Expert?

Whatever

1 Corinthians 10:23–33

OUR COMPETITIVE WORLD of give and take is unbalanced. Too many people are on the take! Selfishness seems to go by various names. The extent of its facade of acceptability seems expressed by the deceptively casual word *whatever*. For example, it's Sunday morning and church bells are ringing. Howie stretches and yawns, thinking his alarm clock sounds awfully far away. His wife rolls over to face him and asks, "Are you golfing or going to church this morning?" He answers, "It's a little late for golf, so I guess I'll go to church." Mrs. Howie says, "Whatever." Then she buries her head in the pillow.

Paul had a "whatever" for the congregation in Corinth, though his was less blasé. In addressing the restrictions some felt necessary for Christians, he said, " 'Everything is permissible'—but not everything is beneficial. 'Everything is permissible'—but not everything is constructive. Nobody should seek his own good, but the good of others" (1 Corinthians 10:23–24).

Christians sometimes wonder what they can and cannot do. Paul proclaims freedom for Christians, but sometimes exercising that freedom might not seem right. Suppose you're invited to play pinnocle, er … peenockle, er … poker. You've played the penny ante variety with friends for years, but a newer friend, one who is a recent convert to Christianity, wonders aloud whether this is proper. What do you do?

A) *Figure out how to spell pinochle?*
B) *Ask your new friend to sit and watch?*
C) *Explain the difference between a friendly game and abject gambling?*
D) *Substitute pretzels, chips (poker or potato), etc. for pennies?*

Getting back to card games, should we even play cards or otherwise socialize with people who don't share the intensity of our values? Can I play cards with people who also deal cursing and dirty jokes?

Within the vast liberty Christians have for living a Christian life, restrictions—motivated by love and concern—sometimes supercede that freedom. We ask, "Will weaker Christians weaken more as they ponder my behavior? Will non-Christians lose respect for Christ because of my actions? How can I balance standing firm in my Christian convictions and maintaining friendships?"

Whatever your answers may be, don't let them be "Whatever!"

222

Popularity

1 John 4:1–6

A RE YOU POPULAR? (If the question depresses you, buy a dog. You'll be popular with at least one breathing being—no matter what you do.) The popularity people enjoy is usually in proportion to how they treat others. The most popular people may be those who treat people often!

As I'm writing this page, editors and anchorpersons have plunged us into tears covering the news of two deaths. Princess Diana was buried today, and Mother Teresa died yesterday. You don't need lengthy background introductions to either woman because both were extraordinarily popular. How fascinating that both women enjoyed reputations of compassion and kindness, though each lived an extremely different lifestyle! Both seemed loved for how they treated others.

As popular as both women were, they certainly weren't above criticism. Photographers ruthlessly hunted Princess Di, seeking to expose the chinks in her values. And Mother Teresa? Her most serious affairs— the ones that drew strongest exposure and criticism—occurred when she voiced her scriptural convictions. It was acceptable for her to mingle with lepers and the emotionally ill, but speak publicly against abortion? Now she was suspected of having a political agenda!

If you've ever wondered how people could accept the gracious gifts and miracles of Jesus and still be reluctant to believe that He was God's Son, think about Mother Teresa in more modern times. The needy loved her and shouted their praise, but many remained unbelievers—satisfied with what they could enjoy in this life. They accepted her earthly gifts and rejected her spiritual gifts.

John commented on this phenomenon too. He said, "We are from God, and whoever knows God listens to us; but whoever is not from God does not listen to us. This is how we recognize the Spirit of truth and the spirit of falsehood" (1 John 4:6).

Only Christians understand the motivation and lifestyle of other Christians. Only Christians find unlimited forgiveness of others sensible. Christians—the strongest variety—accept God's authority (even when they don't completely understand it). Only Christians do good deeds in God's name. Does this mean we curl up and hide in a secluded monastery? No! Get out there and do some good. Do it in the name of Jesus. Even if nobody's listening.

Escape Plan

1 Corinthians 10:11–13

WHEN YOU STAY IN A HOTEL, be sure to plan an escape route in case of fire, spiders, or leaky toilets. (Don't worry much about the latter two. I'm in that room.) Once, while staying in a sprawling motel complex, I diligently plotted an escape route that made two lefts and three rights and covered approximately 6.2 miles of hallway. Perplexed by the complexity of my emergency planning, I gazed out the large sliding door, bemused by all the foolishly unconcerned people gathered around the pool outside my room.

It takes a good escape plan to evade temptation. Temptations engulf us. We could be so much more sinful than we already are, and we could do it with nods or winks of approval. Falling to temptation doesn't have to be public either. Some sins are easy to hide, especially the ones we commit in our minds or behind locked doors and shaded windows. It's enough to make Christians cringe! "Will I fall?" Or more realistically, "How far will I fall?" Is there no way out—no escape plan?

Paul has an answer, one he originally shared with a congregation deluged by temptation: "No temptation has seized you except what is common to man. And God is faithful; He will not let you be tempted beyond what you can bear. But when you are tempted, He will also provide a way out so that you can stand up under it" (1 Corinthians 10:13).

God sends the Holy Spirit to fortify us with His Word. Through Scripture, God reveals how actual people, including Joseph and Daniel, successfully thwarted seduction and conquered fear for personal safety. Of course, their success met with some unpleasant moments on death row and in a lions' pit respectively. But God eventually turned those situations into incredible good.

When we think of temptation, we also think of biblical characters such as David and Peter. They fought to overcome temptation—except they didn't fight hard enough. So what moral can we learn from David's adulterous tryst with Bathsheba or Peter's sworn statements in the courtyard? We learn about Phase II—the alternate route of God's escape plan.

When we succumb to temptation, the only way out is through Jesus. When we can't or won't follow His leadership, then we can request and accept His forgiveness. That's the most wonderful part of God's escape plan. Even those trapped by sin have a sure way out.

224
Relief Pitcher

Joel 2:1–32

YOU KNOW WHAT A RELIEF PITCHER IS. It's someone brought in to replace a pitcher who's suffering whiplash from watching line drives whiz past him or who's been kicked out of the baseball players' union because he doesn't understand the word *strike*. Of course, "relief pitcher" may be familiar to nonbaseball fans too. For example, "It was so hot that Cleve drank all the lemonade, and we had to bring in a relief pitcher."

Relief pitchers in whatever form might remind us of what God said through the prophet Joel: "And afterward, I will pour out My Spirit on all people. Your sons and daughters will prophesy, your old men will dream dreams, your young men will see visions" (Joel 2:28).

God kept His promise on Pentecost when He poured the Holy Spirit into a small crowd of people. Peter, remembering the words of Joel, quoted them to the crowd. Indeed, it was a day of relief and refreshment!

With Jesus returned to heaven, the apostles needed relief if they were to obey God's mission command. It's not like they were baseball players. They weren't that wealthy. Besides that, they were good at what they were doing. But they needed a platoon of "relievers" to swell their ranks as they pitched the Gospel to thousands of eager ears. The Holy Spirit met their needs by empowering others not only to know God's Word, but to continue to spread that Word to others.

The Holy Spirit has worked in similar ways ever since Pentecost. How else could we read God's Word firsthand? How else could we learn at Bible class or grow through sermons? And the Spirit recruits us to pitch in relief also. Who needs to experience God's grace and mercy today? Who needs to know that Jesus cares for them?

The Spirit's pitcher of refreshment is less like baseball and more like lemonade. We sinners feel the heat of sin and the sweat of guilt. Satan parches our souls with his accusations, and we plaintively admit that he's right. But through the refreshing, rejuvenating, regenerating outpouring of the Holy Spirit, we believe that Jesus quenches our thirst for salvation. So go ahead, ask for another drink. The Relief Pitcher is ready and waiting.

225

Knock, Knock. Who's There?

2 John 1–13

HAVE YOU HEARD THE ONE about the grouch who finally gave in to "modern" times? He had a telephone installed. Now he uses modern technology to offend people. He's also the same guy who bought the grump's version of the welcome mat. It says, "Go away."

You probably wish you had a mat like that when those well-dressed people carrying briefcases, brochures, and books go door to door. Once in a while, young children accompany them. Normally, they present no threat to personal safety, but sometimes they're a quiet but spiritually lethal threat. What can we do about them?

A neighbor once suggested that I should welcome these door-to-door zealots into my home. Then, because I'm a church worker, I should set them straight. After all, aren't these people bound for hell unless somebody intervenes? After hearing my neighbor's plea, I acted according to my instincts. When the doorbell rang, I crouched behind the door and barked like a vicious dog. Because my imitation dog bark isn't too good, they quickly left, fearing attack by a deranged maniac.

Although it might sound as though cowardice got the better of me, have you ever refused to answer your door when you suspected the theological persuasions of those on the other side? Maybe, according to John, that's not a cowardly idea after all. John says, "Anyone who runs ahead and does not continue in the teaching of Christ does not have God; whoever continues in the teaching has both the Father and the Son. If anyone comes to you and does not bring this teaching, do not take him into your house or welcome him" (2 John 9–10).

Many door-to-door witnesses are well trained and prepared to answer challenges. They're also capable of questioning and debating your faith. Before you invite them in, find out whom they represent. It will be either Jesus or the devil, though they will never admit the latter because they have personally been deceived. Based on the words from John, our Savior wouldn't be disappointed if you refused to engage in spiritually oriented conversation with such people, especially if you fear the impact they may have on your faith life. You may be equally at risk if you're confident in your faith! These false teachers have reasonable, logical retorts to almost anything you throw at them.

Next time you hear the *knock knock* on your door, find out who's there. Sometimes it's no joke.

Toothless

Job 19:1–22

D ID YOU KNOW the Bible mentions teeth often enough to make some of us jealous? Consider this lover's compliment from Song of Songs 6:6, "Your teeth are like a flock of sheep coming up from the washing. Each has its twin, not one of them is alone." Can you imagine what might happen if you said that to the one you love? (A sweet nothing that tops this is the old "Your teeth are like stars. They come out at night.") Perhaps you're as relieved as I am that the romantic poet didn't peer into your mouth before writing this. If he had, he would have spotted some loners in the crowd.

While we're on the subject of teeth, Job coined a phrase that is still used today. He said, "I am nothing but skin and bones; I have escaped with only the skin of my teeth" (Job 19:20).

Have you ever opened wide in the bathroom mirror in an attempt to discover the skin of your teeth? I hope not. You have undoubtedly experienced the close calls or near escapes that the phrase suggests though.

If you've read Job 19, you've discovered that Job definitely sported an "attitude." He was angry with his friends and with God because of his suffering. He watched as his family and possessions were destroyed—and he had considerable amounts of both. He knew that he himself had escaped termination only by the skin of his teeth.

The "skin of the teeth" syndrome applies to us as well. We might use it to describe our flight from sin's eternal effect. We were lost and condemned. God could have ended the world at any moment, but He waited for us to become believers. He continues to wait, mercifully patient with those who will yet believe. He remains mysteriously silent on when time will end. Given God's concept of time—which is no time at all—believers from the past, present, and future will indeed escape His wrath by the skin of their teeth.

Jesus had no such delay from hellish suffering. He refused to escape death's pains and pangs, though to do so was within His power. Instead, He put some skin on our teeth and pushed us past the devastating destruction we deserve.

Next time you brush your teeth (or send them to the cleaners), thank God for saving you, even if some of the "twins" are absent.

Are You Talking to Me?

Obadiah 1–21

SOMETIMES THE BIBLE is as confusing as a jigsaw puzzle. Perhaps you're one of those patient souls who keeps a "puzzle in progress" on a card table in your living room, sliding and flipping anonymous pieces until they find a home. One old man was like that. It took him three years of retirement to finish one puzzle. Later, he learned that his wife had tossed pieces under his easy chair to keep him occupied and out of her hair.

If you've endeavored to read the Bible from cover to cover without aid from a study guide, you've probably asked God, "Are You talking to me?" One passage that might motivate such a question is Obadiah 17–18: " 'But on Mount Zion will be deliverance; it will be holy, and the house of Jacob will possess its inheritance. The house of Jacob will be a fire and the house of Joseph a flame; the house of Esau will be stubble, and they will set it on fire and consume it. There will be no survivors from the house of Esau.' The LORD has spoken."

Does it sometimes seem the Bible is not relevant to modern life? (You can answer that honestly, even if you don't have lightning rods on the house.) So much of God's Word is history that we're tempted to forget that we're history too. It's just that our history is happening now. But there must be some way to relate the entire Bible to our present life, otherwise why would God leave all those words for us? The answer lies in the fact that perhaps we shouldn't read the entire Bible—or at least not without guidance from trustworthy study guides to help edify us, especially as we traverse the tough, hard to understand places.

Today's selection from Obadiah is just one piece of the Bible. It has a place in God's Word just as a plain blue piece of cardboard fits somewhere in a puzzle. Without that piece the puzzle is incomplete. It's true of Scripture too: Every verse plays a role in the complete story of God's love for sinners and His hatred of sin.

As for the relevance of Obadiah 17–18, a reliable commentary interprets it thusly. Mount Zion was the location of Solomon's temple to God—the home of God on earth. Despite the ravages it suffered, God promised to send the inheritance—His Promised One—to live among the people and to save them. He would be right where they could see Him. And it's really no puzzle at all who that Promised One was.

CROSSwords Puzzle

1 Corinthians 1:18–25

L̲ET'S SEE. Do you know a nine-letter word for "frustration"? Here are some clues: (1) Funk and Wagnal. (2) Sharp pencils with erasers. BIG erasers. (3) Cross words muttered in the general direction of a newspaper page. If you've drawn nothing but empty squares, the title should help. (Sorry if I insulted your intelligence.)

Crossword puzzles have an obvious link with our faith. Jesus spoke seven times from the cross. These statements are often called the "Seven Words from the Cross," though they were actually phrases. Thank God for directing His Gospel writers to record what Jesus said because His words fill what otherwise would be blank spaces—or dark, clotted boxes—in a sinner's life. Yet there remain those who share the sentiments and understanding of many of the people who heard the words uttered on that small hill outside Jerusalem's city limits. For these particular spectators, Jesus' cross words puzzled or frustrated them.

Could the man (they thought in lowercase *M*s) on the middle cross hold the key to freedom and immortality as He gasped a desperate phrase about God forsaking Him? Why would someone presumably so powerful abandon His might to live at the beck and call of someone else? Why didn't this condemned criminal confess His fraud and ambition for the throne with His dying words? Instead, He called out, "It is finished!" Both skeptics and desperate hopefuls probably puzzled the same thoughts, each searching for words to describe their triumph or defeat. The words seemed so foolish, coming as they did from the self-proclaimed Son of God.

"For the message of the cross is foolishness to those who are perishing, but to us who are being saved it is the power of God" (1 Corinthians 1:18). Aha! What's a five-letter word for "power of God"? *Cross*. To those whose bible is the dictionary, the cross means only death. To us who define life by God's Word, the Bible, the cross means just the opposite.

Not that we should become smug about how well we do with cross words! Our understanding comes from faith, and faith comes as God's gift. That faith reveals a two-letter word for sinner. (It begins with an *M* and ends with an *E*.) That same two-letter word describes the object of Jesus' love and sacrifice.

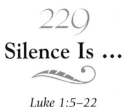

Silence Is ...

Luke 1:5–22

I'T'S OKAY IF YOU HAVE NOTHING TO SAY, just don't say it so others can hear. In fact, if a substitute for intelligence existed, silence would do just fine. Silence truly is what you said it was when you silently inserted a word for "..." in the title. Not that everyone would agree with silence's designation as a precious metal. Take Zechariah for example.

He was a priest who served part-time in the temple at Jerusalem. Like all priests, his duty occupied him only occasionally, though he most certainly was devout all the time. One thing bothered him. He and his wife of many years were childless—a dirty disgrace in ancient Jewish culture. Although he and his wife, Elizabeth, probably prayed often, their prayers seemed to have gone unheard.

When God finally answered the couple's prayer, it was more than Zechariah could handle. He sarcastically questioned the angel Gabriel. Armed with God's power, Gabriel gave a definitive response. He said, "And now you will be silent and not able to speak until the day this happens, because you did not believe my words, which will come true at their proper time" (Luke 1:20). Gabriel imposed harsh consequences for what seemed like logical doubt.

Except when it comes to God and His messengers, doubts are better left unexpressed—especially if they're coming from someone respected as a leader in faith. So it was for Zechariah a personal blessing that he was struck dumb. Now he couldn't question God's Word nor could he utter skepticism or even mild misgivings. Silence, as you probably know, provides plenty of time for listening and thinking.

It might be good if we were struck dumb on occasion. If your faith is active, people know that you're a Christian. Although you might not rank with professionals like Billy Graham or Zechariah or his famous son, people know you believe. They watch and listen too. If they hear you angrily curse your boss or computer or brakes or aching muscles, they wonder about you. They wonder about Christ. Then there may be times when they see how you ignore them when they're hurting. Failure to voice forgiveness—well, that's anything but golden silence.

Pray that God would silence all our doubts and give us golden words for golden opportunities.

No Apologies

2 Corinthians 7:8–13

IF YOU EVER FEEL LONELY and ignored, the fastest way to remedy the situation is to make a major mistake. To err used to be human, but now far too many people are blatantly human! Of course, the best thing about blunders is that we can learn from them. Some of us have a fantastic education! Then there are the others—those who invent creative ways to blame others.

The apostle Paul crammed the postal system with letters addressed to congregations that operated in mistake mode. One such congregation was at Corinth, and Paul minced no words. He called the mistakes of the believers by their proper nomenclature—sins. Paul also said: "Even if I caused you sorrow by my letter, I do not regret it. Though I did regret it—I see that my letter hurt you, but only for a little while" (2 Corinthians 7:8).

Now most of us might not be so bold, which probably is proven by personal experience. When is the last time (unless you're a parent of young children) that you exposed someone's mistakes? Better yet, have you recently called anyone's mistakes a sin? Or if you're in a position to evaluate others—on the job, in the home, behind the teacher's desk— have you found yourself apologetically (sometimes mistakenly called *tact*) exposing one's errors?

I'm not implying that we need to appoint ourselves Accuser General! We need only examine our own lives to observe thriving sin. Admittedly, we would bristle if our neighbor or spouse or sibling or pastor confronted us with the ugly truth, though, like Paul, they would assist us by doing so. If we're afraid or too pompous to identify our own sinfulness, we might just miss the best news of our lives.

Never fear hearing about your sinfulness. Don't feel offended if someone marks your mistakes. (Even if they feel good about it!) Thank them for bringing you to the cross where you can dump your sins. Pile them high. The cross is no longer occupied with gasping and flinching flesh. Jesus' work is done. He took away your sins, and He continues to forgive you.

In the end, when God finally brings you to judgment, you'll need no further apologies. Jesus has completely erased your mistakes—okay, your sins!

Relics

Luke 2:16–20

Y OU KNOW YOU'RE GETTING OLD if others refer to your sweater, your TV, your car, or even your body as a relic. It would be better to call you or your belongings an antique, at least they're valuable. But relics? Often the word and the idea behind the word are spoken with contempt.

At one time, the Christian church was infested with relics. Any church that possessed a bizarre collection of some saint's body parts gained power and influence, members and money. (Today, it probably would gain a coroner's inquiry!) Peter's petrified ear lobe or Thomas' teeth were sure to guarantee some special spiritual blessings (or at least the need to enlarge the congregation's safe). What wasn't funny, however, was that the church misled many believers to trust the "special powers" of worthless relics.

Relics remain today. How easy to venerate the crucifix without honoring the One who hung there. Or perhaps it's the architecture of our favorite church. Could worship really be worship without flying buttresses or arched beams? Maybe it's the liturgy in worship services—an orderly organization of elements sometimes elevated to the authority of Scripture itself. Or perhaps it's that crusty, fragile Bible stuck to the bookcase shelf, the one rarely touched by human hands.

We need no relics. We have Jesus Himself. While we might think of Him when we see crosses or Bibles or pulpits, our loss would be manageable if those were to disappear. We could do what the most famous mother in Nazareth did: "But Mary treasured up all these things and pondered them in her heart" (Luke 2:19).

Like Mary, most of what we ponder about Jesus is pleasant. The dramatic birth announcement, the stunned shepherds under the starry sky, a Baby's cry punctuating the moos and baas and brays. But Mary had piercing ponderings as well. We can only begin to imagine her feelings and thoughts when she heard hammers driving nails through flesh and wood. Then the flash of a sword—and sin—stabbing her Son's side.

The best pondering of all, however, is capturing the essence of Easter in our hearts. It is the greatest treasure ever pondered! We need no splinters of cross nor shreds of burial clothes to remember what was there. Nothing remained of this death because Jesus has risen and lives. For us, His resurrection makes Satan's victory a relic of the past.

Spending Spree

2 Corinthians 9:8–11

MONEY IS LIKE PARKING SPACES (within a half mile of the mall), salted peanuts (small bowl, unexpected company), and time for socializing with a favorite friend. Often, there just isn't enough to go around.

It seems the elusive quality of money affects most income brackets too. The poor can't get any, and the rich have trouble keeping it. Oh, well, as they say, "I'd rather have my health than wealth." Shhh. Don't let the IRS hear that. They might tax it!

What would you do first if you suddenly became vastly richer than you are now? Would your lifestyle change? With whom, if anyone, would you share your fortune? Are there any obligations you have as a Christian? (Oh, there's *that* question again.) Money is never a cure for what ails us—socially, emotionally, psychologically, or economically. But real wealth—that's another story.

Paul assesses our worth this way: "You will be made rich in every way so that you can be generous on every occasion, and through us your generosity will result in thanksgiving to God" (2 Corinthians 9:11).

Genuine God-given wealth is like easy money. It isn't earned; it's inherited. Wealth that comes from God needs no protection either. It's there for the taking and sharing. The "catch," of course, is that God's wealth doesn't always mean dollars—sometimes it's time or talent.

Have you assessed your wealth? Although the Bible downplays the value of wealth, money and possessions are gifts from God. The implications of financial prosperity are obvious. Some of that money will do lots of good for missionaries or hungry children or homeless adults.

Perhaps your greatest treasure is time or talent. Has God blessed you with retirement yet? Are you working at a job that doesn't make strenuous demands on your time? If so, count your blessings and begin sharing them with those who need your presence as opposed to, say, your presents.

Talents? You most certainly have some. Whether it's sewing, carpentry, telling stories, cutting grass, or solving problems, God rejoices when you use those skills to His glory and the welfare of others.

When it comes to giving, Jesus was the perfect example, though we cannot carry it to the extremes He did. He gave until it hurt. Because of that, our giving doesn't have to hurt a bit.

Outside In

Ephesians 1:3–10

OUTSIDE IN IS THE SAME as inside out when it comes to socks, sweatshirts, and underwear. The problem is especially serious with socks, though. While lots of people wear sweatshirts outside in (and those who slip their underwear on inside out keep their situation from public view), socks worn outside in usually get noticed.

You can wear socks the right way and no one will ever look at your feet. But the moment you wear one outside in, you find yourself the center of attention. It wouldn't be so bad if the inside was exactly like the outside. But take it from an expert, it isn't. As I sat waiting for an oil change, I crossed my legs and began twirling a string that was dangling from my ankle. Three people quickly averted their glances when I looked up. You can't tell me they didn't suspect that I had my socks on inside out! At least they weren't backward. So much for the hazards of dressing in the dark!

Outside in is not the same as inside out when it comes to God's grace, however. Inside out is fatal. We cannot rely on inner resources to obtain faith. We're utterly unable to will ourselves into eternal life. When it comes to saving ourselves, we're as desperately lost as a swimmer trying to cross the North Atlantic in a bikini. It just can't be done. God's grace isn't something we can produce from the inside. We can't even pick at the strings. It's all beyond us.

God's grace comes from the outside in, as Paul says in Ephesians 1:7–8: "In Him we have redemption through His blood, the forgiveness of sins, in accordance with the riches of God's grace that He lavished on us with all wisdom and understanding."

God alone gave us faith to believe in the otherwise unbelievable events of His Son's life, death, and resurrection. By His kindness alone, He sent Jesus to take away the sins of the world. (Since we live on the planet, that includes us.) He also sent His Holy Spirit to live in us, constantly reminding us that the cloak of salvation must be worn outside in. Doesn't God dress us well?

A Handful

Psalm 20:1–9

YOU'VE HEARD THIS EXPRESSION generally applied to a young, rather "active" child: "She's a handful!" Given the usual situation that prompts such a phrase, *handful* seems to be an understatement. A few olives or a medium tomato—now that's a handful, but trouble and bad behavior? Even a seven-foot tall basketball player lacks large enough palms to hold sin, evil, wickedness, and other varieties of imperfection at bay.

Scripture often talks about hands, especially God's. Now there's a set of capable hands! Here's how the psalmist portrays them: "Now I know that the LORD saves His anointed; He answers Him from His holy heaven with the saving power of His right hand." (Psalm 20:6). God doesn't even need two hands to keep evil in its place!

Any talk of hands leads us to the cross. Among the excruciating cruelties of Roman-style execution was the piercing of Jesus' hands. The same hands that wiped leprosy from infected limbs and tousled the hair of young children, the same hands that caressed the broken-hearted and beckoned dead bodies back to life, the same hands that endlessly broke bread and served fish were impaled to the cross. The sins of the world were indeed a handful—a bloody, throbbing handful. Those sins of the world included yours and mine, and Jesus had to die to save us.

The most common idea associated with God's hands, however, probably isn't the cross. His hand is a symbol of power. Even as they were nailed to the cross, Jesus' hands were hands of power. Jesus was doing something only God could do and live to tell about it. He was strangling sin's power while His equally pierced feet delivered that kick to the head of Satan promised back in the days of Adam and Eve.

Those powerful hands continue to gently stroke His people. Jesus holds out handfuls of mercy and kindness, sprinkling it generously on us, nudging us into the world each day to share His message and His love with others. We can almost see Him raise those hands in blessing, giving comfort and confidence as we live each day for Him. That applies to good times and bad—times when problems such as conflict, pain, anxiety, or fear are too big a handful for us.

The song is right. God does have the whole world in His hands. And that would be quite a handful for anyone but God.

Stop and Smell the Roses

Matthew 26:36–42

W AS IT SHAKESPEARE WHO SAID, "A rose by any other name means that you don't know your flowers very well"? He probably stole the line from his gardener. Roses are only one fragrant flower in God's bouquet of garden miracles. So important are flowers, that most states adopt one as their own. Even the Department of Transportation has an official flower—the cloverleaf!

People spend millions of dollars each year planting or purchasing flowers. From gas stations to corporate headquarters to concrete planters in the middle of urban boulevards, flowers brighten mundane life. We rejoice that early spring blooms promise the impending death of winter. Summer blossoms soothe our eyes and sweeten the air. Perhaps you've noticed, too, that shortly before the first frost, flowers mellow into their deepest and richest hues.

Gardens, especially one particular garden, meant something different to Jesus. It's something worth remembering, even as we enjoy botanic beauty. Matthew reports this incident involving Jesus in the Garden of Gethsemane: "Going a little farther, He fell with His face to the ground and prayed, 'My Father, if it is possible, may this cup be taken from Me. Yet not as I will, but as You will.' ... He went away a second time and prayed, 'My Father, if it is not possible for this cup to be taken away unless I drink it, may Your will be done' " (Matthew 26:39, 42).

This garden visit by Jesus didn't involve smelling roses. It involved sweating blood. It was as if a shawl of thorns entwined His entire being. Jesus prayed—for Himself, for us. He listened to God's answer as His friends snored in the garden's soon-to-be-shattered serenity. Jesus searched for some other way to take away our sins, perhaps something resembling a garden party to announce victory over sin. But it wasn't in the Father's plan, and Jesus obediently suffered and died for our sins.

Next time you're in a garden, take some time to pray. Oh, you and I are incapable of sweating blood (unless we kneel on a rose bush), and we need not limit our prayers to cries of anguish. Smell the roses, feast your eyes on the petunias, and spend some quality time with the impatiens. Remember how God sent them for your enjoyment, and recall Jesus' moment in the garden. Not the one named Gethsemane, but the one just outside the tomb.

Cheat Sheet

Isaiah 49:13–18

Hᴵɢʜ sᴄʜᴏᴏʟ stimulated four years of intellectual creativity among my friends. Most of that creativity involved obtaining a diploma with as little work as possible.

One friend had a fresh approach to preparing for tests. (Actually, it was a historically proven method, but he wasn't very good at history.) He identified several major math formulas that he then wrote on the palm of his hand. We lectured that such behavior was dishonest. When that didn't work, we warned him about getting caught. He disregarded our lectures and made it through the test with nary a suspicious glance from the teacher. He also failed the test. We had him so worried about getting caught that his palms sweated and the ink ran!

One of the last things we would suspect God of doing is cheating, though this passage might suggest otherwise: "See, I have engraved you on the palms of My hands; your walls are ever before Me" (Isaiah 49:16). While we know that God doesn't "cheat" to remember us, this passage does bring some graphic comfort into the lives of sinners.

The Bible mentions the Book of Life—that record of believers who will be judged righteous for Jesus' sake. In moments when we fail to appreciate the vast and comprehensive knowledge of our Lord, we may wonder how God keeps track of the millions of saints that will join Him in heaven. Will He find our names in the book? Will He remember us? Does He think about us now?

Intellectually, at least, we know that *yes* correctly answers each question. But can't you picture God peering into His hand, looking for your name? And finding it, of course!

Today's Bible passage comforted Isaiah's people as they gazed on the wrecked walls of Jerusalem, wondering if God had forgotten them and their holy city. God used picture language to reassure them that He doesn't forget and that they always will be on His "mind." That same consolation is ours as we gawk at the ruins of our lives, which are wracked by sin and Satan. Through Isaiah, God assures us that He remembers how Jesus repaired our broken relationship and that our names already appear on the roles of heaven. If you're afraid you might forget that Good News, draw a cross on the palm of your hand. Just don't do it in water-based ink!

Pardon Our Dust

Philippians 1:3–10

THE SIGN LOOKED FRIENDLY. What harm could a little dust do? After all, renovation and remodeling keep things up to date. Entering the dust zone, however, we encountered plastic sheets draped from ceiling to floor and heard the din of drills and saws rattling against concrete and wood. Our noses were the first to recognize dust. Our eyes noticed it next, releasing a few tears to float away the grit. We felt it on our hands, too, compelling us to wash them at the nearest sink. This was only the first of 16 more projects scheduled. You know, it's bad enough to visit the hospital, but to pardon their dust? Well …

In a way, the Father, Son, and Holy Spirit Construction Company could hang a "Pardon Our Dust" sign around the necks of all believers. Can you imagine the puff of dust as God took clay from the ground and breathed life into it? Just as babies cry as they are born, Adam probably sneezed. God said, "I bless you," and He did. He's been blessing humans ever since. But Adam and Eve led the fall into sin, thus necessitating constant renovation projects by the original Company.

God had a plan to remodel us, and Jesus was the only one who could implement it. He was born with a dual identity—God and Man—and He grew up learning the carpentry trade. (How appropriate for the one who renovates our life!) He lived as sinners should have but couldn't or wouldn't, and He died to take away our sins. But Jesus came back to life, defeating death and the devil. In the process, He ripped the wall of sin from our lives. Then He sent the Holy Spirit to finish the job.

The Holy Spirit began remaking us. He gave us faith, but He also realized that His work wouldn't end until Jesus returned. The Holy Spirit continues to work, urging us to repent so He can continue perfecting us. He braces us with God's Word so we stand strong against the devil. He polishes us with grace so we have a beautiful luster for the day Jesus returns.

Pardon our dust? Jesus did already. Pardon our dust? There remains much work as the Spirit labors within us. Will the job ever end? Listen to Paul: "Being confident of this, that He who began a good work in you will carry it on to completion until the day of Christ Jesus (Philippians 1:6).

All Natural

Luke 7:11–16

THE MODERN CRAZE for all-natural foods is noteworthy. The foods are nutritious, tasty (???), make you appear health-conscious and fit, and rarely result in any leftovers. That's because it all-natural foods spoil so fast. Natural foods take advantage of God's miracle of nature and all that He intended it to be. Natural foods are also a miracle of modern marketing. It's surprising that anybody buys the stuff with our perverse inclination toward salt, sugar, preservatives—and flavor.

God long has used nature to carry out His miracles. In Old Testament days there were burning bushes, thunder and lightning, fire and water. God often used miracles against His enemies. In New Testament times, Jesus did many miracles, all for the good of His people, which sometimes included enemies. Thus, we see natural water supernaturally transformed into natural wine. We see natural diseases—even death—healed so people could once again live a natural life.

That Jesus healed death is a gracious gift, but it should be no surprise. Along with a large crowd of mourners in the town of Nain, we witness Jesus at work. He met a slow funeral plodding its way to the cemetery. Jesus shared the grief, especially of the widow whose only child was about to be buried. Nature had taken its course in its sinful, tragic way and spoiled the life of a beloved son. But Jesus reversed nature. He commanded the son to arise. Nature yielded, and the young man returned to his mother.

The natural consequences of sin are illness, injury, and death. However, the God who created life and all of nature had power to overcome death. He came to earth as the Man who healed at Nain, and He hung on Calvary's cross as the true Man and true God who suffered, died, and rose to save sinners. How unnatural! And how we might yearn to see a Nain event with our own eyes. Or at least some miracle!

We're tempted to forget that miracles still happen. But considering that God still uses some natural means to accomplish His will, maybe those miracles are now so natural that we fail to notice them? Isn't the birth of a baby still a miracle? Isn't the food we eat, grown from seed, nurtured on sunlight and soil, and able to fuel our bodies still a miracle? Isn't it a miracle that Jesus continues to forgive us despite the suffering we cause? Maybe we should label modern miracles "All Natural!" Natural for a God who loves us in a miraculous way.

Something of Which to Be Proud

Galatians 6:1–10

IF GOD HAD INTENDED for us to pat ourselves on the back, He would have made our elbows bend the other way. Experts advise us to swallow our pride. It's probably healthy advice. Pride is never fattening—unless it goes to our head. We all know—and probably dislike—proud people.

Is it ever proper to be proud? Most philosophers probably would cite statements such as "Pride goeth before the fall" (see Proverbs 16:18) or the once-famous lyrics, "You're so vain, you probably think this song is about you." (If you're well beyond or well under your 50s, you probably won't remember the song, but take my word, those were the lyrics. If I had a better memory, I would remember who sang it!)

Back to the question at hand. Is it ever proper to be proud? Paul, in his letter to the Galatians, said, "Each one should test his own actions. Then he can take pride in himself without comparing himself to somebody else" (Galatians 6:4).

Did Paul really mean you can "be proud of your own accomplishments"? According to this inspired word that came from God through Paul, we can be proud—if our pride doesn't fool us into thinking we're better than others. Paul's "pride" comes from knowing that the Holy Spirit has empowered us to follow God's will and to live a Christian lifestyle.

Most often, pride manifests itself in sinful attitudes of arrogance or exclusiveness. It happens when we forget how sinful we are and how everything truly good about us is good only because Jesus made it that way. It's an especially easy sin for Christians as we get caught up in living according to God's will and absentmindedly give ourselves credit. It happens when we compare ourselves to other sinners and end up feeling good that we're not so bad after all. Good thing this sin, too, is one Jesus readily forgives. Over and over.

Take pride in the truth that God chose to save you for no good reason long before you had any ancestors or tradition of family faith. Be proud that the Holy Spirit works in and through you, though you certainly don't deserve it. Be proud to boast that Jesus died to take away your sin. Let others know they can boast in the same thing because they are just like you.

240

Cookie Crumbs

John 14:25–31

OFTEN WE KNOW exactly what we will leave behind when we go. Property, investments, and cash end up in the pockets of relatives and friends—with a little on the side for the government, of course. There's all the forgotten incidentals too—memorabilia residing in basements and attics that is destined for yet another basement or attic because relatives can't bear to part with it. Besides what we can count and see and lift and dust and toss, there remains even more to leave behind—experiences take up as much space as sentiment allows.

We don't have to die to leave things behind, however. Take cookie crumbs, for example. That's a legacy I leave to the cleaning rag every day after breakfast. Feelings count too. What do we leave behind as we interact with family, friends, acquaintances, and even strangers on a daily basis?

Jesus left some things behind too. John 14:27 quotes Jesus as saying, "Peace I leave with you; My peace I give you. I do not give to you as the world gives. Do not let your hearts be troubled and do not be afraid." Jesus didn't leave any crumbs. He left the whole cookie! Now we enjoy what He left behind.

Don't be deceived. The peace Jesus left isn't the kind discussed at the United Nations. It's not the peace that is shattered nightly in both random and premeditated acts of violence. In fact, it has little to do with external conditions. True peace is a matter of attitude—a condition of trust and contentment that is rooted in God's love for us. This peace exists despite war, domestic bloodshed, climatic terrors, chaotic health, or family feuds. It's a peace that is incomprehensible to all who don't have it.

You and I have the peace Jesus left behind. We know where we've been, and admittedly, we've been some terrible places. We also know where we're going, and we're going there because Jesus sacrificed the peace that was at His command to die a most unpeaceful death on Calvary. It's the peace we have because we know that Jesus waits for us to arrive in a place where tranquility and ecstasy coexist.

Next time you leave behind some crumbs, remember what Jesus left for us. Thank Him for not only remembering you in His will but for making you a living part of it.

Geography Lessons

2 Kings 3:1–19

THIS BEGINS A SERIES of three meditations based on geography. Was it one of your favorite subjects in school? Many students like the subject, probably because it's easy to relate to the main ideas. Most of us have seen geographical features such as mountains, hills, valleys, rivers, lakes, and Uncle Egbert's nose. Like any subject, of course, geography includes many advanced concepts and a specialized vocabulary—such as "diurnal variations," which is easily confused with plumbing terminology.

Valleys are something everybody understands. We've heard of places such as the Hudson River Valley, the Red River Valley, and Rudy Vallee. Valleys are normally fertile places, lower and more temperate than the landforms surrounding them. Exceptions, of course, are places such as Death Valley.

The Bible mentions many valleys. Some of them are more image than reality as in the "Valley of the Shadow of Death" mentioned in Psalm 23. Doesn't this sound like a pleasant place? "For this is what the LORD says: You will see neither wind nor rain, yet this valley will be filled with water, and you, your cattle and your other animals will drink" (2 Kings 3:17). Here's a valley that sounds as though it should be named "Jesus' Valley."

Jesus' Valley is located around every Christian. In actuality, it's more an oasis than a valley. The valley's climate is refreshing, soothing, and nourishing. It stands in stark contrast to the areas outside its boundaries—places where sin has parched all life and decay spreads rampantly.

Sin's blight exists within the valley too, but Christians seem inoculated against its deadly effect. They get sick from it, but they always recover. That's because Jesus' Valley is filled with healing. We know this healing by names familiar to Christians everywhere—grace, mercy, forgiveness, peace, and love.

Life in Jesus' Valley is pleasant, but like valley dwellers everywhere, we need to work too. As we labor for the valley's namesake, we find ourselves spreading the same healing that has so affected us. Grant grace, mete out mercy, frequently forgive, practice peace, and lavish lots of love on those you meet today. Invite them to live in Jesus' Valley with you.

Head for the Hills

Psalm 121:1–8; Song of Songs 2:8

HILLS ARE STUBBY MOUNTAINS. They are easy to climb, but clumsy people are inclined to roll down them as opposed to plummeting off them. Hills may be defined as anything higher than the surrounding terrain. Therefore, my city-dwelling friends and I once belly-flopped our sleds down the hill on Lloyd Avenue. The "hill" was a mound of sooty soil, elevation approximately six feet above the vacant lot it bordered.

David (the king) didn't live on Lloyd Avenue, so when he envisioned hills, he probably had something more impressive in mind. Here's one of his "hill" psalms: "A song of ascents. I lift up my eyes to the hills—where does my help come from? My help comes from the LORD, the Maker of heaven and earth" (Psalm 121:1–2).

David's son Solomon reports on the hills, too, as he repeats the words of a young bride in Song of Songs 2:8. "Listen! My lover! Look! Here he comes, leaping across the mountains, bounding over the hills." David's help and the bride's lover are the same: our Savior, Jesus Christ.

Two basic human needs are love and help. We find both in human counterparts, but they never equal the help and love we receive from Jesus. Only in Him can we find both the quality and the quantity of help and love that sinners need.

Human love, powerful and warm as it is, sometimes wears thin. Our own sinful nature, as well as the sinful natures of those who love us, create defects in love. Sometimes the defect is so deep that love stops completely or it becomes so weak that we're unsure it even exists. When it comes to human help, we're equally limited. We can help in many ways, but often we establish conditions for giving help or are too proud to take it. Then there are those times when no earthly help can help.

How good to know that invincible help and limitless love are available in Jesus! When we're down, suffering in body, soul, or psyche, we can look beyond our problems—even above the hills to heaven itself.

Look for a hill today—even a diminutive one—and remember God's love and help. By the way, isn't it great to know that even if you're over the hill, He is too?

Go with the Flow

Psalm 46:1–7

Our last lesson in geography is about rivers. (Too bad the course wasn't this short when we were in school.) Nearly every great city has blossomed by a river. Early man—and woman too—discovered that rivers offered advantages that improved the quality of life. Rivers made food and transportation readily available. They offered a primitive form of plumbing. Then there was the music—the strains of "Old Man River" wafting above the waves as the showboat passed by—though I don't believe geography books cover that particular aspect. However, life along a river wasn't always idyllic. Floods often obliterated the idylls into a viscous goo of silt and mud.

History has recorded many disastrous floods. Yet cities along rivers still make good places to live. Scripture focuses on that asset as it compares God's care for us to a river at its best behavior. "There is a river whose streams make glad the city of God, the holy place where the Most High dwells" (Psalm 46:4).

The river "flowing through the city of our God" has no history of flooding. Even without dikes, levees, or the Corps of Engineers, it won't flood in the future either. This river is purely beneficial because joy flows along with its currents. Can you imagine bathing in it? How cool and cleansing the water feels as it flushes away our sin and suffering! It's no wonder that John and the disciples took people into a river for Baptism. In this act of washing sins away, believers were free to go with the flow—the flow of the Holy Spirit as He guided them toward God-pleasing words and deeds.

Then there's transportation on God's river of joy. God's river leads us to His city. Not that river travel is completely safe. Yes, there are rapids where the devil tries to sweep us away, shoals where he tries to bash us, and sandbars where he attempts to ground us. Nonetheless, we travel the river in happiness, trusting God to bring us to Himself in His city.

Picture yourself cruising down the river of God. You're sprawled on a lounge chair in the warm sun. A soft breeze coddles you into incredible contentment. A good place to read, isn't it? How about a good book? How about a really Good Book? Just open the pages, and go with the flow.

Get Up and Go

Mark 10:46–52

Have you heard the old line uttered by a tired old man: "My get up and go got up and went"? It's a funny line unless it's your reality! Most people admit to this human twist on the much feared personal energy crisis.

Consider the blind man in today's Bible reading. Bartimaeus was tired of being blind. You might imagine how blindness saps your energy as you summon all other senses to do what sighted persons do so easily. Though Bartimaeus was blind, he had vision enough to recognize Jesus as his healer. He saw what others couldn't see, as we hear from Jesus. " 'Go,' said Jesus, 'your faith has healed you.' Immediately he received his sight and followed Jesus along the road" (Mark 10:52). Indeed, Bartimaeus had a new infusion of "get up and go," undoubtedly praising God as he took in all the sights.

We all suffer an energy crisis, and it's not just on Monday mornings either. Sin saps our strength. Perhaps you remember how a guilty conscience kept you awake nights or how anger disrupted any attempts to relax. Maybe bitterness over past events haunts you, persistently nagging you with unsettling aggravation. Then there's all that energy we waste jumping to conclusions and raising the roof or forging chains of credible lies with which to deceive others. Even feeling sorry for ourselves or imprisoning silent anxiety robs us of energy.

Vitamins offer no help. Health food provides only useless calories. Exercise won't get us back in shape either. Only one way exists to revitalize the spiritually de-energized, and that is faith.

Faith doesn't come by our own striving, so even those suffering the greatest spiritual energy crisis need not worry about "more to do." The Holy Spirit infuses faith into our weak and worn soul. Through His holy energy we see our Savior and believe that He took away our sins. Jesus announces to us the same proclamation He delivered to Bartimaeus so many years ago: "Get up and go. Your faith has healed you—healed you from sin and it's stubborn and dastardly side effects."

So now what? Get up and go where? Where else but along the trail that Jesus walked. Because He healed us from sin, we're free to enjoy the sights of salvation, even as we sometimes stumble along His path. We'll see even better sights someday—angels, saints, Jesus Himself.

What Do You Think?

Matthew 22:34–46

THOUGHTS AREN'T EXACTLY STAPLES OF LIFE. You can live long—an entire lifetime probably—without having an original one. That's probably safer than responding to someone who says, "A penny for your thoughts" and having everyone agree that the investment was worthwhile. Then we find those who persist in offering us food for thought—only it's the diet variety. Me? I get lost in thoughts. Of course, some would suggest it's because I'm operating in foreign territory!

You probably have many thoughts. When you think about it (ugh), it's far easier to be thoughtless than it is to be thought less. Most of us perk up when someone interrupts the conversation with the question, "What do you think?"

Sometimes it's advisable to keep our thoughts to ourselves. If we fail to resist that wisdom, our mouths are usually open long and wide enough to slip in a shoe. But if someone really summons our thoughts, well … why not?

Jesus used the question. Here's one example from Matthew 22:42: " 'What do you think about the Christ? Whose son is He?' 'The son of David,' they replied." Jesus wasn't questioning a friendly crowd here. These were smart-alecks, know-it-alls (no-it-alls too), and other assorted skeptics and rabble. His question successfully confounded them, discouraging them from engaging in further snide and ill-motivated discourse.

How would you answer Jesus' question? Surely you and I would identify Him as God's Son, our Savior. The Holy Spirit placed faith in our hearts that tells us the right answers to such questions, even if we're unsure of other answers. So much of God's Word is difficult to understand. Even with a pile of commentaries, we might find that "experts" disagree on the meaning of certain passages. If Jesus dropped by and asked, "What do you think …?" what would you think?

So much mercy and grace and kindness comes to us! The truth is that even if thoughts fail on certain issues or questions, we always have the answer to Jesus' most important question. It's the answer that identifies us as Spirit-filled, faithful people who know where to take our sins and what to do with them. We know the one answer that yields an eternal 100 percent. We know Jesus as our Savior. That's the thought that counts!

Thanks for Sharing That

Acts 2:22–32

ITS INTENT DIFFERS depending on the circumstances. "Thanks for sharing that" sounds grateful when responding to a tip from a stockbroker. It's less than gratifying, however, when you mutter it to the state trooper who says, "Do you know you were doing 85 in a 45 m.p.h. construction zone?" Christians probably identify similar duplicity when they consider the phrase.

Which tone of voice would you expect in response to Peter's passage from Acts 2:23? "This man was handed over to you by God's set purpose and foreknowledge; and you, with the help of wicked men, put Him to death by nailing Him to the cross."

Wouldn't we much rather hear that Jesus paved our way to heaven? Yet we need to hear precisely what Peter said to the crowd—and to us. We are responsible for Jesus' suffering and death. Our sins, along with the sins of all people, caused the death of the Son of God.

Martin Luther once suggested that Jesus was the greatest sinner of all times as He hung on the cross. Before the devil enjoys that one too much, Luther was referring to the load Jesus bore as He paid for each trespass with His own holy life and blood.

Civilized people live with regret and remorse for years if they happen to be responsible for another's death. That's exactly where we stand as we ponder the cross and what it represents. Surely you're thankful I shared that!

Jesus was great at sharing. Remember how He shared a few groceries with thousands through His miraculous power? He shared His power, too, as He sent disciples out to perform miracles of healing. But when it came to our sins, He kept them all for Himself. We couldn't begin to share the guilt because it would drive us from God's presence and send us to hell. Jesus knew where sharing had to end.

Praise God for sending Jesus to forgive our sins and to restore our relationship with Him. Praising God means more than keeping the Good News to ourselves. It means that we forgive others. Praising God also implies that we tell others why we forgive. Others may not welcome the story of Jesus in your life and theirs, but by the power of the Holy Spirit working through the Good News you share, someday they'll thank you for sharing.

Smile?

James 4:1–10

Smiles are highly overrated if you ask me. Of course, you didn't. Ask me, that is. But I'll tell you why they're overrated, even at the cost of my innermost psyche. A now defunct airline characterized their service by painting smiley faces on the front of their aircraft. Seeing that friendly sight, I was anticipating a pleasant flight. Then a security agent shook me from my reverie. He mentioned something about fitting a hijacker's profile—a one-way ticket, no luggage, and a nervous smile (mine, not the aircraft's). Smiley faces have left me unimpressed and even a bit hostile ever since.

Scripture isn't too keen on smiles either, especially in light of this verse: "Grieve, mourn and wail. Change your laughter to mourning and your joy to gloom" (James 4:9).

Can you imagine what business would have been like for that airline had it painted frowny faces on the jets? It would have left the business sooner than it did! Is it good for Christian "business" to publish verses such as the one above?

Grief must precede joy in Christian life. In more worldly ways, it's the other way around, isn't it? Laughter usually degenerates into tears. Not so for Christians. The sadness and gloom that James encourages originate with how we feel about our sinfulness. It's like James is saying, "Hey! Don't enjoy your sins. Any pleasure you experience is short-lived." It's sort of like the laughter you hear seeping from the local bar. It's often followed by staggering steps, loud words, false bravado, sick stomachs, and throbbing heads.

Sin is like that. James says Christians need to treat sin like the serious matter it is. Repentance involves sorrow—the mourning type—plus a sincere desire to refrain from such sin again. After that believers can smile again, knowing that God forgives them for Jesus' sake.

Are you smiling now? It's okay—go ahead. When you realize how sinful you are, you also realize how forgiven you are. Your smiles can go a long way too—farther than a flight on a failed airline. Send your smiles to those around you—your family, coworkers, antagonists, security agents—all those who need a sunny, or should we say Sonny, smile to brighten their lives. But never smile back at an airplane, even if it smiles first.

News Flash

Psalm 113:1–9

IT'S BEEN AWHILE since any news earned its way into this book, but here's an item on an event that could be hailed as socially redeeming—if we return to the Stone Age. A veterinary scientist, digging in frozen Siberian soil, found the frozen sperm of a woolly mammoth. He wants to extract the DNA and inject it into elephants in hopes of producing woolly mammoths again.

Can you imagine what his mother thinks of his pursuits? "You found *what*, digging *where*? Go to your room immediately and throw out all those filthy science books. Get rid of that shovel too!"

Stories like this prompt us to think about the future (unless you're fixated on the private lives of woolly mammoths). One hundred, one thousand, five thousand years from now, will anyone remember us even as much as some nameless furry beast? Will they discover something about us (or our pets)? What will they conclude about life in the 21st century? Will their mothers be upset about their discoveries?

It might be well that no one "discovers" us in the future. What they are likely to find is a record of sin—greed, depravity, immorality, violence, and other news headlines. They'll have an expert guide to help them identify their discoveries. The devil will still be around, pointing out our sins to everybody in the hopes that God will notice. But God won't listen, and we're assured of that in Psalm 113:7: "He raises the poor from the dust and lifts the needy from the ash heap."

We sinners are poor and needy. One thing on which both the Bible and science agree is that, barring any morbid breakthroughs in mortuary science, we'll return to the ground someday. Perhaps some traces of DNA will remain, but even if that doesn't happen, God will "discover" us. Because Jesus rose from the dead, we will too. While our souls will already be in heaven, our bodies, long turned to dust, will rise perfect in every way to join our souls. We'll live that way forever.

Unlike those woolly mammoths of ancient times, we have something to look forward to. While we may not actually rejoice in our own inevitable passing, we never need worry about extinction. So look forward to that day when Jesus returns to summon us from the grave and take us to live with Him. There's an activity that will surely make His Father happy.

249

Excuses

Deuteronomy 29:22–29

SOME THINGS I JUST DON'T UNDERSTAND. How about you? Take bowling for example. Perhaps it's a reflection of my limited mathematical skills, but I just don't understand the scoring. Would the game have languished so much if bowlers simply counted the number of pins knocked down in 10 frames? A perfect game would be 100—much more sensible than the 300 score now required. Bowlers, of course, don't understand the beauty of this simplicity. In addition, bowlers seem to have a complete inventory of excuses for missed chances—everything from oily lanes to smoke so thick as to limit visibility on the approach. As for me, I know enough to cheer at strikes or moan at gutter balls. Do I need any excuses? Okay, for me, 100 really is a perfect game!

Many people shun or abandon what they don't comprehend. God's Word provides an example. Much of it defies understanding; therefore, dodging it seems appealing and logical. "Why read what you can't fathom?" becomes an excuse. How do you respond?

A good way to respond is to remember Deuteronomy 29:29, which says, "The secret things belong to the LORD our God, but the things revealed belong to us and to our children forever, that we may follow all the words of this law."

In other words, God has secrets that He prefers to keep. That's His business, and we can be certain He has reasons for such secrecy—not that we would understand those reasons anyway. But God revealed all that we need to know. He gave us His Son, Jesus Christ, and the Holy Spirit, who helps us recognize Jesus as our Savior.

Perhaps you know people who avoid God because they don't understand His system of keeping score. After all, "What's fair is fair. The Bible itself points out how good Jesus was to disreputable sinners and how critical He was of good church people."

The deceptive problem, however, was that the good church people only thought they were good whereas sinners seemed to recognize how miserable they made their lives and the lives of others. Sinners were sorry and wanted to change. If that reminds us of us, that's good because the Holy Spirit has worked faith and repentance in us. We know Jesus took away our sins and gave us a new life to enjoy. As for keeping score? God doesn't, so why should we?

250

Excuses

2 Peter 2:1–10

WHO SAYS LOVE IS ELUSIVE? Even if you can't get someone else to love you, you probably can do it yourself! Love is an infinitely popular topic, and it's one of the most basic and pervasive human needs. The Bible says that love is the very essence of God. Scripture urges us to love our enemies and to love our neighbors. (They're probably the same people!)

What do you know about God's love? Undoubtedly, you've experienced it often—probably more often than you realize. Like human love, however, God's abundant love can be misunderstood. Some people think that if God is as abundantly good as we claim, He would never punish anyone in hell. Everyone will go to heaven regardless of whether or not they believe in Him. People who believe this are sincere and open-minded but sadly ignorant or misguided.

God's Word says, "For if God did not spare angels when they sinned, but sent them to hell, putting them into gloomy dungeons to be held for judgment ..." (2 Peter 2:4). The message is quite clear. It seems to paint God's picture in a different light—apparently less loving than faithful believers allege and perhaps even deceptively sinister.

We need not despair though. God truly loved us so much that He sent His Son, who took human form, lived a sinless life, suffered a ghastly death, and returned to a glorious everlasting life so sinners like us—the ones who deserve to join those wicked angels of 2 Peter—might live forever in the glow of His love. God doesn't want a single drop of His Son's blood to be wasted. He wants it used on every person. So what's the difference between those angels and us—between believers and unbelievers or the defiantly depraved who stubbornly follow their own delusions?

Faith is the difference. Evil beings, whether angels or humans, lack the Holy Spirit's work within them, which convinces them not only to believe in a real, loving God, but also to take advantage of His love through repentance and forgiveness. Faith changes life. It drives us to seek God's will, worship Him, and to love Him by loving others. God's love even includes persistent reconciliation. Even better, we can be confident that God's love story won't have a happy ending because *ending* isn't in His vocabulary.

And More Excuses

Psalm 116:1–19

INFLATION IS RESPONSIBLE for many modern woes. You know what inflation is. It's where prices balloon to the bursting point, except they never explode themselves out of existence. Although we may complain about suffering from inflation, we're usually part of the problem—like when we are stranded in the traffic jam that we're part of. Inflation is so bad that if you ask someone to "put in their two cents," it will cost seven dollars. A person could go broke just trying to stay even!

One characteristic of inflation is a proliferation of excuse-making. Commerce excuses higher prices because production and personnel costs increase. Workers excuse demands for higher wages because products cost so much. A vicious circle, isn't it? But something even more vicious exists. It's sometimes used as an excuse for denying the offer of salvation. Psalm 116:12 says it all: "How can I repay the LORD for all His goodness to me?"

The psalmist probably had no intention of attempting a payment plan for God's goodness. It was one of those questions uttered in a mood of gratitude for the incredible and unfathomable love of God. Yet some people mistakenly reason that they must make restitution for their personal drain on God's blessings—including the blessing of eternal life. Perhaps you've even thought about it yourself. "God has given me everything. Now I must repay Him, so I'll go to church every week (maybe I should attend both Sunday services!). I'll also give a little extra to missions, and I'll take my neighbor to church (even if she doesn't want to go!)."

You probably see the error of this thinking. No matter what the sacrifice, our sins have inflated the price of salvation beyond reach. In a moment of weakness, we may want to give up—to make excuses for weak or decaying faith—by saying or feeling that we have nothing to contribute to our salvation. That's when we confess that we're bankrupt and file for protection under the Law.

Jesus gives that protection. He paid what we couldn't afford, buying us a home not only in a good neighborhood but a mansion besides. Inflation doesn't bother Jesus. He's loaded. Loaded with grace and mercy and forgiveness and love and compassion and kindness and goodness and … Well, let's just say that when it comes to blessings, Jesus practices inflation!

Delayed

Deuteronomy 1:1–46

A IRLINES ARE GOOD with terse messages—words that "say it all" and fit in the short space flashed on the arrival/departure screens. *Delayed* is one of those words. Seasoned travelers usually suspect that word because it's often the precursor of another curt communiqué: *Canceled.* This can be especially annoying because air travel is expensive. One might even say that the cost of flying has reached new heights. Then again, flying is probably better than the alternative for long trips. At least in the air you pass bad drivers at a safe distance!

Air journeys will never get as bad as foot travel was in Moses' times. *Delayed* would have been a gross understatement, considering Deuteronomy 1:2: "It takes eleven days to go from Horeb to Kadesh Barnea by the Mount Seir road."

In itself, an 11-day trip would be long by modern standards, but this 11-day trek turned into a 40-year expedition. What took so long? It wasn't bad weather, bomb scares, over-booking, or heavy traffic. The problem was the travelers themselves. They were unruly, rebellious, and untrusting. Besides that, they seemed easily sidetracked and quarrelsome. In other words, they were a lot like us.

We're on our way to a destination where no airline goes. Like the Israelites of Moses' day, we're headed to the Promised Land. While God doesn't encourage us to hurry or hasten the trip by our own means, He has provided everything necessary to make the excursion seem short. Yet we sinners usually make the trip seem exhausting and slow as we give in to all sorts of temptations that lead us to sin. Even if we live a pretty good life, it's neither pretty nor good nor does it elude our suffering from sin in general. Yet there's a way to make travel time seem to fly.

Trust God. Easy to say; sometimes difficult to do. Perfect trust in God would result in anxiety-free life. Can you imagine how enjoyable life would be if we were 100 percent worry free? Can you imagine the joy in a life where every burden would be carried by Someone else? The possibility exists, though a bit beyond the limits of our faith. But don't let that stop you. Pray for more. Faith that is. It'll seem like no time at all until time flies faster than the speed of life.

Bones of Contention

Psalm 42:1–11

HOW DO YOU APPROACH LIFE? Would you characterize yourself as coura-geous or cowardly? Do you bravely hope for the future or dread it? The only hope some people have is hope of avoiding the worst! Sometimes courage to face the future is a matter of body language—knees down and eyes up. Mostly, however, we demonstrate a curious mix of courage and cowardice. How easy it is to boldly stand for some-thing noble and weakly fall for temptations in the opposite direction.

The tension between boldness and timidity are bones of con-tention. We might think of this struggle the next time we observe what's left after a hungry family devours the holiday turkey. What remains is the wishbone and the backbone.

I don't know about you, but I haven't had good experiences with wishbones. In fact, I rarely wished for anything but to crack the bone just right. Even then I often didn't get my wish.

Wishing is futile, especially if we count on it for anything more important than contests inspired by dead turkeys. How much time do people lose wishing they were richer or better looking? How many wish they had a better job, were younger, were older, were smarter, or were closer to retirement? Who doesn't wish they had avoided something in the past? Sometimes we even wish that God was more faithful, espe-cially if life is going badly.

The words of Psalm 42:10–11 give some flesh to the dilemma. "My bones suffer mortal agony as my foes taunt me, saying to me all day long, 'Where is your God?' Why are you downcast, O my soul? Why so disturbed within me? Put your hope in God, for I will yet praise Him, my Savior and my God."

We can replace the wishbone with backbone. Today's psalm explains how that's done. Hope in God differs as much from wishing random wishes as wishbones differ from backbones. We're always win-ners with God, even when we wait to see our hopes materialize. Our future doesn't depend on haphazard circumstances such as cracking a bone just right. We look forward with strong backbones because God Himself is that Bone, holding us up, giving us support, and protecting us. What a good thing to remember the next time we have a bone to pick—with the devil!

Set Up

Philemon 1–25

DON'T LET TODAY'S BIBLE READING INTIMIDATE YOU. The entire book is only 25 verses. Of course, nobody says you have to read the whole thing just because it's the right thing to do, if you know what I mean. If you don't know, the next paragraph will clear it up.

"Therefore, although in Christ I could be bold and order you to do what you ought to do, yet I appeal to you on the basis of love. I then, as Paul—an old man and now also a prisoner of Christ Jesus" (Philemon 8–9). Just what did Paul ask of Philemon? He wanted Philemon to welcome back Onesimus, Philemon's runaway slave.

Paul didn't require Philemon to accept Onesimus without consequences, but when you read the entire account, you get the idea that Philemon's options were somewhat limited. In a way, Paul "set up" Philemon for the benefit of Onesimus. In effect, he said, "Do me a favor. Not that you have to or anything, but don't you think you owe me?"

You probably have some experience with situations such as this. "Here's two box seat tickets to a game for the team that's been sold out since 1950. By the way, I'll be out of town. Could you stop by and feed my 20-foot boa constrictor on the way to the stadium? Of course, if you don't like snakes, that's another story. But if he gets hungry, well …"

In all fairness, some "set ups" are only right. Paul's "cashing in his chips" was one of those situations. God's call to respond to His favor is another.

We can't do a thing to accomplish our salvation. We're like the slave Onesimus—runaways from our true Master. But Jesus wants us to return, and He knows that God will accept us. Although Jesus actually set us free, He also set us up to return the favor by the way we live and interact with others. Not because we have to, but because Jesus did so much for us that we *want* to return that love by serving both God and others. Had Jesus not been set up on the cross for us and had He not made us acceptable in God's sight, we would be lost forever. When you think about that, that's one "set up" that's given us a really good setup.

Nonsmoking Section

Ecclesiastes 1:1–8

Have you been to one of those restaurants that differentiate the smoking and nonsmoking sections by whether they place ash trays on the tables? The practice, of course, meets the letter of the law. In reality it does not affect the intent. Whoever wrote the song "Smoke Gets in Your Eyes" should have included hair, nose, and clothing too! Well-meaning establishments, however, clearly provide environmental barriers between smokers and nonsmokers.

Smoking fell into disrepute when the U.S. Surgeon General stuck his nose into the act, though he probably wasn't the one who first called cigarettes coffin nails—or at least coughin' nails. In reality, smoke got a bad name already in Solomon's day.

While smoke fills the air and permeates certain objects, it's still just smoke. Wave at it and it billows away. Give it some time and it disappears. Perhaps that's why Solomon, the wise Old Testament king, described much of life as little more than smoke. " 'Meaningless! Meaningless!' says the Teacher; 'Utterly meaningless! Everything is meaningless' "(Ecclesiastes 1:2). Solomon wasn't just "blowin' smoke" either! Then again, maybe he was. In the original language of the Bible, the word for "vanity" is *smoke*.

Isn't that a good description for all the things in life that don't really count—the things of little genuine value? In our sinfulness, we value things such as dollars, cars, houses, golf clubs, toys, jewelry, and the like. But those things are like smoke, eventually dissipating in purchases, rust, sagging foundations, drowning, dead batteries, and clasps that mysteriously break only to be noticed too late. More smoke? How about friendships, family, and accomplishments? Treading on some traditionally sacred ground here, aren't we? Not that any of those things should be minimized. They are gifts from God. But friends separate, family members die, and accomplishments fade. Like smoke, they don't last.

Only one thing lasts. Only one thing is not smoke. That's God's love for us. Through that love He gave His Son to take away our sins—in a sense removing all the stinking ashes of life. Even better, God continues to forgive though we continue to sin. His love fills us to overflowing so we might love both God and others. Finally, His love will someday take us to the ultimate in smoke-free living!

Make Over

Colossians 3:1–4

I SUSPECT THAT SOMEDAY people will come with service schedules just like new cars. Instead of new tires at 40,000 miles, we'll be scheduled to have our arches raised at 40. Then at 50, we'll get our retinas and corneas tuned to eliminate blurs and floaters. Original equipment hair can be replaced as early as 55, and after that we'll be eligible for prorated charges on make-overs of bent backs, expanded stomachs, and shriveled faces. Of course, we really don't have to wait because much of this is currently available through surgical alteration of our bank accounts.

Cosmetic make-overs provide only a temporary fix. Real change comes from deeper inside. Paul says, "Since, then, you have been raised with Christ, set your hearts on things above, where Christ is seated at the right hand of God" (Colossians 3:1). The remainder of Colossians 3 provides details of the kind of favorable changes—the spiritual and moral make-overs—that take place when we come to faith.

Before we're "made over," our hearts are set on things below. Way below. Sin dragged us down even before we were old enough to sin on our own. Sin makes us ugly, perhaps not so much in looks but surely in attitude and behavior. Talk about needing a make-over! It's the sinner's foremost need because without it, God won't give us a second look before sending us off to hell.

Thank God we don't have to pay for the alterations that make us acceptable. Jesus paid the price. Paul reminds us that the make-over really makes us different. Now our hearts are set on higher things—things that beautiful people like us can do. Now we hate sin (though not enough to avoid dabbling in it daily). We want to do what God wants; therefore, we seek to learn His will through studying His Word. The Holy Spirit works in us to help us grow in Christ and increasingly put our faith into practice until that day when our make-over reaches full maturity.

Although Jesus did a complete job, the Holy Spirit keeps us working to maintain our beauty. Avoiding sin is difficult. Growing in faith takes time, energy, and effort. While we're doing all that, we remember how we got this far. We owe it all to Jesus, the One and only Creator of the perfect faith-lift.

Antiques

2 Thessalonians 2:13–17

UNLESS YOU'RE A SPECIALIST, you probably can't tell the difference between antique and just plain old. It's similar to the difference between priceless and worthless. Antiques are what you leave in the basement for the next generation to complain about and the following generation to fight over after you're gone. "Just plain old" is something you get rid of immediately before it's deemed an antique.

However you view the issue of old versus antique, we're probably at the end of an era. Will anything today last long enough to become an antique? If we have something old, we better take care of it. A well-preserved antique increases in value the older it gets. (Don't you wish the same were true of us?)

Each of us owns an antique. No, it's not our favorite tie or wallet or shoes. (If we wait long enough, they'll be back in style before they become antiques!) The Bible says: "So then, brothers, stand firm and hold to the teachings we passed on to you, whether by word of mouth or by letter" (2 Thessalonians 2:15).

Historic letters are sometimes worth much, and treasured old sayings remain quotable for years. Then there are family stories passed by word of mouth from generation to generation. While they might not carry the price tag of Ben Franklin's notepad, their worth is nothing short of a fortune. It doesn't take the average Christian long to determine that his or her special antique—God's Word—isn't just plain old. God's Word is beyond ancient, and its value is inestimable.

Sinners that we are, we sometimes leave this precious antique wedged on a dusty shelf or—perhaps worse—still encased in its original wrapper. We think that someday it'll be worth something if only we don't wrinkle any pages. Of course, God's Word is more than a collection of sentences, paragraphs, and chapters. Its words belong in our hearts where they come alive through the power of the Holy Spirit. How good to hear and believe all that God has done for His people! How wonderful to know that He sent Jesus to take away our sins! Isn't it beyond comprehension to have these blessings just because He loves us?

Treasure your antique, but don't baby it. Don't display it only on Christmas or Easter. Keep it right there in your heart and everywhere else. As old as it is, it will never be too old.

Proverbs

Proverbs 8:1–36

SCRATCH AROUND the recesses of your memory. What are some of your favorite proverbs? Here are some of mine, though I suspect my memory is incapable of perfect wording: "A penny earned makes for little bacon in the piggy bank." Or how about this: "A stitch in time hurts a lot more than a butterfly bandage." Other memorable proverbs—well, almost memorable—include: "A watched pot boils over anyway" and "An ounce of prevention probably costs more than your medical coverage provides."

Proverbs are wise sayings. They date far back in history. The ones with which we're most familiar seem to come either from early American history or a time somewhat further removed—the time of King Solomon. The biblical book of Proverbs preserves Solomon's God-given wisdom.

Solomon's proverbs are valuable because he took them from a higher source of wisdom. While we may feel humble compared with a king long remembered for good judgment, Solomon's "source" remains available to us.

Here's one of my favorites (and this time I got it right): "For whoever finds Me finds life and receives favor from the LORD" (Proverbs 8:35). The "Me" in this Proverb is wisdom personified, a.k.a. Jesus. Earlier in Proverbs 8 we discover how easy it is to "find" Jesus. It says that He calls to us. Now if you've ever played hide-and-seek, you normally don't call out to the one trying to find you. It's different with our loving Savior. He says, "Wisdom isn't elusive if you're looking for the right kind. I'm right here, and I want you to have My wisdom. Take it. It's free!"

The best wisdom ever is not only the knowledge that Jesus died to save sinners like us, but it is the faith to believe it—to inscribe it in our souls just as Franklin's students might have carved his sayings into desk-tops. And we don't have to worry that we might lose some of God's proverbs. They're safe in the Bible, even if we take them out and use them in everyday life. You know what they say—"A little knowledge is better than a lot of stupidity."

Whatsisname

2 Chronicles 13:12; Job 16:19; Psalm 32:7; 33:20; 71:5; 140:7;
Isaiah 9:6; Jeremiah 8:18; John 8:12; Revelation 19:11

MY FATHER ALWAYS HAD TROUBLE WITH NAMES. Whenever he started a conversation that involved news about someone, he said something like, "You know, whatsisname bought a new car, and it looks a lot like the one whatsisname bought—only a different color."

I'd reply, "Who, Dad?"

"Oh, you know, whatsisname."

A few weeks later, I might remark I saw Mr. Smith driving a new car. Then Dad would say, "I told you about that a few weeks ago. It's the same kind as whatsisname's."

Everyone gets a name—whether they want one or not. As proof of how heartless modern people can be toward the helpless, just read some of the names parents give to babies! This despite the fact that a good name is worth more than money. (It's tax free!) Good names, however, have little to do with the letters that spell them. A good name comes from the person who wears it.

God has many good names—as well He should. The Bible passages at the top of page identify some of them, so when you have time, start paging. Among them is this famous and beloved passage heard most often at Christmas: "For to us a child is born, to us a son is given, and the government will be on His shoulders. And He will be called Wonderful Counselor, Mighty God, Everlasting Father, Prince of Peace" (Isaiah 9:6).

Great names, aren't they? But consider this one: "Even now my witness is in heaven; my advocate is on high" (Job 16:19). How often have you called Jesus your "witness"? Sounds legal rather than merciful, but it is a good name nonetheless. We sinners need a witness, but not the kind who testifies against us.

God knows we sin. We need testimony in our favor, and we have it! It comes from Jesus Christ Himself, a star witness who tells God that He knows us. We're one of the faithful, made that way by the Holy Spirit. We belong in God's eternal kingdom because Jesus took away our sins and we have His grace and mercy.

Even if you get old and forgetful, you'll never forget Jesus' name. He has so many! But in case your memory really fails, you can call Him Whatsisname. Just be sure to use a capital W.

The End

2 Peter 3:11–18

A N ENGLISH TEACHER SAID never to do this—end a written piece with "The End." He said, "If the reader doesn't know to stop reading when he runs out of pages, something is wrong with him or her. Or the writer." So how does the greatest book ever written end? If you check it out, it doesn't end with "The End." In fact, we may even say it ends with "The Beginning."

If we think of the Bible as God's history of salvation, the story doesn't conclude with Revelation 22:21. Salvation's history continues as alive and vibrant as it was 2,000 years ago, 4,000 years ago, or even an eternity ago because God loved us even before we began. If we dare think of an end to salvation's story, we must remember what happened about 21 centuries ago when Jesus took the sins of the world to an intimidating cross. He pronounced the end in a dying gasp late one Friday afternoon. Then He did it again with a victorious shout early the following Sunday morning. It was the end of sin's power to kill us. The end of Satan's power to claim God's children. It was the end of the end and the beginning of the beginning.

Like many readers, you probably feel a sense of accomplishment, triumph, or at least closure when you come to the final pages of a book. If you read these devotions one by one each weekday, it's been about a year since you began. The book seemed long then. Now it probably seems even longer. No wait! I hope not. With all those pages behind you, the book remains in the last minutes of its useful life. How unlike life is this book!

Life never ends. At times it's as unpredictable as the trajectory of a grapefruit's squirt, but life goes on—not as a trite phrase spoken to ease those temporary setbacks, disappointments, failures, and sorrows, but as a real moment on a timeline that began on our birthday and continues infinitely.

Praise God for making us His own—for including us as a name to remember in His history of salvation. Praise Jesus for the new beginning He earned for us on the cross. Praise the Holy Spirit for giving us faith. And now, since it's not really the end, I leave you with this:

But grow in the grace and knowledge of our Lord and Savior Jesus
Christ. To Him be glory both now and forever! Amen. 2 Peter 3:18

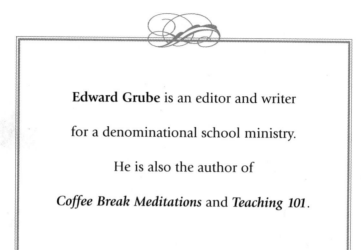

Edward Grube is an editor and writer

for a denominational school ministry.

He is also the author of

Coffee Break Meditations and *Teaching 101*.